Fred Turoff

Head Coach of Men's Gymnastics
Temple University

Artistic Gymnastics

*A Comprehensive Guide
to Performing and Teaching
Skills for Beginners and
Advanced Beginners*

 Championship Series

Wm. C. Brown Publishers Trade and Direct Group
Vice President, Publisher *Thomas E. Doran*
Managing Editor *Edward E. Bartell*
Senior Editor *Chris Rogers*
Media Assistant *Karla Blaser*
Production Coordinator *Peggy Selle*

Cover design by Sailer & Cook Creative Services.

Cover illustration by Jeff Olsen

Library of Congress Catalog Card Number: 90-82240

ISBN 0-697-10745-0

Printed in the United States of America by Wm. C. Brown Publishers,
2460 Kerper Boulevard, Dubuque, IA 52001

10 9 8 7 6 5 4 3 2

This book is dedicated to the coaches who had the greatest influence on me in developing my love for and commitment to gymnastics.

Bill Coco

Ginny Coco

Tom Gibbs

Abie Grossfeld

Karl Kogel

A. Carl Patterson

John Peasenelli

Don Tonry

Table of Contents

v

Contents

Contents

Preface

The tremendous successes of our teams at the 1984 Olympics spurred a growth of interest in artistic gymnastics. Artistic gymnastics is different from rhythmic gymnastics and sports acrobatics in that we perform on apparatus; rhythmic gymnastics utilizes small hand apparatus (a ball, clubs, hoop, ribbon, rope) and excludes acrobatics; sports acrobatics includes partner skills, team skills, and tumbling. As more new students are exposed to artistic gymnastics, public interest grows, physical fitness is promoted, and some young students seek further training toward competition, and so build up the base of future participants in our national program. Although there are many books on gymnastics training, none that I know of are as complete as this text is concerning lower level skills. This book was written to give physical educators, coaches, beginning gymnasts (both young and old), and parents a set of comprehensive guidelines for doing and teaching beginning skills in artistic gymnastics.

Not every student will want to train for years to become a competitor. Some are interested in an experience, many learn as part of a general physical education program, and some learn that this is what they would like to pursue. There are many more skills presented here than can be covered or learned in a semester, a year, or even two years. Yet I consider all to be basic skills, for beginners and advanced beginners. Any skills that should be covered in an elementary or secondary school unit on gymnastics, a university activity class, or the first years of serious training can be found here. A safe foundation for later mastery of intermediate and advanced skills is a firm foundation of basic skills.

Every gymnast, no matter what level, must practice basics. Skills are rated A, B, C, and D, with A-level skills being the easiest and D-level skills the hardest. With the exception of a small number of B-level skills that I feel are necessary, just about all skills presented here are rated as A-level skills—some are too easy to receive even an A rating, but are necessary for a movement background. You who are the beginning competitive gymnasts must strive to learn as many of these as you can. Training should take place in a proper setting such as a gymnastics gym, not at home under improper conditions. When you practice these skills, try to learn them with good form so that keeping form becomes a habit. This means that your legs are straight when they should be, your toes are pointed as they almost always should be, and that your body is in good alignment for the skill that you are attempting. Your teacher/coach will provide you with feedback concerning these points. In many cases, skills can be done to the left or the right. For simplicity, I describe only one direction. You should try both to see which is best for you. Also remember that whenever you land on a mat, you should absorb the landing in your ankles, knees, and hips to dissipate the force of contact with the ground. Do not ever land with your knees locked! Dance training and landing practice will help here.

Each skill is presented with a description of how it should be performed (what I would say to my student), with a short list of common problems, and with suggestions how a teacher can spot—that is, assist—his or her student to learn the skill. The gymnasts pictured doing the skills are relative beginners in many cases, and they do a good job of illustrating how the movements are done. Where a mistake is made, I point it out so that you can see it. You will also see a way in the photographs to hand spot most skills. I discuss spotting in chapter 1 (**Safety in Learning and Teaching**). If you have access to an overhead spotting rig, this can help with many skills, but if you do not, you will be able to spot these skills by hand with the hints I give. I describe where I would stand, which hand/arm motions I would use, and how I would follow or assist my student for each skill that may require spotting. For clarity, unless otherwise noted, any spotting that is done from the side is described as done from my student's left side. The figures, for the most part, show this as well.

I generally present skills in each chapter in order of increasing difficulty. However, where a family of moves is discussed, the moves within that family are presented in order of increasing difficulty, so the final move in that family may be more difficult than the next move discussed after that family. Keep this in mind as you work your way through the skills introduced in each chapter.

There are often many ways to teach gymnastics skills, and those described here are ways I have found successful. Other teachers/coaches may have different approaches to these skills. If you hear of another way, listen to it and weigh its merits. It may work for you, or may provide a clue in a different fashion that makes a point clear that was not so before. By the way, teachers are not only adults. In a gymnastics practice, each gymnast can be a teacher/coach. If you see something that will help a fellow gymnast, tell him or her as long as you do not interfere with the main teacher.

Once skills are learned singly, you should try to combine them with other skills in sequences. With the exception of vaulting, gymnastics routines are composed of at least 10–12 movements (depending on the event) that must be combined in a rhythmic, harmonious way without unnecessary intermediate movements. I briefly describe the current combination requirements of competition routines at the beginning of each chapter so that you will know what you are working toward. As you progress you will learn the rules of gymnastics and learn how to compose and choreograph your routines, and may eventually learn how to judge them. At the end of each event chapter I suggest sequences to be tried (with increasing difficulty as you go down the list) to give you some ideas of how skills are drilled and combined.

Gymnastics has a history that can be traced back to the ancient civilizations of China, Greece, and Rome. However, our modern form of artistic gymnastics was pioneered in the mid-1800s by Friedrich Ludwig Jahn, who developed it in Germany as a way to build a stronger, sounder youth.

The events seen in competition today—floor exercise, pommel horse, rings, vault, parallel bars, and horizontal bar for boys, vault, uneven parallel bars, balance beam, and floor exercise for girls—were not all invented back in those times. For instance, the uneven parallel bars event for women was introduced internationally around 1950. Prior to that women competed on even parallel bars as the men still do today. The events themselves have evolved as well. Newer materials and technologies have brought changes in the equipment used to allow safer training and performance along with augmented performance. Routine composition has changed as the sport has evolved. Each generation of gymnasts masters current requirements and goes on to challenge new frontiers. Rules governing competition are reevaluated at regular intervals to try to keep up with the ever inventive gymnasts and coaches.

In a meeting I attended, a fellow coach gave a talk and declared, "Gymnasts are the future astronauts. Who else is better at spatial orientation than we are? We are the future." These words have truth in them. NASA has recently tested gymnasts to see if they are more resistant to space-orientation problems and motion sickness than people of other backgrounds. Although gymnasts turned out to have similar problems with motion sickness, they proved to be more mobile in a weightless condition, that is, better in orientation and maneuvering and quicker to adapt to weightless conditions than others tested. At any rate, the kinesthetic (body position) awareness, strength, and flexibility derived from gymnastics practice can enhance training in other sports and in everyday life.

The national governing body of gymnastics is the United States Gymnastics Federation (USGF), currently located in Indianapolis, Indiana. The international governing body is the Fédération International de Gymnastique (FIG), headquartered in Switzerland. The USGF is responsible for many functions in connection with artistic and rhythmic gymnastics and sports acrobatics: educating the public and the gymnastics community, promotions, running an age-group developmental program, selecting teams for international competition, and sanctioning and conducting domestic competitions.

It is my hope that all who read this text will better understand the building blocks of artistic gymnastics and be able to learn them and/or pass them on to the thousands of students who will benefit from a firm foundation of beginning artistic gymnastics skills.

I would like to thank the following friends who had a chance to review this material and offer their suggestions:

Ken Anderson, Janet Cantwell, Mark Cuyjet, Tom Gibbs, Winnie Grimes, Muriel Grossfeld, Dave Rosenberg, Jeff Rosenberg, Toby Towson, Rick and Graceann Tucker, Russell Warfield, Debbie and Jay Whelan.

Thanks go to the following coaches and gymnasts who donated their time and appear in the photographs:

Leslie Abate, Christine Amodei, Michelle Amodei, Ken Anderson, Stella Bednar, Danny Beigel, Courtney Bogart, Shannon Bogart, Fred Brannon, Stephan Choiniere, Susan Cianflone, Lara Cohen, Melanie Dorwart, Mike Dutka, Anthony Galasso, Cindy Gonzalez, Winnie Grimes, Benji Karetny, Eli Karetny, Maureen Kealey, Tracey Kohl, Lindsay Kravitz, Cheryl Mascio, Angela Pale, Jim Pietrafitta, Jaime Rosano, Bill Sell, Lenny Shaw, Sonya Vargas, Carlos Vazquez, Macey Watson, Meggan Watts, Jill Zimmerman, Dawn Zukowski.

Finally, I thank Harry Saffren for his constant encouragement and suggestions, Temple University for providing me with the facilities and lighting for the photography, and Temple University gymnasts Mike Dellapena, Anthony Galasso, and Jim Van de Zilver for taking some of the photographs.

Fred Turoff
December 21, 1989

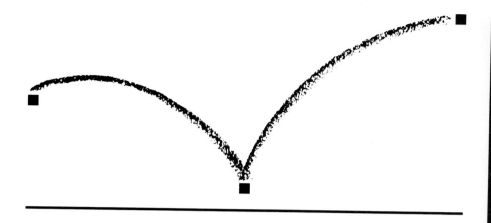

Physical Preparation

Artistic gymnastics is a sport that everyone can practice to some level. However, to be successful at accomplishing goals, it is necessary to make preparations to insure that your body is ready to challenge and overcome the rigors that gymnastics places upon it. Strength and flexibility are the two key physical properties necessary to master skills. The stronger your muscles and joints are, and the greater your joints' ranges of motions, the easier it is to learn skills. Other characteristics are also helpful—timing, balance, and perseverance, for example. But the need to constantly improve strength and flexibility cannot be emphasized enough.

How do you prepare? To start with, be active—take part in regular exercise. General exercising will give you a basis to build upon. Beginning gymnasts can be tested for physical preparedness to sort them into readiness levels, and they can be brought through a gradual strengthening and stretching program to help their quality of learning and of life in general. A teacher/coach can suggest ways to improve any areas of weakness. Physiology and kinesiology can be taught to even young gymnasts through instruction on how to tense certain muscles, how to assume certain shapes, and how to accomplish certain movements.

Since artistic gymnastics involves moving your body around apparatus or in near-earth airspace, it is important not to be overweight. Accomplished gymnasts are superbly muscled, lean, and conditioned athletes. Obviously not every student will be, but that does not mean that gymnastic progress is not possible for the heavy student, only that it is not as easily done as by those who are trim. Training in gymnastics itself provides plenty of stimuli for muscle development for all of your body's major muscle groups. However, there are many supplemental exercises that training gymnasts should be aware of to enhance the development of particular motor functions and physical qualities and therefore increase the likelihood of learning skills. These are almost always skill or movement specific—to gain strength in a certain movement pattern, do exercises in that pattern.

Clothing and Personal Gear

When you train, you must be appropriately dressed so that your clothing and personal gear do not interfere with anything you are working on. Loose clothing is to be avoided, as is jewelry. Leotards, tights, T-shirts or heavier shirts (not loose), tank tops, close-fitting shorts, socks and/or gymnastics shoes, and close-fitting warmup suits or sweat suits are all appropriate. (Note that bare feet are permissible for some events—floor exercise, balance beam, and vaulting.) If you have long hair, it should be tied back so it does not get in the way. Glasses should be held on to your head by an athletic strap. If you are ready to use gymnastic handguards, your coach will instruct you in their use, and they always come with a set of directions. I discuss handguards at the beginning of both the **Rings** and the **Horizontal Bar and Uneven Parallel Bars** chapters. Some performers wear handguards on pommel horse and parallel bars as well, but this is not as common.

Using Gymnastics Equipment

Equipment should be checked regularly for correct setup and wear. Even the bolts holding parts together occasionally loosen, so once in a while they should be checked. Matting should be appropriate to the event and the skill being taught. (Competition matting requirements and a complete discussion of mats are found in the *USGF Gymnastics Safety Manual*.) When you are learning dismounts, it is a good idea to use a skill/safety cushion (which is a thick, absorbent mat) for your landing at first, and then move to a regular landing mat (which is still quite absorbent but not as soft). Any time there is the chance of a fall, extra matting may reduce the possibility of an injury and may allow you another opportunity to perform the move. Also see if supplementary equipment is readily available, such as gymnastics chalk (discussed next section), emery cloth or another device to clean off chalk buildups, or spotting equipment. The safety of the student is always paramount in the teacher's mind as well.

Using Gymnastics Chalk

Whenever you work on an event that requires a secure grip with your hands, you must use gymnastics chalk, which is magnesium carbonate (sometimes called "mag"), and comes in block or powder form. Gymnastics chalk should always be applied to your palms (and to your handguards if you use them), as it will help you get a more secure grip and absorb sweat and oils. It is better to overdo it when putting chalk on your hands rather than to use too little. Some women use it on their feet for balance beam. It is also used on floor exercise and vaulting when performers go barefooted.

Landings and Uncontrolled Falls

During training the student will be faced with many landing situations. To avoid injuries it is helpful to go over landing techniques and how to fall without getting hurt. Anyone with a dance background will be familiar with *pliés*. This is how to land for any skill where a stand is required. When your feet contact the mat, the force should be absorbed in your hips, knees, and ankles, rather than absorbing the force in only one or two of these joints. The more the force of the landing is spread out, the less force any one of these joints will have to experience. Keep your trunk and head somewhat upright, and let your arms drop as you contact the mat to further disperse force and to lower your center of gravity—where your weight is centered—for greater stability. (Once you have control, you will lift up your arms to show a good finish position.) Sideways landings must be avoided, as these place stress on the collateral ligaments of landings must be avoided, as these place stress on the collateral ligaments of your knees, and your knee is not constructed to move in this way. In fact, sideways landings are outlawed by the International Gymnastics Federation.

Figure 1.1a, b, c, d

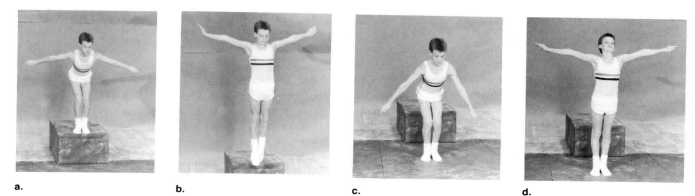

a. b. c. d.

Figure 1.2

Figure 1.3

Practice jumping from various heights and absorbing the landing. This training will become useful as you begin experiencing the thrill of gymnastic flight and then have to return to mother earth.

Figure 1.1a–d shows one landing drill.

Occasionally you will experience an uncontrolled fall. To correctly dissipate the force of such an occurrence, it is **very important** to remember not to try to break the fall by extending a limb in the direction of the oncoming mat or apparatus. A much safer method is to roll forward, backward, sideward, or over your shoulder. Forward and backward rolls are covered in chapter 5. Sideward or over-your-shoulder rolls are recoveries and are not covered there. For a sideward roll, simply roll over sideways in a tucked or stretched position. (If you are in a straight body position, this is called a log roll, which is often taught to young students to introduce them to twisting motions.) A shoulder roll looks like it will be a forward or backward roll, but instead of going straight over your head, you roll obliquely over your shoulder. This way your head hardly touches the mat, if it touches at all. Should you ever fall so that you think you will land on your head, it is a good idea to put your arms overhead (not extended or locked out!) so that they can absorb some of the force of contact. Protecting yourself during any uncontrolled fall requires fast thinking. The use of proper matting will certainly help lessen the possibility of injury in the case of an uncontrolled fall, but it does not remove that possibility. It must be stressed often to not reach out with an extended limb in an attempt to break an uncontrolled fall. Try to avoid the actions shown in figures 1.2 and 1.3 when falling.

Teaching Progressions

To make teaching as safe as possible, it is necessary to have a current knowledge of methodology, equipment, and sources of information. The generally practiced method of teaching gymnastics skills is the progressive method where a student must master certain preliminary skills before moving on to more difficult ones. The number of basic skills it is necessary to master before moving on to intermediate skills in a particular movement pattern is sometimes quite large. Moving too fast through a skill progression or skipping steps can have detrimental effects down the road. The stumbling block to learning a hard skill later could be those basics that were neglected.

All the skills presented in this book I consider basic or beginning skills. Some are so easy for most gymnasts that they are not even given a difficulty rating in the rule books. It is not necessary to master every skill covered here to be able to attempt and master intermediate and advanced skills, but the more the student is able to do, the more complete the student's background will be.

Spotting

Spotting serves three functions: (1) to allow manipulating a student through a skill to provide the feel of the skill if needed; (2) to prevent injury in case the student misses; and (3) to provide moral support—just being there makes some become brave. Those of you who undertake the role of a spotter, which at times can be a potentially hazardous duty for you if you are hand spotting, will have to learn from experience or other teacher/coaches when to back off from spotting to allow your students to feel a movement without your help. This is an important point. Gymnasts must be allowed to perform free from your support when they are ready. You must be careful not to allow your students to become so dependent on your spotting to perform skills that they do not do them if you are not there—even if they are ready. Be careful of your health when you spot, too. For instance, **NOTE**: (1) Do not reach over a bar that is around your shoulder height; (2) if you put your hand on the abdomen of your student who is tucking or piking, be sure to keep your thumb next to your hand to avoid having it bent the wrong way; and (3) if your student has a loose shirt on and you are spotting a series of backward handsprings, I will bet dollars to donuts that your hand will become wrapped up in the shirt!

When you spot a skill, remember to spot the finish/landing as well, especially moves that show speed or flight. Be sure that you and your student understand what you are supposed to do. If you have a question, ask someone who has more experience than you do. Gymnastics coaches freely share knowledge. Keep in mind that an incorrect spot may impede the safe development of some skills.

If you have access to spotting belts, as are pictured in figures 1.4a and 1.4b, you will be able to stand away from your student a bit and see what is going on. These belts can be supported by short ropes that you and an assistant hold in your hands, or they can be used with an overhead spotting rig, as seen in figure 1.5. Whenever you use an overhead spotting rig, be sure both you and your student have a clear idea of what will happen, where the ropes will be, and where you will provide assistance or support. A practice run of the spot and performance can be done at slow speed to check your procedures. If the overhead rig is not used correctly, it could lead to an accident or impedance of performing and/or learning a skill. Learning to use these belts and spotting rigs takes a bit of practice, but I prefer them for many skills because they allow me to support my student as well as have a clear view of what he/she is doing.

Figure 1.4a
A spotting belt for rotation such as doing handsprings or saltos.

a.

Figure 1.4b
A spotting belt for rotation and twisting.

b.

Figure 1.5
An overhead spotting rig for horizontal bar dismounts.

Safety Pits

A state-of-the-art training device is a loose foam pit. This area allows gymnasts to perform repetitions of skills without having to be overly concerned about the consequences of a fall or missed landing. These are often found in private clubs or universities, but I know of none in public schools. A discussion of safety pits is found in the *USGF Gymnastics Safety Manual*. Note that these are not fail-safe devices. Careless or incorrect use of any safety devices can negate their intended purpose, so be sure that if you use one you know how to do so.

Teacher, Are You Ready?

When teaching a skill, the teacher should always ask himself or herself two questions after determining that the teaching area is ready. These are:

1. Is my student ready to learn the skill? Does my student have the necessary physical characteristics, understanding of the skill, and confidence to perform safely?
2. Am I prepared to teach this skill? Do I understand the skill, and have I clearly described the way to perform the skill? Do I know how to spot in case of a mistake or in case my student needs to be guided through the skill?

If everything is ready, then go ahead and have fun.

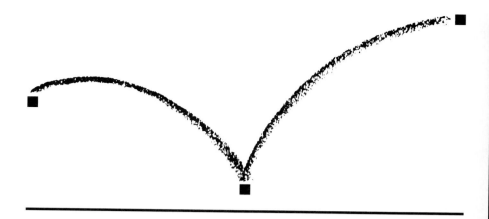

Some terminology is necessary to communicate gymnastic ideas clearly. To help you understand the many body positions that are often mentioned, refer to the illustrations below for some examples. Sometimes a literal description is used—for example, an L support is a support in a piked position that looks like the letter L, and a V seat is sitting with your body balanced on your seat in the shape of the letter V. Good form refers to the correct positioning of the legs, feet, arms, hands, and head. Terms used once are explained in the text, and if a term is used several times for a particular event, it is explained in the introduction to that event.

Positions

A variety of positions seen in gymnastics is shown in figures 2.1–2.12. These positions are referred to often in this text.

Figure 2.1
Tuck (hips and knees flexed).

Figure 2.2
Cowboy tuck (hips and knees flexed but legs spread—this is bad form, as are the hooked feet).

Figure 2.3
Pike (hips flexed at or greater than 90°).

Figure 2.4
Open pike (hips flexed less than 90°).

Figure 2.5
Arch.

Figure 2.6
Layout—stretched body or back slightly arched.

Figure 2.7
Hollow (rounded) chest.

Figure 2.8
Straddle (this is a straddled stand).

Figure 2.9
Piked straddle (this is a piked straddled stand).

Figure 2.10a, b
Front support—your front is facing the apparatus/event.

a.

b.

Figure 2.11
Stride position or support—one leg in front, one behind.

Figure 2.12a, b
Rear support—your rear is facing the apparatus/event.

a.

b.

Figure 2.13
Hooked toes (ankles dorsiflexed).

Figure 2.14
Bent (flexed) knees—when they should be straight.

Figure 2.15
Split legs—when they should be together.

Figure 2.16
Legs split and hooked toes (ankles dorsiflexed).

Figure 2.17
Bent knees and hooked toes.

Figure 2.18
Good hand/arm alignment for boys (girls have much more freedom in this respect).

Figure 2.19
Poor hand/arm alignment for boys.

Figure 2.20
Poor hand form for boys.

Form

Examples of poor form (form breaks), which are mistakes in the position of your arms, hands, legs, feet and head, are illustrated in figures 2.13–2.17, 2.19, 2.20 and 2.22, whereas figures 2.18 and 2.21 point out desirable positions.

Terms Seen Often

NOTE: Some terms describing moves are interchangeable, such as backward = back, forward = front, sideward = side; also, when describing a gymnastic element, skill = move = element.

Arabesque   A dance position, this is a stand on one leg with your other leg lifted up behind your body (also called a **scale**).

Beat Swing   A swing that utilizes a rapid change of body position (for example, pike to arch or arch to pike) to generate power for lift or rotation—also called a **tap swing.**

Figure 2.21
Excellent handstand alignment with an ideal toe point.

Figure 2.22
Examples of poor handstand alignment: (a) too much arch (only a bit is acceptable); (b) lower back arch and hip pike; (c) way too much arch, a shoulder angle, and a raised head.

a.   b.   c.

Blind Landing   A landing from a move that is rotating forward, so called because you cannot see the floor below you as your feet approach the mat at the end of the move.

Blocking   Usually, pushing downward and opposite to horizontal movement with your arms or legs, ahead of your center of gravity, to affect the horizontal movement, lift, or rotation of your body—mostly to add to lift.

Center of Gravity = CG   The point where all of your weight is concentrated; the line of action of your weight always passes through your cg—it can be within your body or outside of it depending on your body shape.

Extension   Movement term describing the following positions: wrist—hand in line with forearm; shoulder—arm down by your side; elbow—straight; hip—thigh in line with your trunk; knee—straight. **Extend** means move toward extension from flexion.

Flexion   Movement term describing the following positions: wrist—palm pulled toward your forearm; shoulder—arm overhead in line with your trunk; elbow—bent; hip—thigh up in front of you; knee—bent. **Flex** means to move toward flexion from extension.

Flyaway   A somersaulting dismount done from the rings or horizontal bar or uneven parallel bars.

Forward Lunge   A standing pose or transitional position with your legs in a stride position with your front knee flexed and your back knee extended; arm position is optional. See figures 2.23a–c.

Figure 2.23a
Forward lunge with weight on the front foot, as if you were kicking into a handstand.

Figure 2.23b
Forward lunge with even weight distribution over the feet, as in a landing.

Figure 2.23c
Forward lunge with even weight distribution and both feet turned out for stability (good dance technique), as in a pose.

a.

b.

c.

Frontways Facing the apparatus with the front of your body, or moving with the front of your body leading.

Hold Move A move that is held in a specific position for 2 to 3 seconds.

Hurdle A transition step, skip, or jump between a run and a skill.

Hyperextension Movement term describing the following positions: wrist— back of hand pulled toward your forearm; shoulder—arm up behind you; hip—leg up behind you. **Hyperextend** means to move toward hyperextension from extension.

Kip Any movement that utilizes a rapid opening from a pike to either a lesser pike, a straight body, or an arch (that is, a rapid hip extension, possibly coupled with spine extension) for the purpose of going up and/or turning over.

Pirouette A turn, usually referring to a turn in a handstand.

Plié (Pronounced: plee-áy) a dance term referring to flexing (= bending) one or both knees in landing, posing, or takeoff (with hip and ankle movement as well); ***demi plié*** is a partial flexion.

Pose A move that is held in a specific position for less than a second (just to show the position).

Press A strength move done to a final hold position.

Pronate A movement term describing forearm rotation: If you hold your hands in front of you with your palms facing up, by turning them in and down, you are pronating.

Rearways Facing the apparatus with the rear of your body, or moving with the rear of your body leading.

Salto A somersault.

Shoulder Pike Having an angle between your upper arm and trunk, usually referring to a position between full and half flexion.

Figure 2.24a
Sideward lunge with weight over flexed leg,
as if you were going into a cartwheel.

Figure 2.24b
Sideward lunge with even weight
distribution over the feet, as in a landing or
a pose.

a.

b.

Sideward Lunge   A standing pose or transitional position with your legs
straddled, one knee flexed and the other extended; arm position is optional.
See figures 2.24a,b.

Sideways   Facing the apparatus with the side of your body, or moving with
the side of your body leading.

Supinate   A movement term describing forearm rotation: If you hold your
hands in front of you with your palms facing down, by turning them in and
up, you are supinating.

Turn-out   This is a common dance term referring to an outward hip rotation
(which is emphasized in classical ballet): If you stand with your feet together
and parallel, by rotating your legs so that your toes separate but your heels
remain together, you are turning out.

Note that sometimes international terms are used when describing moves
or positions; you will find this more and more as you read the available publications of gymnastics. For example, an eagle grip on a bar is called an *elgrip,*
and a loop on the pommel horse is called a *Schwabenflanke.* In some cases, we
have adopted the international term into our everyday gym lingo, such as a
Stütz, or *Stützkehre* (translation: support turn) on the parallel bars. As you
get better and begin to learn some of the harder moves, you will learn that
some of them are named after their creators, or named after those who either
first performed them in the international arena or popularized them, such as
the Thomas flair described in chapter 7 or the Yamashita vault described in
chapter 10.

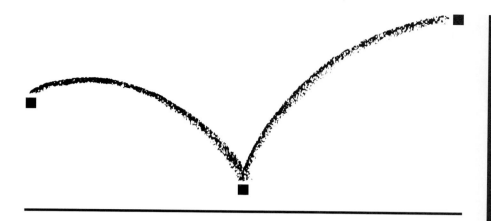

Purpose

Before beginning any training session a warmup is recommended. This is a preparation of your body for the oncoming stress that training will place upon it. You want to raise your body temperature a bit and promote increased blood flow to your muscles and joints. The warmup may consist of general movement, a series of stretches, mild strength exercises, and a review of some skills previously learned. It is also often a social period that precedes the training period, which demands concentration. Often people gather in an area and warm up together, and talk amongst themselves about the day's events, the coming training, later plans, etc. The teacher can use the warmup period to go over the plans of the training session as well.

Examples of Warmup Exercises

As an example of a warmup, let's look at a "head to toe" warmup, so called because your joints and muscles are stretched and worked in order from the top to the bottom of your body. DO NOT BOUNCE IN ANY OF THESE STRETCHES. A slow and forceful stretch is safer. To be effective you must feel a light discomfort due to the stretch, but do not stretch so hard that you injure yourself. Each exercise can be done for about 30 seconds, and exercises can be repeated, as often the first careful use prepares your muscles and the second or third warms them up well. Most of these exercises are illustrated in figures 3.1–3.18.

1. Begin with a light exercise such as jogging around the gym or jumping to get your heart beating faster and to warm your body. By warming your body, you will be able to stretch more easily. Exercising for a few minutes will do the trick.
2. Roll your head around and stretch your neck in all directions (figure 3.1).
3. Swing your arms back and forth and circle them around (figure 3.2).
4. Stretch your shoulders in a flexed position on the floor (figure 3.3a), on the apparatus (figure 3.3b), or on a block or mat pile with your back arched (figure 3.3c) or rounded (figure 3.3d).

Figure 3.1

Figure 3.2

Figure 3.3a

Figure 3.3b

Figure 3.3c, d

c.

a.

b.

d.

5. Stretch your shoulders in a hyperextended position (if you use the apparatus you can hang this way) on the mat (figure 3.4a), or on the apparatus (figure 3.4b).
6. Go through a dislocate motion using a broomstick or parallel bar—this starts with an undergrip (palms facing forward) behind you and finishes in an eagle grip overhead (figure 3.5).
7. Stretch your wrists in all directions. Flex (bend) and extend (straighten) your elbows as well while stretching your wrists (figure 3.6).

Figure 3.4a

a.

Figure 3.4b

b.

Figure 3.5a, b, c

a.

b.

c.

8. Do a few pushups.
9. Jump a few times from your hands and feet (with straight arms) up to a piked handstand position where your weight is supported on your hands (figure 3.7). If you have control, extend your hips to a handstand.
10. Twist your trunk side to side (figure 3.8).
11. Stretch the sides of your trunk with your top arm overhead to add to the stretch (figure 3.9).
12. Roll back and forth on your back a few times, then push up to a bridge (figure 3.10a,b). Try to extend your elbows and knees. Then rock back and forth gently to increase the stretch (figure 3.10c,d,e). You can lift a leg as a further challenge (figure 3.10f).

Figure 3.6a
You can stretch your wrists this way . . .

a.

Figure 3.6b, c
Or this way.

b.

c.

Figure 3.7a, b

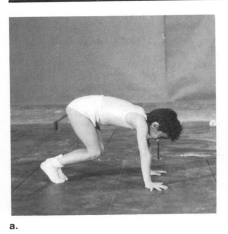

a.

b.

Figure 3.8

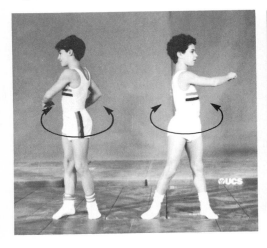

Figure 3.9

Figure 3.10a, b

a.

b.

Figure 3.10c, d, e

c.

d.

e.

Figure 3.10f

f.

Figure 3.11

Figure 3.12

Figure 3.13

Figure 3.14

13. Sit in an L position. Flex your hips (pike tighter) and bring your trunk to your legs (figure 3.11). You can pull on your legs to help this stretch. Do this with your trunk in both hollow (rounded) and arched positions. This piked position is so often used in gymnastics skills that it has great importance. Try it with your feet/toes both pointed and hooked. Your legs must remain straight or the stretch will not have its full effect.

14. Sit in a straddled L position. Flex your hips and bring your trunk to the mat in both hollow and arched positions (figure 3.12). Your hands may hold onto your legs or feet if necessary. Go as low as you can, but keep your legs straight.

15. Push up to a straddled stand and move forward to a straddled front support. Press your pelvis toward the mat to increase your hip stretch (figure 3.13).

16. Push back to a straddled stand and try to lower to a straddled split (figure 3.14).

17. Turn to a stride split one way, then the other (left leg in front, right leg in front). If you cannot go all the way down, start with slightly flexed knees and extend them as you feel the stretch starting, or just go as far as you can and keep your legs straight (figure 3.15a). You can support yourself with your hands if you can go down close to the full split position. If you cannot go down that far, do your split

Figure 3.15a

a.

Figure 3.15b, c
Overstretch methods.

b.   c.

Figure 3.16a, b

a.   b.

between some mats or books or any raised surface so that you can support yourself. To work further flexibility, you can overstretch using a raised surface or wall/mat pile (figure 3.15b,c).

18. Stand up and do some leg lifts forward, sideward, and rearward (figure 3.16a,b). Do a few *pliés* (figure 3.16b).

19. Stretch your calf and Achilles' tendon by leaning against a wall or a piece of apparatus or a partner for support, placing one leg behind you so that your back foot is pointing forward, and then moving your body so that your ankle is extremely bent up—the opposite of pointing (this is called dorsiflexing)—and your heel just about comes off the mat (figure 3.17). As an alternative, you can do both legs at the same time.

20. The last stretch—work on a good foot/toe point by pressing the top of your foot to the mat while standing on your other foot (this is called plantarflexing your ankle, which is the position of a pointed foot/toe). Do not let your foot turn out to the side—keep it in line with your lower leg (figure 3.18a). As an alternative, have a partner push down on your feet while you are seated on the mat (figure 3.18b).

Figure 3.17

Figure 3.18a

a.

Figure 3.18b

b.

If this warmup is completed in about 15–20 minutes, your body will be warmed to the point of light sweating, and you will be ready for gymnastic activities. There are other exercises that can be done as well. This is only an example of a successful warmup technique. When dealing with young students the teacher may have to invent games to encourage stretching behaviors. Be as inventive as you wish. There is no one correct way to go about a warmup as long as the body is prepared for activity.

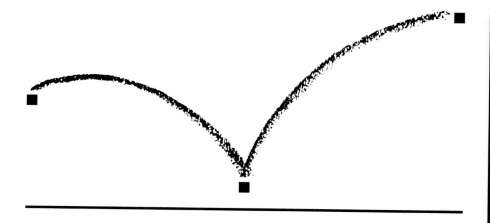

Use for Gymnasts

More and more gymnasts are finding the benefits of dance training in their performances. A dance curriculum can be found in the US Gymnastics Federation's training program for both boys' and girls' artistic gymnastics (and women's rhythmic gymnastics). Girls compete in dance in addition to their other four events at the lower levels, and boys are tested for dance skills at the regional and national levels. The two arts are closely related. Gymnasts are dancers with more degrees of freedom, plus they have apparatus to work on. Rhythm, correct alignment, position awareness, and landing techniques are practiced constantly in the course of dance training. I encourage any of you who are interested in artistic gymnastics as a competitive endeavor to begin dance training at some early point in your career, and to continue throughout your career. In addition, dance skills can easily be introduced in school units or courses for beginners. As I have often heard pointed out in dance classes, you practice dance moves every day. Each time you stretch up on your toes for a high object, you are doing a *relevé*. Each time you raise your hand in class, you are doing a *port de bras*. Of course, in these cases you are not stressing specific techniques, but the point is made.

There are many books on the market that discuss dance technique. One that is written specifically for gymnasts is *DANCE IN GYMNASTICS—A Guide for Coaches and Gymnasts* by Denise Gula, published by Wm. C. Brown Co. Publishers. If you read this book you will have a good idea of the relationship between dance and gymnastics, learn dance terms, and learn how to perform many dance movements that will help you in your gymnastics.

Skills to Learn

Some of the things you will want to know are: foot and arm positions; how to perform a *plié, relevé, tendu, dégagé, battement, développé, rond de jambe*, various *ports de bras, chassé*, various jumps (plain, tucked, straddled, split, *sissonne*, twists) and leaps (stride, split, stag, *assemblé*); and various combinations of these movements. A number of dance skills are introduced in chapter 8 (**Balance Beam**). (Most dance terms are in French as dance movements were codified by the French, and the terminology has been passed down from the seventeenth century, but these terms have been assimilated into each culture that practices classical ballet and the modern and jazz styles that evolved from it.) Many of the skills can be practiced free standing or at a ballet *barre* (pronounced: bahr), which could be a balance beam or parallel bar or even a wall in a gymnastics gym. If you use a *barre,* do not lean on it for support, just hold it lightly to help with balance if you need to.

You can practice any movements to music to get an idea of beat and rhythm. A source of rhythm is often a beating drum. These movements do not have to be complex. If you watch any dance class, you will see that dancers begin with basic skills, just as gymnasts do, and practice them before going on to more advanced skills and combinations. You can make up a series of skills or have someone such as a teacher or a fellow student present you with one to work on. I recall reading articles in two issues of *Gymnast* magazine (May 1975, pp. 60–61; June 1975, pp. 56–57) called "I've Got Rhythm" that were addressed to boys and described many rhythm drills that have been used in the USA boys' program. *International Gymnast* magazine often has dance articles aimed at gymnasts' education. In any dance class I have attended, there were various combinations of basic skills interspersed with more complex movements that made me feel quite uncoordinated at first, but were fun after a few tries and became progressively smoother as they were practiced.

Rhythm Exercises

Try walking or swaying your body to different rhythms and music. Surely you will not want to walk to a classical piece the same as you would walk to a reggae number. Try moving your arms in a set pattern for, say, eight counts. Then try moving each arm through the pattern. Finally, try moving your arms independently, that is on different counts, perhaps moving one through the sequence on the first count and the other on the second count. This will bring a lot of levity to a class as students try to coordinate their movements. Be careful not to elevate your shoulders when moving your arms—keep your shoulders depressed (down) and relaxed to avoid several bad consequences: (1) this is a source of fatigue and balance loss on both floor exercise and balance beam; and (2) it will cause your neck to appear shorter, which is not desired.

These days we are surrounded by a variety of music and rhythms, and most of us can move with a sense of timing that is useful to dance and gymnastics.

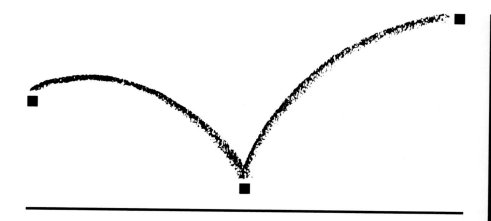

Tumbling is often the first activity of artistic gymnastics to which students are introduced. Floor exercise, which consists of tumbling and transitional skills such as balances, leaps, flexibility, dance, and acrobatics, plus (for men only) strength and hold moves, is performed on a 12-meter by 12-meter area, which these days is usually carpet over foam resting on some sort of spring-supported floor system. Tumbling skills may be learned on this type of surface, but it is not necessary for beginning skills. A mat placed on the gymnasium floor is often all there is on which to perform tumbling skills. Many types of mats are available for this activity, which is often the first type of gymnastics activity to which students are exposed. In fact, many begin to tumble on playgrounds or house lawns, as I did. Some even tumble in the streets, but this is not to be encouraged as the street is an unforgiving surface on which to perform.

This chapter deals with tumbling; the next covers transitions. Beginning tumbling skills progress from rolls through various springs and kips. All should be taught from a stand before a run is introduced. For some students, the use of an inclined mat can help in learning many skills. This is a mat that looks like a wedge of pie on its side, so there is an inclined surface to roll down or spring down. An alternative is to put a soft mat such as a skill cushion on a vaulting board, thus creating an inclined mat. Be sure that there is a soft mat at the end of this inclined surface, in case your student goes beyond it.

Both front saltos (tuck and pike) and back saltos (tuck, pike, and layout) are rated as medium difficulty skills (B value) in the current men's rules, but the women's rules rate them as beginning (A value) skills. Since a feeling for saltoing (somersaulting) is necessary for many skills on other events, I have included tucked saltos here. It is interesting to note that, as of this writing, a salto dismount from the rings, parallel bars, or horizontal bar is a beginning skill in men's rules, while on the floor it is rated higher.

A competition floor exercise for boys is composed of at least three different tumbling passes composed of various tumbling moves, a strength part, and a balance on one hand or foot. Girls must show more in terms of dance and choreography connecting at least three tumbling passes, and perform to music (this is the only event that has musical accompaniment). They must have rhythm changes in their exercises corresponding to their music, and show leaps of great amplitude for maximum effect. Both girls and boys are required to utilize the entire floor area, but girls do so more as they have more freedom of movement in their routines. There are minimum difficulty requirements for the moves shown as well. A girl's routine lasts 70–90 seconds, while a boy's lasts 50–70 seconds.

Organization of This Chapter

Forward Roll

Tucked (Figure 5.1)

Figure 5.1a, b, c, d, e

a.

b.

c.

d.

e.

Squat down with your feet together and place your hands on the mat about shoulder width just in front of where your knees would go if they touched the mat. Look at your toes to help duck your head forward and to make your neck and back rounded. Push your body over your head by extending your legs as you lower your head, barely touching the mat with the back of your head, then roll on your back from your shoulder blades to your seat, and up to your feet, returning to the tucked position that you started in. Reach forward as you finish your roll to help you to get up. (Some find that holding their shins in the tucked position helps maintain the tuck.) You can wind up exactly as you started, ready for another, or you can stand up directly.

Common problems are not maintaining a rounded shape when rolling (especially at the end of the roll), straightening your legs before rolling up to your feet, and looking to the side when starting the roll, which makes you go crooked. You can practice the end of the roll by rocking back and forth on your back in a tucked position and rocking up to your feet (you will open and close your tucked position a bit to develop roll momentum—open as you start to move down and close as you approach your feet).

To help a student who has trouble starting the roll, hold his head in place with your left hand and lift his left thigh or knee with your right hand. If he has trouble completing the roll, grasp his waist and help him up at the end of the roll, provided he has not opened his body or legs to prevent the completion of the skill.

■
Spotting

Variations of a Tucked Forward Roll   There are a variety of ways to perform even a simple tucked forward roll. Four of these are shown in figures 5.2–5.5. When you come from a handstand, at first you may bend your arms as you lower to the mat and lean forward into the roll. As you get better, keep your arms straight as shown.

Figure 5.2a, b, c, d
This is a step-in entry to a no-handed roll with a one-leg-tucked roll position.

a.   b.   c.   d.

Figure 5.3a, b, c
Here is a step-out finish.

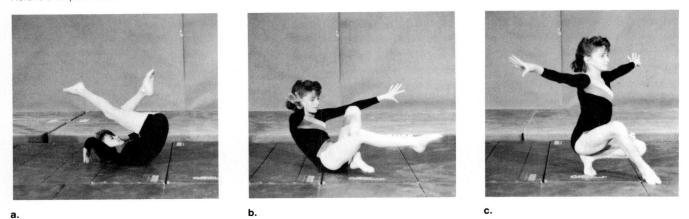

a.   b.   c.

Figure 5.4a, b, c
This is a finish in a kneeling lunge.

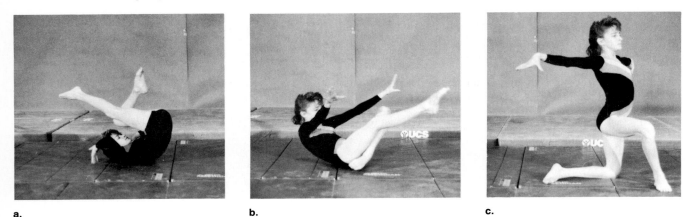

a.   b.   c.

■

**Spotting the Roll
from a Handstand**

If your student falls over excessively, giving him too much momentum for a smooth roll, block his legs a bit and guide him to the mat (note that when he progresses to a straight-legged roll he will want that extra momentum).

Tucked Forward Roll to Various Jumps   To use the momentum generated by a roll, there are a few exercises that we practice to use in floor exercise performance later on, and to get landing practice from a low height. These jumps,

Figure 5.5a, b, c, d
Rolling from a handstand.

a.   b.   c.   d.

shown in figures 5.6–5.11, proceed directly from your roll, after first doing them from a stand to get the feel of them. First off, simply jump up after completing a roll and land in a partial squat (*demi plié*) to dissipate the force of landing. You can then vary the jump by trying a tucked jump, a straddled jump, a straddled toe touch, a piked jump, or a twisting jump. In all cases, jump with your body upright and go straight up. When doing the twisting jumps, you can experiment with different arm positions to see how this affects your ability to twist. Start with your arms wide and then, while in the air, keep them there, or put them overhead, or put them by your sides, or wrap them close to your chest or abdomen. As an alternative, start with your arms narrow and open them as you are in the air. Which way works best? It does not matter which direction you twist; just jump up and twist.

The common problem with these jumps is that you are not upright and aligned when you begin your jump. Even though you are bent over when performing the straddled toe touch, you will finish upright if you start upright. If you do not start upright, your landing will be askew and will be difficult to control.

You can aid with all of these jumps, if necessary, by following behind to provide support by lifting your student at the waist where practical. NOTE: Watch which direction your student twists (do not give instruction). He will usually twist in the direction that is most comfortable for him, and this is a signal which way he should learn subsequent skills that require a twisting action.

■

Spotting

Figure 5.6
A straight jump.

Figure 5.7
A tucked jump (slight form breaks).

Figure 5.8
A straddled jump.

Figure 5.9
A straddled toe touch (feet slightly hooked).

Figure 5.10
A piked toe touch (bad foot/toe form).

Figure 5.11a, b, c, d, e, f, g
A jump to full turn—note Eli looking for an
orientation spot and opening his arms to
slow his twist.

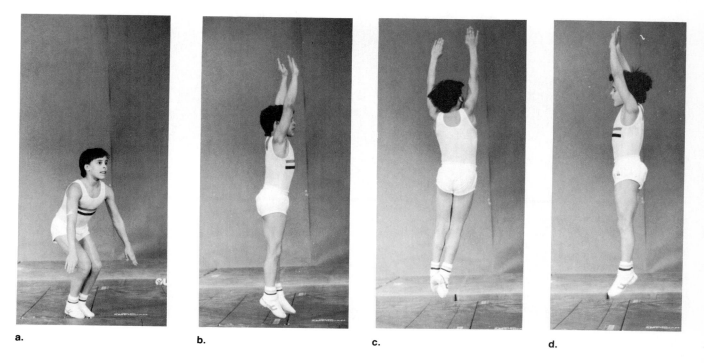

a.

b.

c.

d.

e.

f.

g.

Floor Exercise—Tumbling

Figure 5.12a, b, c, d

a.

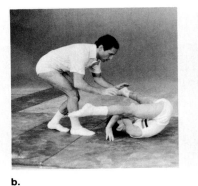

b.

c.

d.

Piked Straddled (Figure 5.12)

The starting position is a piked straddled stand, with your hands placed on the mat directly below your shoulders. As you begin the roll by lowering the back of your head toward the mat, round your back. If you maintain this body position, you should have no trouble coming back up to your feet. As soon as your hands leave the mat, bring them around to reach for the mat between your legs so that you can push down on the mat to help you get up. If you have good straddle flexibility you may not need to push on the mat to get up to your feet.

Common problems are not being able to straddle widely enough to get up easily, and not having the flexibility to push down on the mat between your legs far enough to help you get up. You can practice the end of this roll as I explained in the tucked roll, by rocking back and forth on your back in a round-backed piked straddle. Reach for the mat between your legs and push down on it. If you do not get up at first, keep at it—you will soon.

■

Spotting

Since your student's legs are straddled, you cannot spot this skill from the side. You have to move behind him and follow closely as the roll proceeds. You can reach over him to aid in the start of the action. Grasp his waist to help in the completion of the roll.

Figure 5.13a, b, c, d, e

a.　　　　　　　b.　　　　　　　c.

d.　　　　　　　e.

Piked (Figure 5.13)

This is the most difficult of the simple forward rolls, as your legs are together and you must have good hip flexibility and a strong push on the mat to complete the roll. This roll is most often done from a handstand as you can develop momentum falling from the handstand to help complete the skill. To perform it from a stand, begin by squatting partly and reaching out a bit from your feet. Push off from your feet into the roll and into a pike, and as your hands contact the mat duck your head forward and round your back. As soon as your hands come off the mat, reach for the floor beside your thighs and push down hard. This will make you pike tightly and enable you to come to your feet. Keep your toes pointed during the roll, and this will help you to get up. Practice the end of the roll as you did the previous two rolls.

Common problems are not rolling fast enough, reaching in the wrong place for an efficient push, and not having enough hip flexibility (usually due to tight hamstring muscles).

■

Spotting

Stand to the side, and lift your student's seat or waist to aid in the completion of the skill.

Dive (Figures 5.14 and 5.15)

To get the feel of the end of a dive roll you can stand on an elevated platform (a mat, a spotting block), lean over, and roll to the surface below. Build this up gradually and you will learn how to reduce the force of contact with the mat. You will also learn why you do not want to hit your head hard when doing forward rolls. Imagine how it would shake you up if you landed on your head

Figure 5.14a, b, c, d, e, f
A dive roll from a stand.

a.

b.

c.

d.

e.

f.

when you were supposed to roll past it—you could get hurt. CAUTION: This move involves a head-under landing from a height and must be approached with good preparation! Now to do a dive roll, stand on the mat, squat slightly, look at a spot far enough in front of you so that you cannot reach it, and jump so that your hands land in that area as your body goes over your head (figure 5.14). Watch your hands hit the mat, then duck your head and bend your arms to reduce the force of contact. Assume a tucked position as your body passes over your hands. This roll can be done in other body positions but you should try the tucked roll first as it is the easiest. The end of the roll is just like the roll from a stand. You can do several roll-to-dive-roll combinations in a row to get used to the move. After you are competent at a standing dive roll, add some running steps and a hurdle to two feet ahead of it so that you can fly through the air a bit (figure 5.15). Eventually you will want to do this skill with a slightly arched body at the height of your head when you are standing. Get spotted at first as this approach has much more momentum to deal with plus a greater drop to the mat.

Common problems are not rotating enough to get your body past your hands and head, and assuming a tuck position before rotating enough.

Figure 5.15a, b, c, d, e, f
A dive roll from a run and hurdle to two feet.

a.

b.

c.

d.

e.

f.

■

Spotting

Stand to the side and support your student by reaching under his body. For low rolls you may have to kneel rather than stand in order to reach under him. In this way you can adjust his flight path and can affect his rotation. Be sure to follow the student all the way into the roll.

Backward Roll

Tucked (Figures 5.16 and 5.17)

This skill requires a bit of care when attempting it, as you can put pressure on your head that forces your neck into flexion and can cause possible injury if not performed correctly. However, most everyone learns it with a minimum of trouble. To begin, squat down and put your hands by your ears with your fingers pointing down and your palms facing back. Your elbows are flexed and close to your forehead. Look down at your toes and keep looking at them throughout the roll to promote good position. Simply sit back and pull your feet over your head. As your hands hit the mat, push against the mat to keep pressure off your head and to push up to your feet. The faster you do this roll, the easier it will be. Keep tucked and you will land in a squat just as when you started. To help you learn how to push on the mat when doing this roll, a drill is to stand in a pike with your hands and feet on the mat (like figure 5.19d), duck your head, and do a type of pushup, lowering the back of your neck toward the mat and then pushing back up to your piked stand with your hands still on the mat.

Common problems are opening from the tuck when going backward, reaching back late, not pushing hard enough with your hands, and rolling off to the side.

Figure 5.16a, b, c, d
Spotting a first backward roll very closely—
note a hand under Lindsay's neck to keep
her full weight off it.

a.   b.   c.   d.

For a first-time beginner, kneel next to your student and place your right hand under her neck to lift up and keep pressure off it (figure 5.16). Your left hand goes under her lower back and lifts as well to get her over. If she knows how to push down on the mat to keep pressure off her neck, then stand to the side and help her to move smoothly into the roll. As she becomes inverted, it is helpful to lift up on her hips to relieve pressure on her neck and head, and to allow her body to go over this sticking point. Small children with proportionally large heads may have trouble with this skill.

Figure 5.17a, b, c, d, e

a.

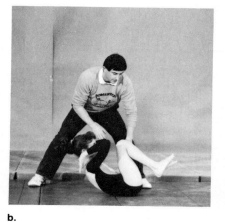

b.

c.

d.

e.

Figure 5.18a, b, c, d, e

a.

b.

c.

d.

e.

Piked Straddled (Figure 5.18)

This roll looks like the piked straddled forward roll in reverse. You begin in a piked straddled stand and reach between your legs (which increases your pike) for the mat as you sit back. This pulls you into a rounded-back position to enable you to roll, and absorbs some of the momentum of the fall. As your seat hits the mat, bring your hands up by your ears and reach for the mat that is coming up behind your head. Pull your straddled legs over and outside of your shoulders. Push on the mat to finish in a straddled stand. When doing this roll you generally do not want to be in a wide straddle, as that will cut down on your momentum.

Common problems are going too slowly, opening your pike during the roll, bending your knees, and not pulling your legs over your shoulders forcefully enough.

Figure 5.19a, b, c, d, e

Note knee bends in figures b and d.

a.　　　　　　　　　　　b.　　　　　　　　　　　c.

d.

e.

You cannot spot this close to your student's side, so it is necessary to follow her as the roll is performed or wait until she goes by and then reach in quickly (do not get hit by her leg). Lifting on her waist is the usual aid, as most who have trouble will get stuck trying to get past the inverted position.

■

Spotting

Piked (Figure 5.19)

As with the piked straddled backward roll, this looks like the piked forward roll in reverse. Begin by bending over and reaching for the floor behind your thighs. As you sit back, your hands will contact the mat and act a bit as shock absorbers to somewhat cushion the contact with the mat (just a bit—otherwise you could injure your wrists). As your seat touches the mat, bring your arms up and reach behind your head. Pull your legs over your head and push down on the mat to arrive at a piked stand.

Common problems are not going fast enough, reaching back late, not pushing hard enough, and opening from your pike.

■

Spotting

Stand by your student's side and watch that she does not fall out of control into the roll. As with other backward rolls, lifting her waist will help in the completion of the skill where necessary.

Extension (Figures 5.20 and 5.21)

Figure 5.20a, b, c, d
A bent-armed back extension.

a.

b.

c.

d.

Figure 5.21a, b, c, d
A straight-armed back extension.

a.

b.

c.

d.

This is the backward roll most often seen in competition, and it has many variations. It is usually done from a tucked or piked position. Having a good handstand will make this easier to perform. To learn this from a tuck or pike, begin a backward roll. As your legs pass over your head, extend your body to a straight position and press down on the mat vigorously. Watch your toes at the start of the opening to avoid throwing your head back, which would cause you to arch excessively. As you reach the handstand position, look at your hands out of the tops of your eyes. You can then pike down or step down to the mat, or stay up and pirouette (see chapter 6). You will have to experiment to find exactly when you should extend your body to achieve the handstand. Once you become proficient with this movement, you can try to upgrade it by performing it with straight arms. To do this you must move faster into the roll, and bring your legs farther over your body. Keep your hands in one of two positions at this time: with your fingers pointing toward each other and your wrists hyperextended (the backs of your hands are pulled toward your forearms), or with your palms facing back toward the mat (forearms supinated) and your wrists extended (hands in line with your forearms). Be careful to keep your fingers together since a loose finger can jam into the mat. Pull your arms back hard as you go into the roll, and keep pushing against the mat as you go up. If you make a thud as your hands hit the mat, you probably reached back late—a good one is relatively quiet.

Common problems are extending at the wrong time so that the handstand is missed and having poor position in the handstand.

Grasp your student's legs from the side and pull her to the handstand. A good drill is to put her on her back in a pike and have her go through the extending action while you guide her legs on the way up.

■

Spotting

Cartwheel

Monkey Jump (Figure 5.22)

This is a lead-up skill if you have trouble learning a cartwheel. This often happens if you are weak in the upper body and do not feel comfortable holding your weight on your hands. (It is a good idea to practice kicking up from a lunge toward a handstand and lowering to a lunge as described in the next chapter to get a feeling of supporting your weight on your hands.) To learn this low cartwheel motion, find a line to learn it on. Decide whether you want to put your left hand or your right hand down first (eventually you will learn both). I have found that if you prefer to twist to your left (left shoulder back), then you usually prefer to put your left hand down first. Squat down on the line with your feet on it, turned out, and spread a little wider than your shoulders. If you are going to your left, look to your left and put your left hand on the line with your fingers facing to the left of the line about a shoulder width away. Jump around so that your right hand lands on the line about a shoulder width away from your left hand and with the fingers of your right hand facing the same way as your left hand. Looking at your hands will help. You must lean on your hands so that your legs come around and your feet land on the line one at a

a.   b.   c.   d.

time, your right foot first, followed by your left foot. As you shift your weight to your feet, your hands will push off the line, and you will end up as you started. If you can do this skill, you just start working up toward a cartwheel by kicking your feet higher and higher until you go over the top of your hands and can straighten your legs.

Common problems are not landing on the line due to not putting your weight over your hands, and not putting your hands and feet down one at a time (left hand, right hand, right foot, left foot).

■

Spotting

Stand behind and to the side that your student will move toward. Lift up on his waist to guide him to the line.

Two-armed (Figure 5.23)

Now that you are ready to do an upright cartwheel, you should know that there are several varieties (side-to-side, side-to-back, front-to-side, and front-to-back). When we say front-to-back, we mean that you start facing forward and finish facing where you started from, facing backward. Each cartwheel has its uses, and you should learn them all. To begin a left side-to-side cartwheel, which is the kind you will do to perform a series of cartwheels, begin in a sideward lunge with your arms over your head. If you can do this on a line, it will help you to learn a straight cartwheel, which will help your future tumbling. Keeping your arms in the same position throughout the movement, push off with your right leg, reach for the mat along the line you have selected, and put your left hand down with your fingers facing where your back is facing. As you shift your weight to your left hand, pull your right leg up and over your body so that you split widely. Your left foot pushes off the mat just before your right hand contacts the mat. The fingers of your right hand may face the same as your left, or may point toward your left hand. I find the second choice helps me in fast cartwheels and relates directly to a later skill, the roundoff. At the midpoint of the cartwheel, you will pass through a straddled handstand. You should be

Figure 5.23a, b, c, d, e, f, g
A side-to-side cartwheel.

a.   b.   c.   d.

e.   f.   g.

looking at your hands. Once you pass this position, bring your right foot down to the line as your left hand comes off the mat. The move is completed by pushing off with your right hand (both arms are still overhead) and by bringing your left leg to the line, passing through another sideward lunge to a straddled stand.

Common problems are not kicking directly overhead, going off the line, arching, piking, and changing leg or arm positions (especially reducing your straddle as you go over or dropping an arm).

Stand on the back side just ahead of your student and touch your right hand to his left side. As he moves into the cartwheel, reach over with your left hand, grasp his waist, and help him over the top and down to the line. Watch out for bent legs, which will hit you.

■

Spotting

Figure 5.24a, b, c, d, e
A one-armed front-to-back cartwheel using the first arm.

a.

b.

c.

d.

e.

One-armed (Figure 5.24)

Once you have mastered the two-armed cartwheel, moving to the one-armed variety should not be difficult. You have a choice here. You may put your first hand or your second hand down. Each has its uses. I like to teach the first-hand-down cartwheel as a lead up for a roundoff, and ask my students to do them as front-to-back cartwheels. This teaches you to do a pirouette (a turn) on your first arm. However, in girls' gymnastics on balance beam and floor exercise, the second-hand variety is more commonly seen.

Common problems and spotting are the same as for two-armed cartwheels.

Series (Figure 5.25)

This can be a fun set of skills because you can go quite fast. Your hand contact will not be as noticeably one-two as for slow cartwheels, you will push off with your hands much harder than for slow cartwheels, and your legs will not be as

Figure 5.25a, b, c, d
This is the transition between cartwheels.
Note that Coach Winnie can keep her right
hand in contact with her student during the
fast cartwheels; Stephan should keep his
arms overhead as he stands up.

a.   b.   c.   d.

wide upon landing as you will need to make a fast transition between cartwheels during your foot contact phase. As you finish one cartwheel, instead of pushing up to a straddled stand you stay a little low and pass from the finishing lunge position directly to the starting lunge. Be sure to keep your arms overhead and look where you are going. Straight cartwheels are necessary unless you plan to explore the area off the mat.

Common problems: the same as for slow cartwheels.

It takes a bit of sidestepping to spot these fast-moving skills. You can keep contact with your student throughout the series with one hand, but the other will have to change between cartwheels. For left cartwheels, I keep my right hand in contact with my student's left side by his waist.

■

Spotting

Dive (Figure 5.26)

Just as you added a dive to a forward roll when you mastered it, you can add a dive to a cartwheel. This is often done with an underreach, which means that you start with your arms down and behind you and reach out into the movement. It is also usually done from a run and hurdle where your arms are not held overhead during the hurdle as most other skills demand (hurdles are described next), but are held behind you. To become airborne, as you step onto your bent front leg (through a lunge) and into the cartwheel, push hard into the movement with your back leg and then push down on the mat as hard as you can with your front leg while swinging your arms from behind to in front of you (this is the underreach). You will contact the mat with your body upside down and find it easy to complete the skill.

Common problems are reaching out too far so that the completion of the skill is hindered, and going around the side rather than overhead.

a. b. c. d.

■

Spotting

The same as for the slow cartwheel, but of course you have to move with your flying student.

Hurdle (Figures 5.27, 5.28, and 5.29)

Several kinds of hurdles are used to connect a run with a tumbling skill that begins with a step into a lunge. They all wind up in the same lunge position. It is important to learn an efficient hurdle as you cannot run forever before tumbling to build up speed. At this writing, boys are allowed only three steps before beginning a tumbling pass in floor exercise, and girls are allowed as many steps as they can fit into their tumbling pass, often as many as six. Although you may hurdle fairly upright, it is very important to maintain forward velocity during your hurdle and to push your whole body as a unit into the following tumbling skill, not just reach down with your arms. And when you hurdle, your feet are relatively in line as if you were working on the balance beam—they step on your running line.

The first uses a stretched skip step (figure 5.27). As you run down the mat, take a skip out of one of your steps. As you skip, lift your arms overhead. If you put your right hand down first for a cartwheel or a roundoff, you will skip on your left foot—step on your left foot, hop on your left foot bringing your right leg forward—then step out on your right foot into a lunge with both legs bent. Note that your legs stay fairly straight during the airborne phase of the skip, and your arms stay overhead. As you go into your next skill, it is important to push forward with your back leg. I prefer this hurdle to the others.

The second hurdle (figure 5.28) looks similar to the first in that it, too, is a skip step, but in this case the leg that you bring up in front of your other one is bent (sometimes both legs are bent). I do not think it is as pretty as the previous one, but it is often used.

Figure 5.27a, b, c, d, e

a.　　　b.　　　c.　　　d.　　　e.

Figure 5.28a, b, c, d, e
Compare figures b and c to the previous hurdle.

a.　　　b.　　　c.　　　d.　　　e.

The third hurdle uses a *chassé* action (figure 5.29). The difference between this one and the previous two is that during this hurdle your legs do not cross. So if you put your right hand down first for a cartwheel or roundoff, you will start your *chassé* on your right foot—step on your right foot, hop from your right foot to your left foot while traveling forward (but do not bring your left leg forward), and then step out into a lunge with your right foot leading. Your left foot will trail behind your right foot throughout the hurdle.

Figure 5.29a, b, c
A *chassé* hurdle—note the legs do not switch position.

a.   b.   c.

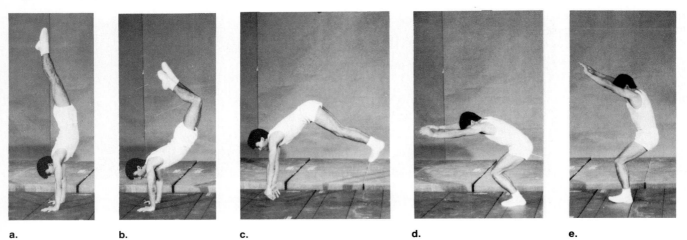

a. b. c. d. e.

Snapdown (Figure 5.30)

This skill is the finishing action of a roundoff and a backward handspring and is an action used in other skills on other events. From a handstand, you sag in your shoulders a bit and arch your back. You may even bend your legs, but eventually you should do it without knee flexion. Start to fall toward a front support and rapidly pull your feet down to the mat as you push hard on the mat to thrust your trunk up. I explain this as a snap up of your upper body along with a snap down of your legs. As your hands leave the mat, lift them forcefully so that they are overhead as soon as possible. Think of putting your feet right where your hands were to help you turn over. Your knees will be slightly bent

Figure 5.31a, b, c, d
Using a vaulting board as an elevated surface to start from.

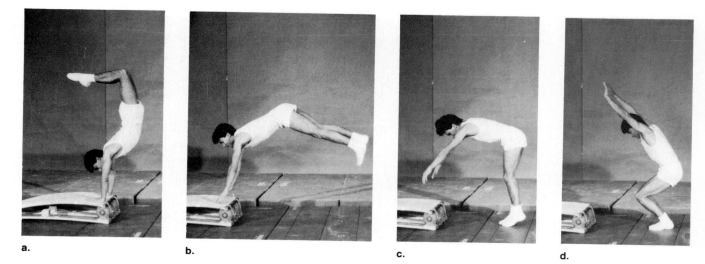

a.   b.   c.   d.

on contact with the mat. You can do one at a time, or several in a row by rebounding from the mat back up to a handstand and then snapping down again (called mule kicks). If you have trouble rotating to an upright position, do the snapdown from a slightly elevated surface such as a vaulting board to help you to get the feeling (figure 5.31). If you are a beginner who has little pushing power, you should cover the board with a mat in case you land on it.

Common problems are not pushing down hard, not trying to pull your feet under you, and leaving your arms down at the finish.

Roundoff (Figure 5.32)

This is one of the most important skills to learn, as the roundoff is the usual skill that converts a forward run into backward movement. If you have mastered a front-to-back cartwheel, and can do a first-arm cartwheel, then you will have little trouble with a roundoff. For a left roundoff, as you step into the roundoff, which begins exactly like a fast front-to-back cartwheel, push vigorously off your right foot (your right knee flexes and then extends) and pull your right leg directly over your body. Reach for the mat with your arms and body aligned, not just with your arms. Turn on your left hand just as you did for the front-to-back cartwheel. In this way, your right hand will help push you to a good finish position. Remember to put your right hand down with those fingers facing your left hand, and put it somewhat in line with your left hand (you will see your hands when you are upside down—do not close your eyes). As you turn upside down, bring your feet together as soon as possible (this will happen on the way down), pull them down, and push down hard on the mat. This is the snapdown part of the roundoff. You want to land with your arms up over your head, your knees and hips slightly flexed, and your body fairly upright. The skill that follows your roundoff will determine the optimum place for your feet to land (blocking angle) and the position your body should be in.

Figure 5.32a, b, c, d, e, f
Courtney's landing position in figure e is too low, and note the spotter switches his hand position quickly between figures d and e to catch her to prevent a backward fall.

a.

b.

c.

d.

e.

f.

A variation of hand placement is to put your hands on opposite sides of your running-direction line—your left hand goes on the right side (with your hand turned more so that your fingers point somewhat back to where you just were), and your right hand goes on the left side. This requires more of a trunk turn as you lower your trunk toward the mat, but gives more of a two-handed push into your snapdown.

An excellent drill for a roundoff is to do a one-armed roundoff using your first arm only. This will teach you to turn on your first arm (pirouette), to go directly overhead with your legs, and to tumble in a straight line. Another excellent drill is to start in a stride-squat (like figure 5.32a but lower—about halfway down) and do the roundoff from there. This teaches you to push with your back leg as well as your front leg, and to get your body down to the mat with your arms aligned.

Common problems are not maintaining good arm-trunk alignment, not pushing off either or both legs to get past your hands forcefully enough, not kicking your lead leg hard over the top, jumping onto your hands rather than putting your first hand down while you still have your front foot on the mat, putting both of your hands down on one side of your running line, hurdling crooked, and not pushing hard enough on the mat.

Done just as for a cartwheel, and in so doing you can help to twist your student's body. Stand or kneel on her leading-hand side and next to where her hands will go on the mat, so if she does not kick over the top you will not get kicked.

■

Spotting

Limberover

Backward (Figure 5.33)

This skill takes a good bit of shoulder and back flexibility. You have practiced the lead up if you have incorporated bridging in your warmup (see chapter 2) and are able to do one with straight arms and legs—with your arms, trunk, and legs forming a continuous arch. If you are able to rock back and forth in a bridge, you should feel where your weight is transferring from center to over your hands or to over your feet. In fact, if you are able to rock sufficiently to push up forward to a stand or push up backward to a handstand, you will have done a lot of preparation for both limberovers.

Begin in a stand with your hands overhead and feet together. Reach back with your hands for the mat behind you, and shift your hips forward to counterbalance. As your hands go down, you will come to a point where your weight will shift back and onto your hands. (This portion is called a backbend.) At this point, push off with your feet to move your shoulders past your hands. Your body will follow so that you can lift your feet up to a handstand. Your shoulders will shift forward a bit while you are on the way to the handstand. Once you reach the handstand, pike down to the mat and stand upright with your arms over your head. Keep your eyes on your hands from the start of this skill until you are on your way to a stand.

Common problems often stem from a lack of flexibility, which will prevent the correct execution of this skill. If your shoulders and/or back are tight it will be difficult to place your hands on the mat properly during the backbend or shift your weight over your hands in the middle of the limberover. Obviously, the closer you can put your hands to your feet, the easier this skill will be. If you do not shift your hips forward when reaching back you will fall backward.

Support your student's lower back on the way down, and lift his lower back and legs to help complete the skill. Be sure he passes through a good handstand position.

■

Spotting

Figure 5.33a, b, c, d, e, f
In figures d and e Benji's shoulders should
be a bit farther past his hands.

a.

b.

c.

d.

e.

f.

Forward (Figure 5.34)

Like the backward limberover, this skill requires great flexibility to perform it
easily. Begin in a stand with your feet together and arms up and step into a
lunge. Kick through a handstand slowly and begin to overarch. As you do this
you must shift your shoulders to counterbalance your legs, which are going over
your body and toward the mat. As you continue to arch, your shoulders flex as
far as possible and your back arches to allow your feet to contact the mat. At
this point, keep looking at your hands, push on the mat with your hands (all
the way through your fingertips), and shift your weight onto and past your feet.
(It is allowable to flex your knees slightly during the second half of this skill,

Figure 5.34a, b, c, d, e, f
Benji's weight should be shifted more over
his feet in figure d.

a.

b.

c.

d.

e.

f.

but not as you finish it.) Continue the movement up to a stand, straighten your legs, and keep your eyes on your hands until an upright position is achieved.

Common problems are similar to the backward limberover in terms of flexibility requirements. If your shoulders and/or back are tight it will be difficult to shift your weight to your feet at the end of the movement. Lifting your head before the finish of the skill often pulls your hands off the mat early, preventing a complete push. And the closer you can put your feet to your hands, the easier this skill will be.

Figure 5.35a, b, c, d, e, f

b.

c.

d.
e.
f.

■

Spotting

Assist from the side by supporting your student's shoulders and lower back during the execution of the move.

Walkover

Backward (Figure 5.35)

Whereas limberovers are performed with your legs together, walkovers are performed with your legs in a stride position, and ideally in a stride split. This skill starts as you lift your lead leg up in front of you as high as you can while holding your arms overhead. (If this is difficult, start in a slightly staggered stance with no weight on your front toes—which in dance is called a *tendu*—and do not worry about holding your lead leg up to start.) When your leg is as high as it can go, reach back with your hands for the mat (while watching them and looking for the mat), and shift your weight forward over your support leg (which will bend a bit). You bend backward in sequence—arms and head, then back, then knee (just as much as is necessary). As you touch the mat, push off with your foot and shift your weight over and a bit past your hands, moving to a split handstand. As you pass through the handstand, bring your lead foot to the mat while you hold your trailing leg as high as you can. Bring your body up while holding your trailing leg up (in an arabesque position). Finish by stepping back onto your lowered trailing leg so that you can do another. For variations, you can put your legs together when you reach a handstand, or switch your legs so that you step down on the foot that left the mat last.

Common problems are similar to the backward limberover, but here you want to be sure to keep your hips square—facing forward—as you lift your leg and begin the move. As you pass over the top, your split should be in line with your line of movement.

Done as you would for a backward limberover. You can help your student emphasize the split of her legs by helping her lift her lead leg with your left hand while supporting her lower back with your right hand at the start of the walkover, by shifting both hands once the handstand is imminent and pushing down on her legs to promote the split, and by holding her trailing leg up with your right hand while supporting her abdomen with your left hand as the move is completed. Or, as in figure f, you can help her lift her chest at the end of the walkover.

■

Spotting

Forward (Figure 5.36)

Begin the forward walkover by stepping into a lunge with your arms overhead. Kick through a handstand but do not join your legs—try to split them as far as possible throughout the skill. As you pass the handstand, you will shift your shoulders back a bit so that you do not fall forward. Bring your lead foot down to the mat as far under your body as possible, but hold your other foot as high as you can. Push smoothly off your hands through your fingertips and shift your weight onto your lead foot. Continue holding your trailing foot as high as possible and bring your body up to an upright position with your arms overhead. You can then step forward into a lunge and perform another forward walkover. As a variation, switch your legs as you pass through the handstand so that you step down on the foot that left the mat last.

Common problems are the same as for a limberover. Because you come up on one leg only, it may be more difficult to stand up. And keep your hips square so that your split is along your line of movement.

Done as you would for a forward limberover, but you can help your student emphasize the split of her legs by pushing down on her legs with both hands to promote the split once the handstand is imminent, and by holding her trailing leg up with your left hand and supporting her back with your right hand as the move is completed. Or, as in figure e, you can help her to lift her chest as she finishes.

■

Spotting

Figure 5.36a, b, c, d, e, f

a.

b.

c.

d.

e.

f.

Neck Kip (Figure 5.37)

The neck kip is not seen too often in a floor exercise as it is difficult to work out of, but it is useful for developing pushing power and timing. Begin the skill by lying back on your shoulders in a deep pike with your hands on the mat by your ears and your fingers pointing toward your shoulders. This position is reminiscent of the hand placement for a backward roll or a bridge up. Lift your hips so that your weight is over your shoulders and hands. Move your hips forward just before you begin to open rapidly from the pike, so that your flight path will be forward and upward, not straight upward (you will wind up in a handstand if you do not move your hips forward). While this rapid opening is occurring, push down hard on the mat behind your head. As you finish opening into an arch, you should become airborne. Keep your head back and watch your hands—but do not pull your arms forward. If you are fairly limber, you will have no problem pulling your feet under you to allow you to stand up. The finish position

a.   b.   c.   d.

is an upright stand with your arms overhead. If you have trouble getting to your feet, you can do this skill from a raised surface such as a folded mat. This will allow you a bit more time to turn over if you need it. You can drill the first half of this move by kipping to a bridge from your inverted pike, learning how to open rapidly and to push backward on the ground.

Common problems are not pushing hard enough on the mat, pulling your hands off the mat rather than pushing off with them, pulling your arms forward, not arching enough to get your feet under your body, and opening too slow.

On your knees by your student's side, put your right hand behind his neck or upper shoulders and your left hand under his back. As the opening is initiated, lift up. Be careful if he drops his arms on the way up! This can give you a good whack on the head.

Spotting

Headspring (Figure 5.38)

Before you try a headspring (or head kip) it is a good idea to try a piked press to a headstand, then arch over to a bridge, and push up to a forward limberover. This way you will have an idea of what it feels like to go through the headspring in slow motion. However, the placement of your head in relation to your hands is different here than for a headstand, as we are not concerned with a stable base of balance for this skill. Begin by squatting down and looking at the mat in front of you just beyond your outstretched, shoulder-width arms. Reach for the mat with your hands and put the top of your head on the mat between them as you extend your legs forcefully. This will drive your seat over your head and put you in a pike position. When you feel your seat is past your head, open your body rapidly into an arch—kip—and push down hard on the mat. You should become airborne. Keep your eyes on your hands until you finish the skill. Land with your arms overhead in an upright stand rather than in a squat stand. Your knees will flex slightly as you land. To perform another headspring, squat partially after landing and you are set up for the next one. These can be done quite rapidly. You can also do a roll to a headspring in series.

Figure 5.38a, b, c, d, e, f

a.

b.

c.

d.

e.

f.

Common problems are not pushing hard enough with your legs into the headspring, misplacing your head, rolling onto the back of your head rather than putting the top of your head down, kipping before your hips are sufficiently past your head, not pushing hard enough with your hands, pulling your hands off the mat rather than finishing your push off with them, pulling your head and/or arms forward once you leave the mat, and landing in a squat.

■

Spotting

Kneel to the side and just in front of where your student will put his hands. Your right hand reaches under his left shoulder, and your left hand reaches under his lower back. Both hands lift and guide.

a.   b.

c.   d.   e.

Forward Handspring Skills

Landing on Two Feet (Figure 5.39)

Before trying this skill you should be familiar with kicking to a handstand. In fact, if you can do a forward limberover, you will have almost done the forward (or front) handspring in slow motion (limberovers do not leave the mat; handsprings do). Although you seldom see this performed from a stand, it is a good training technique. Once you learn the feeling of the move, doing a jump and hurdle or run and hurdle will give you plenty of extra power to do more advanced tumbling work involving forward handsprings. Begin with your arms up and step quickly into a lunge with your back leg bent. Push off with your back leg onto your hands as if you want to pass through a handstand as fast as possible. Your arms may bend just a bit. Look at your hands throughout the move—from the moment they hit the mat until you attain a stand. As your first leg goes up, push off quickly with your second leg and bring it to your first leg. Push down on the mat with your hands as your legs pass overhead. You will be airborne in an arch with your arms overhead and will land in this position with your feet side by side.

Common problems are not pushing into the move forcefully enough, not continuing to kick over hard enough, letting your shoulders buckle forward during the hand contact phase so that you cannot push on the mat effectively, diving onto your hands, pulling your head forward before attaining a stand, and not arching enough. If you are quite flexible, be sure you are not just doing a fast front limberover, which does not get airborne as a front handspring does.

■

Spotting

Stand to the side and just ahead of where your student puts his hands on the mat. Your right hand reaches for his left upper arm, your left hand reaches under his back. Both hands lift and guide.

Step-out (Figure 5.40)

The forward handspring step-out is like a fast version of a forward walkover. It is performed just as a forward handspring is except that you do not join your legs, so that you land one foot at a time. Keep your legs split wide to allow you to pull your lead leg under you to help finish the skill. As a variation, try to switch your legs in midflight so that the foot that left the mat last is the first to land.

Common problems are similar to a front handspring, plus not pulling your lead leg around far or hard enough to make the landing easy.

The spot is the same as for a forward handspring.

Series

The step-out puts you in the position to go directly into another forward handspring (or a roundoff or a cartwheel). As you land on your lead leg, push forward into a lunge, look at the mat where you will put your hands, and do another handspring.

■

Spotting

You must sidestep rapidly to keep up with your student. It is possible to keep contact with her back with your left hand throughout the series. Your right hand will have to regrasp, however.

Tinsica (Figure 5.41)

The tinsica is a forward handspring done with your hands in a staggered pattern. As you reach for the mat, put one hand down before the other. You will not be able to push off this as well as with a regular handspring.

Figure 5.40a, b, c, d

a.   b.   c.   d.

Figure 5.41
Compare the hand placement of the tinsica to figure 5.40b.

From Two Feet (Figure 5.42)

This skill (also called a bounding handspring, bounder, mounter, or forward flip flop) requires a run and hurdle onto two feet to get the momentum necessary to perform it, just as you learn to do for a high dive roll. The differences are that for a high dive roll you go up, whereas here you go forward and reach directly to the mat, and when you do this bounding handspring, you jump into a pike rather than an arch. Coming from the run and hurdle onto two feet with your arms overhead, reach forward and jump through an inverted piked handstand—your body will be about halfway piked. As your hands hit the mat—your elbows may be flexed slightly—and your seat passes over your hands, kip into an arch and push off the mat with your hands. Land in an upright stand

Figure 5.42a, b, c, d
Jump into this skill from two feet. Dan's
elbows flex a bit too much in figure b.

a.   b.   c.   d.

with your arms overhead. An excellent power drill is to try to do these in series,
starting from a small run and building speed as you go along. You can also do
these from a front handspring—in fact, that teaches you to turn your front
handspring over so that you can develop forward power.

Common problems are not piking enough, not driving your seat overhead
and forward, allowing your shoulders to buckle forward, not pushing hard on
the mat with your hands, and pulling your head and/or arms forward before
finishing the skill.

■

Spotting

Stand where you do for the other handsprings. Be careful of dropped arms at the
end of the skill! For a series of front flip flops you will have to sidestep rapidly to
keep up with your student.

Backward Handspring Skills

Single From a Stand (Figures 5.43 and 5.44)

Here we have the basic building block of backward tumbling, which is seen in
practically every floor exercise. If you have done the backward limberover, you
have done a slow-motion version of a backward handspring (also called a flip
flop or flic flac). To begin the skill, stand with your feet together and your arms
overhead. Turn your hands so that your fingers face toward each other. Squat
halfway and look up at your hands. Jump backward into an arch and pull your
hands to the mat behind you. As your hands contact the mat, your elbows may
flex a bit. Once your body passes over your hands, snap your legs down forcefully as you push down hard on the mat to get your trunk up. Land in an upright
position with your arms overhead and your knees and hips flexed a bit. Once
this method is learned, you can do the move from a different starting position—
with your arms down. As you begin to squat, pull your arms back. When you

Figure 5.43a, b, c, d, e, f

a.   b.   c.

d.   e.   f.

Figure 5.44a, b, c, d
Using an arm throw into the flip flop.

a.   b.   c.   d.

start to jump backward, swing your arms forward and upward rapidly, and throw them overhead and back to the mat. The rest of the move is the same. The second method provides more power from a standing start due to the arm throw, but the first method teaches the move from the position that it usually starts from—out of a roundoff or another backward handspring—and emphasizes the leg push, an important consideration. It is also safer to spot.

The most common problem is not jumping back hard enough. If you shift your hips forward at the start of the move rather than push back, you will go up and often wind up undercutting the move, that is, pulling your hands under your body rather than contacting the mat well behind where your feet were and behind where your body is while in the air. Without a strong backward push it will be difficult to stand up quickly at the end of the move. If you do not fully extend your knees as you fly back you will not push as much as is necessary. Other common problems are pushing off from your heels rather than through your toes, a lack of rotation, snapping down before your body passes over your hands, not pulling your arms back hard enough, letting your shoulders buckle forward when your hands contact the mat, bending your arms excessively, and letting your arms drop at the end of the skill.

If you have soft mats available, jumping backward to a seat without throwing your arms can help you to get the idea of pushing back. If you have a large pit mat (several feet high) or can stack mats up, stand next to the mats with your arms overhead and jump backward onto the mat, going as far back as you can. If your hands hit before your back, you are reaching around well. Finally, if you have a trampoline, you can do this skill over and over with less effort (although it will differ a bit due to the spring of the trampoline bed). Be sure to get spotted at first as the trampoline can throw you a good distance.

■

Spotting

Assume a kneeling position beside and just behind your student. This skill is famous for teachers getting hit in the face by a student's errant arm in the arm-throw method! BE CAREFUL. Your left hand is by his lower back, and your right hand reaches for his abdomen as he goes over. As he goes through the skill, follow along with the action, providing support where needed. If you have a heavy student or are more worried about the first flight phase, an alternative spot is to have your left hand by his upper left thigh and your right hand by his lower back, so you can lift with two hands rather than one.

If you do not have safety cushions available, to get a student used to jumping backward, which is the first hurdle to overcome, have him stand with his arms overhead and jump backward onto your outstretched arms (which you first show him so he knows they are there). As he lands on your arms, turn him over to his hands and place them on the mat so that he is in a handstand. He then finishes by piking to the mat. If he can do this without a problem, then the skill should be taught from a stand without heavy assistance like this.

Series and From a Roundoff

Once you learn a single backward handspring, you should try to learn a series of flip flops. Since you land in the position necessary to start another flip flop, it is just a matter of pushing back and going ahead with the second, third, and so on. You want to accelerate backward, so push hard to the rear as you go. Do not drop your arms between flip flops. A good drill is to do a flip flop from a

Figure 5.45a, b, c, d
Spotting for a series—reaching in with your
right hand (you have to move quickly).

a.   b.   c.   d.

Figure 5.46a, b, c
Spotting for a series—reaching in with your
left hand.

a.   b.   c.

snapdown. This will build up your strength as it takes a good push and leg snap
to get moving into a good flip flop. As you go faster you will flex your elbows
on contact with the mat less and less.

Common problems are the same as for the standing flip flop, but it is easier
to let your hips shift forward, thus cutting your power and performance, when
trying to accelerate unless you concentrate on pushing back.

Stand up and be ready to sidestep rapidly to keep up with your student. One hand
(refer to figures 5.45 and 5.46) can stay in constant contact with his back
throughout the series.

Spotting

The same goes for doing a roundoff flip flop. The finish position of the roundoff is the same as the start position of the flip flop. Do this from a standing roundoff before you run and hurdle into your roundoff.

The most common problem is not pushing hard enough into your roundoff, which results in an undercut flip flop. If your roundoff is not straight, your flip flop will continue crooked and emphasize the problem.

■

Spotting

Stand up as above, but it is suggested that the spot be on the side of your student's first hand, so that if his roundoff is piked over the top, you will not get hit by his legs.

Step-out (Figure 5.47) and Mixed Tumbling

You should be able to step out of a flip flop just as you step out of a backward walkover. If you plan on doing mixed tumbling—combining the skills covered in this chapter in both slow and fast combinations—you must know which foot to bring down to the mat first. If you do a left-hand-first roundoff or cartwheel, which also means you put your left foot out in front for those moves and for a forward handspring, then you must step down on your right foot and turn around on it so that you wind up stepping out to a left-foot-first lunge for the following skill. This is the position that you finish in when you step out of forward handsprings. You can think of the step-out and turn as stepping down with a one-quarter turn onto your right foot and then another one-quarter turn into the lunge for your next skill. The number of different combinations that can be done using forward and backward handsprings, cartwheels, roundoffs, and the other skills you have learned up to now is quite large, so you can be inventive and try many of them.

Figure 5.47a, b, c, d

a.   b.   c.   d.

Diving Backward Handspring (Figure 5.48)

Another variation of a flip flop is a high flip flop, called a diving flip flop, where height is emphasized rather than pushing back (so it is not useful in fast series tumbling on the mat). These are often done from a step-out and to a step-out. You can do several of these in a row, which can look spectacular, and which has uses on floor exercise and balance beam. The timing of the leg split varies with the purpose. You can split early, or wait until hand contact.

Figure 5.48a, b, c, d, e, f

a.

b.

c.

d.

e.

f.

Figure 5.49a, b, c, d, e
From a stand: Eli kicks out of his tuck before landing—a beginner should land as shown in figure e.

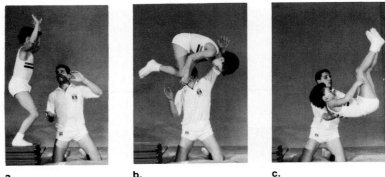

a.

b.

c.

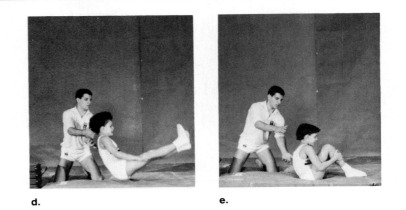

d.

e.

Forward Salto Tucked (Figures 5.49, 5.50, and 5.51)

A front salto (also called a front somersault or front somi) tucked can be done from a run, from another skill such as a front handspring, or from a stand. When you first want to get the feel of this move (figure 5.49), stand in front of a soft mat on a raised surface (such as a folded-up mat) with your arms overhead, and do a tucked salto onto your seat or feet by jumping off the mat so that your seat comes over your head as you pull your body into a tight tuck—but be sure in this early stage to keep your knees separated so that if you land short you do not bash your head into your knees. Later, when you get control and height, you will learn to keep good form. As you finish the salto, look for the wall in front of you to regain an orientation point. Front saltos are tough to land because the landing is blind, that is, you do not see the mat directly below you. It is difficult to do a good front salto from a stand; that is why you should do it onto a soft mat. Once you get the feeling of how to do it, you can add a run,

Figure 5.50a, b, c, d, e, f
Overarm throw into a front salto tucked.

a.

b.

c.

d.

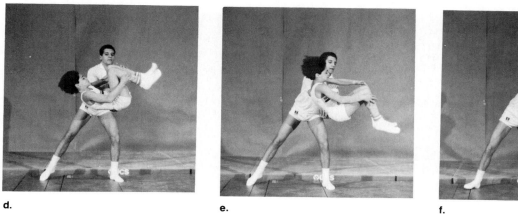

e.

f.

jump to both feet, and punch from both feet to add power to your salto. Your trunk will have a slight forward lean and your feet will be in front of your hips—giving you a slight pike—at contact with the ground just prior to takeoff. This blocking action of your legs will allow you to go up and rotate. Punch down on the ground with your feet as hard as you can.

Several arm motions are used to help in performing this skill. Here are two of them. The overarm throw (also called overarm reach or overreach) is what I ask you to do when you first begin to learn this salto since it is the simplest (figure 5.50). As you jump to your feet, lift your arms overhead and throw them forward as you punch into the salto. Your hands will grasp your shins to help pull into a tight tuck. Another arm motion is called a Russian lift, as the Russian team popularized it many years ago (figure 5.51). This utilizes an arm swing up and behind your body, which adds momentum to your rotation and jump. It can be used from a stand, but is most often seen from a run. On the step just

Figure 5.51a, b, c, d, e, f, g, h
A Russian lift to a front salto tucked.

a. b. c. d.

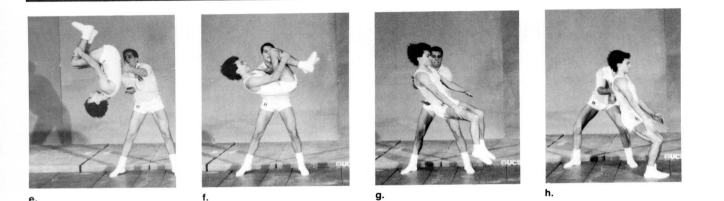

e. f. g. h.

before you jump to both feet, begin to swing your arms in a circle so that they are moving down in front of you as you are in the air during the hurdle to your feet, and as you contact the mat they are swinging back and up so that just before you leave the mat going into the salto your arms are about horizontal behind you where you stop them. Immediately pull your hands to your shins as you become airborne and begin the salto (some grab behind their thighs, but I prefer the shins, which promotes a tighter tuck).

Common problems are leaning too far forward, which gives you rotation but little height, being too straight on contact or leaning back when you punch the salto, which gives you height but little rotation, tucking poorly, throwing your head down at takeoff, which pulls your trunk down, punching from your heels rather than the balls of your feet, and lacking leg strength to get over enough. For the Russian lift, a common flaw is timing your arm swing incorrectly so that your arms are not up behind you at takeoff.

Use an overhead belt if available, or reach in below your student with both hands as the salto is completed (figure 5.51)—you will have to do this for a Russian lift, or have him do a front hip circle around your right arm while your left hand helps support (figure 5.50). To do this, put your right arm by his abdomen as he begins the salto, and have him close into a tuck around your arm (be careful of your thumb—keep it next to your index finger). You can lift him with this arm and reach under him with your left arm.

Backward Salto Tucked (Figure 5.52)

As with the front salto, the backward salto (also called a back somersault or back somi) tucked can be done from a stand or from another skill. It is easier to do a standing back salto than a standing front salto, however, and easier to land as you see the landing area once you have turned over halfway. When you do the salto from another skill such as a flip flop you can get much higher than from a stand because of the added force you get from the preceding skill. Doing standing back saltos is good sticking practice, which means you can practice orienting yourself at the end of a somersault and learning to land without moving, preferably in good posture. It is also an excellent exercise to develop power for tumbling and landing.

Simply described, to do a standing back salto you jump up and pull your knees over your head, but of course it is a bit more difficult than that. You throw your arms up and back and jump up hard, but do not throw your head back right away (try to look at something in front of you). As your feet leave the mat, pull your knees to your chest directly to get to a tight tuck, grab your shins with your hands, and look back to see the mat where you will land. As you complete the salto, open from your tuck (if you are high enough) by extending your hips and knees, and *plié* to land (that is, bend your knees to land). You can practice a free tuck position by using your leg muscles only, rather than your arms and legs, to keep in a tuck. That is, do not hold your legs with your hands, put your arms by your sides, and pull your tucked legs around.

Common problems are leaning back too much, jumping too weakly, jumping off your heels, tucking loosely, throwing your head back from the mat, throwing your arms too late, and not looking for the landing.

An overhead spotting rig may be used for this skill, but it is also easily hand spotted. Stand or kneel to the side of your student. Touch her back with your right hand, and give support if needed. Your left hand can be used to supply her with rotation, if necessary, by pushing up on her seat. Your hands switch position at the end of the salto to stabilize the landing. Put one hand on each side of her body, and be careful if she puts her arms to the sides at the end—do not get poked in the face. Alternatively, you can put your left hand by her back and support her in flight with that hand, reaching by her abdomen with your right hand (figure 5.52). If you are worried that your student does not jump well, the first method is better as you will have both hands under her at the start, when you can boost her over if she is in trouble. Either way, be sure to spot the landing as well—watch for overrotation.

Figure 5.52a, b, c, d, e, f

a.

b.

c.

d.

e.

f.

Sequences to Practice

1. Tucked forward roll to straight jump, tucked forward roll to tucked jump, tucked forward roll to straddled toe touch, tucked forward roll to jump with full turn and stick the landing
2. Dive forward roll, jump with one-half turn, back extension
3. Straight-armed back extension, step-out with one-quarter turn into cartwheel to dive cartwheel
4. Roundoff, rebound with one-half turn, dive forward roll finishing in a straddled stand

5. A series of front headsprings
6. A series of front handspring step-outs
7. Front handspring, punch into a series of bounding front handsprings (forward flip flops)
8. Snapdown to a series of backward handsprings (flip flops)
9. Roundoff, flip flop step-out with one-half turn, roundoff, flip flop step-out with one-half turn, front handspring
10. Front handspring, forward flip flop step-out, roundoff, flip flop step-out with one-half turn, front handspring, dive roll, straddled toe touch

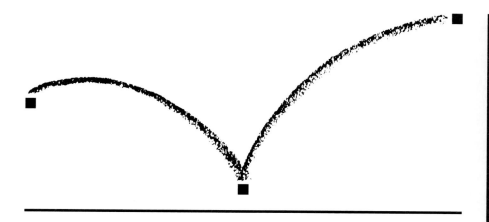

Tumbling passes in floor exercise have to be tied together with various transition movements. These take the form of balances, strength moves, acrobatics, dance parts, and flexibility moves. The use of these moves allows you to cover the floor area and tumble in different directions.

Women's floor exercise uses dance skills much more extensively than men's and is the only gymnastics routine performed to music. The routine must be coordinated with the music and should express a story or feelings to the viewer. There are no 2–3-second-hold parts in women's floor exercise as there are in men's, although there are poses and momentary holds.

Each hold part in men's floor exercise (and all of men's gymnastics) must last 2–3 seconds, and the movement to such a position must be done rhythmically. Throughout these skills the position of your arms, hands, head, trunk, legs, and feet should be considered to bring about a pleasing look to the movement and possibly express a feeling.

Both boys and girls are encouraged to take dance classes so that they learn techniques and rhythm that will help them in their gymnastics training. A number of dance skills are introduced in chapter 8 (**Balance Beam**), and these can be done on the floor as transitions as well. These include poses, leaps, and turns.

Here are some beginning floor exercise skills that will, in many cases, be useful on other events as well.

Organization of This Chapter

Balances on One Foot
Balances on the Hands and Head
Headstand
Handstand
Handstand Skills
Balances on Other Body Parts

Controlled Falls
Connecting Floor Movements
Valdez
Neck Kip With Half-Turn
Sequences to Practice

Balances on One Foot

Forward Scale (Figure 6.1)

The forward scale (also called a front scale or arabesque) gets its name because the forward or front part of your body faces the floor. Begin in a stand with your arms raised a bit higher than your shoulders and to the sides. Look at a point perhaps 20 feet in front of you at eye level or just below on the floor

a. b. c. d.

throughout this move for orientation. Step out on one of your feet and transfer your weight to that foot. This leg is turned out slightly. As your back foot comes off the floor, turn your back leg out and lift it as high as you can to the rear and do not drop your chest. The turn-out tension in your legs should be equal. As you lift your leg farther, it will make your trunk go down. Your body position will be an arch, mostly in your upper back. Keep your hips pressed down and feel as if you are lengthening your support leg. This will help your hips stay square to the floor. Both the heel and the front of your support foot stay in contact with the mat, but you should feel your weight more over the front of your foot, with your toes pressing down and controlling your balance. Try to lift your foot at least as high as your head. If you can go up higher, do so. The arm position that I have described here is one of many positions to use. Another way to vary this scale is to slightly flex one or both knees. Learn this move on both legs.

Common problems are dropping your chest before you lift your leg, jumping around, turning your support foot in, not having your chest and hips facing the floor directly, and having your arms uneven when you intend to have them even.

■

Spotting

Stand next to your student and guide him through with voice and manipulation.

Side Scale (Figure 6.2)

This scale is a bit more difficult to balance than the front scale. Begin by standing with your arms raised just above shoulder height and to the sides. Look at a point about 20 feet from you throughout the move for orientation, like you do for a front scale. Turn both legs out (with equal turn-out tension), place them about shoulder width apart (second position in dance), and shift your weight sideways onto one foot. Feel as if your support leg is lengthening. Keep your weight over the front of your support foot as described for a front scale. As your other foot comes off the mat, lift it sideways until it can go up no farther. At this point, lift it more by allowing your trunk to drop over to the opposite side, but do not let your trunk change alignment so that your belly sticks out. When your trunk is a bit above horizontal, and your leg is at least as high, you are in

Figure 6.2a, b, c, d
Bill's head is out of line in figures b, c, and
d; otherwise his position is good.

a.

b.

c.

d.

Figure 6.3

good position. If you can lift your leg higher, it will be more impressive. Your
trunk can be held higher if your leg is higher, too. Various other arm positions
are used.

Common problems are dropping your trunk too much, dropping your head
out of line with your trunk, and not maintaining an upward V shape of your
leg and trunk, piking, and jumping around.

The same as with the front scale.

■

Spotting

An often seen variation is the Y scale (figure 6.3), so named because the
shape of your body is the letter Y. This is a side scale showing an extreme of
flexibility, as your leg is held up alongside your trunk either with the help of a
hand or, in the most impressive case, by sheer hip-muscle strength alone. Balance becomes tougher as your leg goes up since this raises your center of gravity,
so until you can do it well, move slowly into your final position.

Figure 6.4

Figure 6.5

Figure 6.6

Figure 6.7

Figure 6.8

Balances on the Hands and Head

These moves are close to the mat and are not particularly dangerous. The most common problem, other than a lack of strength, is trying to move into them too fast. When learning balance skills it is necessary to proceed slowly until you develop the feeling for the balance.

■

Spotting

Kneel near your student and give verbal or manipulative help.

Frog Stand (Figure 6.4)

Begin this balance in a squat with your knees spread. Put your hands on the mat directly under your shoulders with your fingers apart and pointing forward. Flex your elbows slightly, and squeeze your knees inward so that they press in on your arms just above your elbows. In this way they will sit on your arms there. Look directly down. Lean forward slowly, putting your weight on your hands and taking it off your feet. Your arms will bend a bit more, and your feet will come off the mat as you rock forward. This is a lead-up skill for a headstand and handstand.

Tripod (Figure 6.5)

This starts as if you are going to do a frog stand, but as you shift onto your hands you lean a bit farther forward and put the front of the top of your head on the mat directly below where your head was, where you were looking all of the time. Note that you will be making approximately an equilateral triangle with your hands and head. Your elbows will be directly above your hands, and the length of the sides of your triangle will be the length of your upper arms. This will be important when you do a headstand, as this is a good base of balance. As your head touches the mat, push down with your hands to lift your seat up so that it is as high as possible, but with your knees still resting on your arms just above your elbows.

Baby Planche (Figure 6.6)

Begin by kneeling on the mat. Place your hands on the mat just below your shoulders with your fingers facing more forward than out. Lean forward and push down on the mat to lift your legs off the mat. Try to keep your seat at the same height as your shoulders.

L Support (Figure 6.7)

Begin by assuming an L shape on the mat, called an L seat. Put your hands on the mat just in front of your hips and push down on the mat. Lift your body up in the L shape without bending forward. If you have trouble doing this, lean a bit forward and push your seat off the mat with your heels still on the mat, then move your shoulders back slowly until your heels come up off the mat. If you still have trouble, then lift up to a tucked position and see if you can hold your seat off the mat. You can gradually extend your legs to the proper position. A good L support has a flat, upright back and horizontal legs.

This is more easily practiced on a set of parallel bars and can even be practiced on two chairs or books to provide a bit of height off the floor, which allows those with weak hip flexors to see where their legs are in relation to horizontal.

Straddled L Support (Figure 6.8)

This is tougher than an L support because the flexibility demands are greater and the strength requirement is as well. Begin in a straddled seat. Place your hands on the mat just in front of your hips and lean forward. Press down on the mat and lift your legs off the mat. You will be leaning forward a good bit. Some find it easier to do this with their fingers facing sideward or even backward. Try them all.

Headstand (Figure 6.9)

If you have mastered all of the low balances on your head and hands, then you will be able to move smoothly into a headstand. To perform this skill, it is easiest to proceed from a tripod. If you feel comfortable in the tripod, just lift your legs off your arms, straighten your trunk vertically, and slowly extend your legs upward toward the ceiling and bring them together. As you do this, you will be aware of small shifts in balance that are necessary—your body will lean a bit, you will feel the weight distribution over your hands and head. Keep the front of the top of your head on the mat, and keep your neck stiff so that your head does not wobble around. Your body should finish in a slight arch or be straight in your headstand. To come down from the headstand, there are a variety of ways that you should practice, and they will be directly applicable to the handstand as well. First of all, you can lower your legs just as they went up, finishing

Figure 6.9a, b, c, d

a.

b.

c.

d.

in a tripod. You can also keep your legs together and lower them directly to the mat, either with bent or straight legs. If you fall over toward your back by mistake, or if you intend to go that way, here are two ways to do this. First, as you fall over, duck your head and do a forward roll. Second, you can go into an arch and land in a bridge position. If you are flexible enough you can then stand up by straightening your arms and doing the end of a front limberover. You can practice this skill against a wall to get the feeling of being upside down. Be sure to put your head right next to the wall, and be careful that another student or object is not nearby that might be hit if you fall.

Piked Press to a Headstand (Figure 6.10)

As a variation on going up, you can do a press, which is a slow, controlled strength move, into a headstand. Do this in a piked position (you can straddle as well, which makes it easier). Begin in a front support. Put your head down (just as you did for the tripod) on the mat directly below where it was and slowly push your seat up as your feet drag on the mat toward your head. As your seat gets overhead your toes will come off the mat. Lift your legs slowly up to a head-stand. As a drill to increase strength and balance, you can stop for a few seconds just as your feet come off the mat, balance there, then proceed upward.

Common problems are moving too fast, putting your head in between your hands rather than in front of them, not distributing your weight between your hands and head, and rolling onto the back of your head.

■

Spotting

Stand or kneel next to your student and assist him in getting his legs up and/or finding the correct vertical position.

a.   b.   c.   d.

Handstand (Figures 6.11 and 6.12)

This is the most used skill in all of gymnastics, so mastery of it is absolutely essential if you want to get ahead. It is also fun to do! To kick to a handstand, step into a lunge and place your hands on the mat at shoulder width with your fingers apart. You can hold your arms overhead, as in figure 6.11a, or just put your hands directly down without thinking about arm-trunk alignment (until you kick up to your handstand). Look at your hands when they are on the mat out of the tops of your eyes to help keep you from lifting your head too high (out of good alignment). Kick your back leg up and push off with your bottom leg so that both legs go overhead. Join them as soon as possible. As your body becomes inverted, push down hard on the mat to make your body as long as possible. Work toward performing your handstand as straight as possible so that you have the maximum extension from your hands to your toes. Good alignment here means that your arms, trunk, and legs all line up straight (see figures 2.21 and 6.12). You will find that you make small adjustments in balance with your fingers and wrists once you learn this skill. When you are just beginning to learn it, you will be making bigger adjustments than you need and will probably make adjustments in your shoulders, trunk, and hips as well. This will pass as you become stronger. (You learned to do the same kind of balancing adjustments when, as a baby, you learned to stand on your feet. To feel these adjustments that are second nature to you now, stand with your eyes closed and be aware of the small movements that you make with your ankles and toes to retain your balance.)

If you fall out of your handstand, recall that you learned several recoveries when you learned the headstand. They are used here, too. Another recovery is to perform a pirouette (a turn) if you go over. Once you turn you can step down to the mat. To get used to staying upside down, you can practice this skill against a wall in the same fashion that you practiced the headstand. Just put your hands

Figure 6.11a, b, c

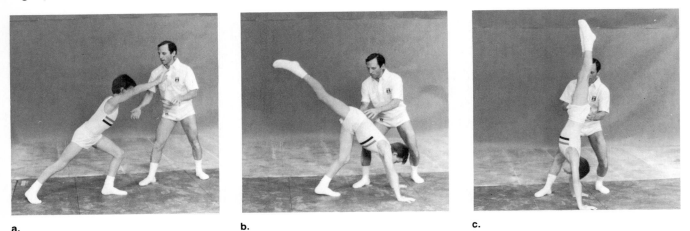

a. b. c.

Figure 6.12

This handstand has very good alignment—if Lindsay's shoulder-trunk line was better, her handstand would be excellent.

Figure 6.13a

Figure 6.13b

Figure 6.13c

Figure 6.13d

a few inches away from the wall to start so that you have room for your head to be up a bit to allow you to see your hands. When you feel good about being upside down, slowly move your feet away from the wall to learn the balance.

There are many other drills to build handstand strength. If you walk on your hands rather than hold one place, you can move forward, backward, and even sideward to learn to control your balance while inverted and in motion (handstand races are a fun way to do this). Just kicking up toward a handstand, returning to your starting lunge, and then kicking up again over and over will give you a good idea of supporting your weight. You can switch your legs during this drill so that you land on the opposite leg that you pushed off with each time. If you are quite weak yet, pushing off from the mat only a small distance will start you on the road to handstand strength. To begin developing the strength for a press to a handstand, if you can put your palms on the mat while standing in a deep pike (or a straddled pike if you are not so flexible), you can push down on the mat and lift off from your toes, learning the balance shift needed to initiate a press (described shortly). See how long you can stay there. When you have mastered a handstand, you will be able to kick up to it any time you wish, and you will be able to stay in one for at least one minute. Do not be discouraged if it takes a long time to learn this—most gymnastics skills take hundreds of repetitions to achieve competency, and more to gain mastery.

Learn various handstand positions—split (figure 6.13a), stag (figure 6.13b), double stag (figure 6.13c), and straddled (figure 6.13d).

Common problems are not doing enough handstands to build up enough strength to do the move, arching, having an angle in your shoulders and/or hips, lifting your head, not pushing down hard enough, and kicking up too strongly or too weakly to attain the correct vertical position.

Stand next to your student's hands. Put one hand on either side of his legs to provide stability once he has kicked toward the handstand. If he has control of the inverted position, you can adjust other parts of his body if they are in incorrect position by hand if verbal feedback is not working.

■

Spotting

Handstand Skills

Pressing to a Handstand With Bent Arms (Figure 6.14)

Just as you learned to press to a headstand, you can learn a simple press to a handstand before you challenge the more difficult ways of getting to a handstand using strength. This press is done with bent arms and piked hips, with your legs either tucked or straight together or straddled. I will describe a straddled press. Begin in a piked straddled stand. Put your hands on the mat at shoulder width with your fingers spread and pointing forward. Bend your arms, shift your weight over your hands, push up onto your toes, and push down on the mat to lift your seat up over your head. Keep your legs pointing down and close to your body until your seat gets over your head, then lift your legs up to the side as much as possible until they meet overhead. Your arms will straighten as your legs move together. If you do this in the piked position, you will find that you will lean forward more while lifting your legs, and that it is a little tougher to lift your legs overhead. Remember to move slowly through this

Figure 6.14a, b, c, d, e

a.

b.

c.

d.

e.

movement. Pressing from a frog stand to a handstand is another challenge—you have to go up a bit farther, but you have an easier time lifting your legs when they are bent.

Common problems are moving too quickly to allow control, and not pushing down hard enough on the mat.

■ **Spotting**	Stand directly in front of your student, so that in the handstand his back is in front of you. Lift his hips if needed, then shift your hands to his legs. If the press is done without a straddle, you can spot from the side as well.

Figure 6.15a, b, c, d

a.   b.   c.   d.

Straddled Straight-armed Piked Press From a Piked Straddled Stand (Figure 6.15)

This press takes more shoulder strength than the bent-armed one, and will require lots of practice to learn well. The warmup drill shown in figures 3.7a and b is actually a lead up for this. Interestingly, many girls find this easier to do than a bent-armed press. Begin in a piked straddled stand and put your hands on the mat below your shoulders. Push down to lift your seat over your head. Bring your straddled and piked legs at first toward the plane of your hands and then outward and upward in that plane. If you can straddle wide you will have less of a balancing problem in going up. Do not lean too far forward, and align your hands, shoulders, and hips before lifting your legs over your seat. Keep pushing down until you reach a handstand, and then continue pushing down to attain a good, stretched position. If you are too weak to go up, you can do the move in reverse—start in a handstand and lower through a straddled handstand, then pike down to just touch your pointed toes to the mat. Do this slowly.

Common problems are leaning too far forward, not straddling enough, and being too weak to push your body up.

The spot here is the same as for the bent-armed straddled press.

Pirouettes (Figures 6.16 and 6.17)

If you feel comfortable in the handstand, you are ready for a two-step pirouette (turn). To do a forward pirouette starting on the left, shift your weight to your left a bit by pushing down with your right hand, pull your right shoulder back, and do a one-quarter turn on your left hand so that you move your right hand directly in front of your left hand with your fingers facing each other. Then complete the pirouette with another one-quarter turn by shifting your weight onto your right hand, pulling your left shoulder forward, and moving your left hand into a normal handstand position. A backward, or reverse, pirouette is done similarly, but the turn is started behind your right hand—like the second half of the front pirouette—and the heels of your hands face each other, not your fingers. To turn the same direction, if you turn first on your left hand when you do a forward pirouette, you will turn first on your right hand when doing

Figure 6.16a, b, c, d, e
In this forward pirouette, Danny lets his body get out of alignment in figure d, and it would be better if his fingers were pointing toward each other in figure c.

a.

b.

c.

d.

e.

Figure 6.17a, b, c, d, e
In this reverse pirouette, Danny has a similar body alignment problem in figure d.

a.

b.

c.

d.

e.

a backward pirouette. The finish is like the first half of a front pirouette. You should learn to turn both forward and backward, and both to the right and to the left, but generally you will perform both pirouettes turning in the same direction. It is very important to push down hard during your turn to maintain good alignment. Later on you can do these pirouettes in one step.

Figure 6.18

Figure 6.19

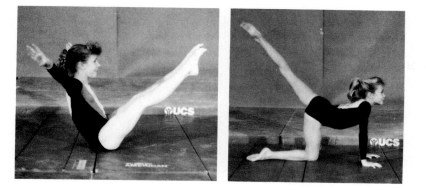

Common problems are not pushing down hard enough during the turn, letting your chest sag, lifting your head to look for the turn (like a handstand, your head should stay in line and you should look out of the tops of your eyes), not shifting your weight over your support hand, and not completing a one-half turn in two steps.

The same as for a regular handstand, providing support if needed.

Spotting

Balances on Other Body Parts

These are low balances that require no spot.

V on the Seat (Figure 6.18)

This is an easy balance. You simply lift your legs off the mat from an L seat to attain the V shape by keeping your back straight and lifting your legs up as high as you can. You may touch the mat as you start if you need to. The higher you go, the harder it is to balance. If your legs go up high enough, you can pull them in close to you with your hands. The only part touching the mat is your seat. The stronger and more flexible you get, the tighter your V becomes. As a variation, begin in a tuck and open slowly to a V.

Forward Knee Scale (Figure 6.19)

This scale is first tried with your hands touching the mat for stability. Begin on your hands and knees with your hands directly below your shoulders and lift one leg up and to the rear as you did for a front scale (with your leg turned out). Keep your hips square to the mat—your hips should not swivel as you lift your leg. Keep your hips tucked in (do not let your belly sag) and arch in your upper back. To add a challenge, lift your hands off the mat one at a time. It is more difficult to balance this way than on your foot, isn't it?

Figure 6.20a, b, c, d

a.   b.   c.   d.

Controlled Falls

These two methods are ways that gymnasts often connect tumbling passes with floor movements. They usually require no spot.

Prone Fall (Figure 6.20)

From a stand, keep your body straight and reach out ahead of you for the mat. Lean forward and fall until your hands contact the mat. At the point of contact, your elbows flex to absorb the fall. Resist all the way down to the mat with your arms close to your sides. If you are worried about the fall, begin on your knees instead. Just keep your body straight from your knees to your head and do the same motions as you would from your feet. You can build up to a stand by next falling from a straddled stand, then putting your legs together more and more until they are touching. As a variation, start in a stand and begin to fall backward. Do a one-half turn and then a prone fall.

A common flaw is piking on the way down. DO NOT HIT THE MAT WITH YOUR ELBOWS LOCKED!

Swedish Fall (Figure 6.21)

This is a variation on the prone fall. As you fall, lift one leg up behind you so that it is pointing straight up when you finish the fall. Turning out will help you to avoid bending your upraised leg. Your body will probably show a little pike in the end position to facilitate lifting your leg to the vertical unless you are quite flexible.

Common flaws are not lifting your leg to vertical and bending your top leg. Again, DO NOT HIT THE MAT WITH YOUR ELBOWS LOCKED!

Connecting Floor Movements

These are a few of the many connections used in floor exercise. They are performed close to the floor and usually require no spot.

Pinwheel (Figure 6.22)

For the pinwheel (or single-leg circle), begin in a single-leg squat with your hands on the mat under your shoulders. To go counterclockwise, put your straight right leg out to your right side. Your left leg will be bent with your left foot under you. Begin the move by lifting your right leg so that your right foot does

Figure 6.21a, b, c, d

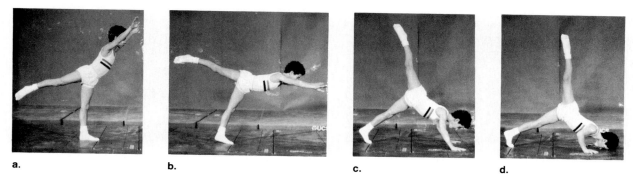

a.   b.   c.   d.

Figure 6.22a, b, c, d, e, f, g, h
Lenny has a right knee bend in figures f and g—his right knee should be extended throughout the pinwheel.

a.   b.   c.   d.

e.   f.   g.   h.

not touch the mat, and swing it forward. Lifting your hands one at a time and then putting them back on the mat in the same sequence, pass your right leg under your right hand and then your left hand. As your right leg continues to swing around, shift your weight onto your hands and jump over your right leg with your left leg (this feels like the beginning of a press momentarily). Complete the move by bringing your right leg back to the starting position. Face in

Figure 6.23a, b, c, d, e
A squat-through that can finish in a rear support, L seat, or L support.

a. b. c. d. e.

Figure 6.24a, b, c, d
A stoop-through to a rear support—Benji has two form breaks: knees and feet.

a. b. c. d.

one direction during the leg circle. As a variation, you can turn around either way while doing the pinwheel. You can also try switching legs and directions.

The usual problem is not putting your weight on your hands so that you do not jump over your right leg well. Another is not keeping your bent leg under you.

Squat-through (Figure 6.23) and Stoop-through (Figure 6.24)

From a front support, lean forward on your arms a bit, arch your back and sag down in your shoulders, then lift your seat up and push down on the mat. Pull your feet forward between your hands with your legs either bent, which is a squat-through, or straight, which is a stoop-through. Finish in a rear support, L seat, or L support (easier). The stoop-through is much tougher as it requires greater hip lift and more flexibility. As lead-up drills, you can start in a front support and lift to a tucked or piked balance on your hands with your toes barely touching the mat and return to your front support, then repeat that but push through into an L seat. You will probably find it tougher to stop momentarily in a tucked or piked support before going through than to do the whole movement. These drills are good strength builders.

Figure 6.25a, b, c, d, e
Eli's toes should be pointed in figures b and
c, and a stronger push would bring his
chest around more in figures b–d.

a.　　　　　　b.　　　　　　c.　　　　　　d.　　　　　　e.

Straddled Cut (Figure 6.25)

This begins just as the squat- or stoop-through does, but you have to push down on the mat much harder as you must become airborne a bit to allow the straddled cut to be performed. As you begin to recoil out of your body arch and shoulder sag, shove down and pull your straddled straight legs around to the front of you. Your hands will pass over your legs, then reach for and push down on the mat as you complete the move. Try to land in a rear support, although just landing in an L seat may be sufficient if it is your first try. Eventually, you want your hands to contact the mat before your feet do. This can also be done from a bent-armed front support, which looks like the down part of a pushup. You may find that you have more power from this position.

Common problems are not straddling widely enough, not pushing down powerfully enough, and not rotating your chest around early enough.

Jump to Chest Roll (Figure 6.26)

This is another way to get from a stand to a front support. As a lead up, kick to a handstand or three-quarter handstand, then bend your arms and lower your chest to the mat as you arch hard. Shift your shoulders forward and roll on your front to an arched front support (figures e-h). Then do the whole move from a stand. This move is most often done using a Russian lift (which is also described in the front salto section—it is useful for helping you to rotate). Begin with your arms in front of you and let them drop as you squat partially. Your arms continue to swing up behind you as you jump up and lift your seat up so that your trunk rotates down to the mat with your body in a piked position. Your arms stop their motion just before you leave the mat and reverse their direction, so that you are reaching for the mat as you are coming down to it. At the highest point of your jump with your hips up high, open from your pike into an arch. When you contact the mat with your hands, flex your elbows to absorb the force of contact, and shift your shoulders forward a bit for control. Allow your chest to touch the mat and roll down your body to your feet, keeping your hands on the mat. The end position is an arched front support. As a variation, as you open from your pike to an arch, if you add a one-quarter turn, then this move is called a Japanese jump.

The common problem is not shifting your shoulders forward to control the roll down your front.

Figure 6.26a, b, c, d, e, f, g, h

a.

b.

c.

d.

e.

f.

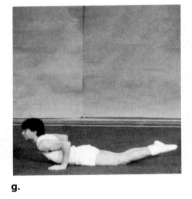
g.

h.

Valdez (Figure 6.27)

This movement is used to get from a seated position on the mat to a handstand or stand by going through a backward walkover-type movement. You begin in an L seat on the mat. Pull one leg up so that that foot is by your seat with that knee pointing up. The choice of which hand you put on the mat behind your seat is up to you, but if you use the hand that is on the same side as your bent leg, you may find it easier to complete the skill, as this is not as demanding on your flexibility or leg push power (that lifts your hips) since it allows you to turn your body a bit and possibly do a cartwheel-like action to finish the Valdez rather than a pure walkover action. (I know at least one coach who separates these moves, calling the cartwheel type a Valdez and the other a sit-start back walkover.) If you are flexible, it hardly matters. Whichever hand you use, when you put it on the mat behind your seat, turn it out and around completely (forearm supinated and shoulder rotated outward) and then hyperextend your wrist so that your palm is on the mat. Your fingers and elbow are facing in. At this point you reach overhead and back with your other hand and push down on the mat with your bent leg, while lifting your hips and straight leg overhead. Your other hand will land on the mat to the side of your hand that was back there, and you will notice that your hand that was on the mat can shift around a bit to a regular handstand position. If you do this successfully, the end will

Figure 6.27a, b, c, d, e
Note Melanie's hand placement is for a
balance beam drill—in line.

a. b. c.

d. e.

feel just like a backward walkover. You can finish in a split handstand or one
with your legs together, or step down directly. If you practice this for the balance beam, you will want your hands to finish in line as if they were on a beam
(as shown in the figures), rather than parallel to each other.

Common problems are not pushing on the mat hard enough to get your
body up and over your hands, and not being flexible enough to compensate for
a lack of push.

This is done much in the same way as for a back walkover. Kneel on the right side
if your student's right leg is her straight one (as shown). If she has not done a
Valdez before, place your right hand under that leg, and put your left hand behind
her back. As the move is begun, lift to help her get to the handstand. If she has
experience with this move and/or a back walkover, you can spot as the figures
show, with your right hand under her back and your left hand nearby for stability.

■

Spotting

Figure 6.28a, b, c, d
Eli has a leg split in figure b, and could turn
a bit more sharpely to finish earlier.

a.

b.

c.

d.

Neck Kip With Half-Turn (Figure 6.28)

Here is a variation of the neck kip discussed in chapter 5 that is useful for getting from a seated or back-lying position on the mat to a front support. As you begin your neck kip, do not drive your feet down as hard, rather twist your body as you open so that you wind up facing the mat. Your hands do not push as hard either, but will slide around to a front support. Your feet and toes may be pointed or hooked in the front support. The more weight you have on your hands, the easier it will be to finish with your feet pointed, as you will not smash into the mat with your feet. This twisting action can also be done at the end of a headspring, finishing in the same manner. As you get better, finish your turn higher and higher, eventually getting to a handstand.

Common problems are not twisting hard enough, and dropping your hips too much so that your turn is low and your feet hit hard.

■

Spotting

Kneeling by your student's side, put your right hand under his back. As the movement is started, help him twist and support his weight to facilitate the turn. Reach under his legs at the finish with your left hand to lower him down.

Sequences to Practice (Hold positions should last three seconds.)

(Some tumbling skills are used as well.)

1. Front scale, Swedish fall, turn to a straddled stand, press to a headstand (hold)
2. Two pinwheels, extend backward to a front support as you finish the second pinwheel, squat- or stoop-through to an L seat, lift to a V seat (hold), straddle your legs and push up into a straddled L support (hold)
3. Side-to-side cartwheel, side scale, kick sideways to a handstand, one-half back pirouette (one-quarter turn), step-down with one-half turn to a front-to-back cartwheel, finish in a forward lunge
4. Dive forward roll, jump full turn, fall to a front support, turn to a straddled stand, press to a handstand (hold)

5. Jump to a chest roll, turn over to a rear support, lower to an L seat, lift to a L support (hold), lower to an L seat, Valdez to a handstand, forward pirouette, straight-legged forward roll

6. Valdez, back walkover, diving back handspring, step-out, finish in a forward lunge

7. Front handspring, fall to a front support, start a slow, piked forward roll but as your shoulders touch the mat do a neck kip with one-half turn to front support, bent-armed press to a handstand with straddled legs (hold)

8. Roundoff, flip flop, jump (punch out of the flip flop) with one-half turn to front support, straddled cut to rear support, one-half turn to front support, pike up to a stand

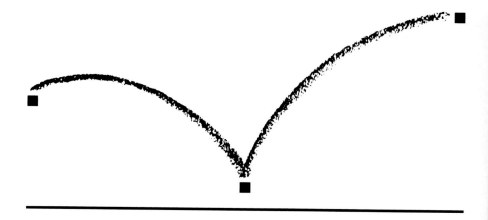

Pommel horse is the most difficult event for most male gymnasts to master. Your routine must be performed without stops and with your body constantly changing position over the horse. Your hands are also constantly in motion, as your balance shifts rhythmically from one hand to the other as your body swings around, above, and by the horse. Wherever your legs are, your trunk leans to the opposite side. If you fall off the horse doing a particular skill, you did not lean in the opposite direction enough (unless you first collapse on the horse and then fall or if you hit the horse while swinging). A good hint for all horsework is to try to keep two hands on the horse as much as possible—that is, do not leave a hand in the air when it could be on the horse. With two hands on the horse you can have control, whereas one hand offers little control.

What you want to show on the pommel horse is circular swings that cover a great area—that look wide or big—and pendular swings that go high. You will learn to dip and push out of your shoulders on pendular skills and a few circular skills. For circle work, you will learn to push your toes in as wide a circle as you can without dipping your feet below the level of the horse body, unless you intend to do a skill that requires this, such as a loop dismount (described later). During almost all circle work, you will not allow yourself to sag down in your shoulders. Circles should look stretched, high, and free, with no body shape changes when you perform skills. Getting the strength to do this takes thousands of circles. A number of training programs now keep their students on low horses (with and without pommels) and mushrooms (described shortly) until the students exhibit strong circle work, and only after lots of this training are they allowed to work on high horses.

A competition routine must cover the three parts of the horse—the left end, the middle, and the right end (also called the neck, saddle, and croup)—and must show changes of the direction that your body faces. Both pendular (scissors) and circular skills must be performed, with double-leg circle work (circular swings with your legs joined) predominating. Skills are done both on the pommels and on the leather (the body of the horse). The width of the pommels can be adjusted to a degree.

Skills can be learned to the right or the left, and should be tried both ways. Once you find which way you prefer to do double-leg circles (described as clockwise or counterclockwise as seen from above the horse), you will concentrate on learning skills that use that direction of swing. As a convention in this chapter, all circling skills are described going clockwise.

There are several devices that are used to help learn pommel horse skills. Most often seen are a short version of the horse without pommels (handles) called a buck, a low horse, and a mushroom—it looks like its name. You will find pictures of these devices in the section on learning double-leg circles. One other device (that is not pictured) is a bucket in a twisting belt that hangs at about the height of the horse from a rope attached to the ceiling over the center of the horse. The bucket is placed in the twisting belt so that its opening points horizontally, and you put your feet in the bucket. A lightweight but sturdy plastic bucket works best. As you swing your body around with your feet in the bucket, you can go through many of the circling skills to get the feel of them. The bucket supports your feet and so supports a portion of your weight.

It is a good idea to wear some form of close-fitting pants when performing on the horse, as this will allow your legs to slide on the body of the horse rather than scrape your skin off when you graze the horse (or pommel by mistake).

Spotting is seldom performed on this event, so whenever it is useful I will point it out.

Terms Used in This Chapter

Counterturn   Turning your body opposite to the way you are circling.

Double Overgrip   In a front support on one pommel facing the long axis of the horse, to have both hands on the pommel so that your knuckles are pointing away from you—your forearms are pronated.

Double Undergrip   In the support described above, to have your knuckles pointing toward you—your forearms are supinated.

Mixed Grip   In a support with both hands on one pommel, to have your hands facing opposite ways.

Turn In   Referring to hip axis position, when your body goes back across the horse from rear support to front support, you rotate your body so that your front turns toward your support hand.

Turn Out   Referring to hip axis position, the opposite of the above.

Organization of This Chapter

Strength Exercises
Pendular Swings and Cuts
Scissor
Simple Travel
Simple Reverse *Stöckli*
Simple *Czechkehre*
Simple Swiss
Pendular Swiss
Single-leg Circle
Double-leg Circle

Getting Out of Circles into Leg
   Cuts
Loop
Thomas Flair
Side Travel Frontways
Kreiskehre
Czechkehre
Loop Dismounts
Sequences to Practice

Strength Exercises

The novice pommel horseman can do a number of exercises on his hands to build up his support strength.

Walk around the horse in a front support (figure 7.1). Go from one end to the other, then go around the end, and then repeat this. Try to keep your body from touching the horse. You can walk up on the pommels or choose not to. Do both.

Figure 7.1a, b, c

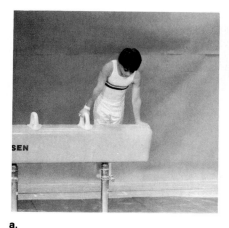 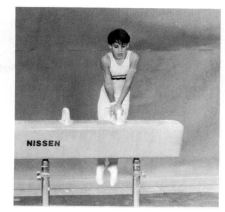 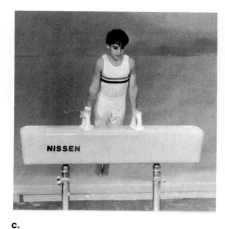

a.   b.   c.

Figure 7.2a, b, c

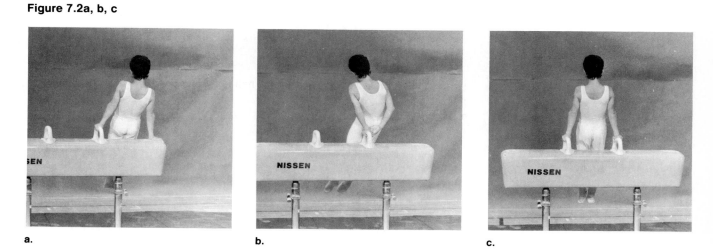

a.   b.   c.

Walk around the horse in a rear support (figure 7.2). This will be much more difficult than the front support, as we are usually much stronger pushing in front of ourselves than behind ourselves. Follow the same guidelines as for the front support.

Walk from one end of the horse to the other in a straddled L position (figure 7.3). When you get to the end, turn around without sitting down and go back again.

If you have access to a set of parallel bars, support swings there will help you. You can do these forward and backward with much freedom. However, small side-to-side swings will get you used to one kind of shifting that pommel horse requires.

Holding yourself in a front support, swing your body side to side. Swing from your shoulders so that your whole body shifts and has a long appearance. Do this both with your legs together (figure 7.4) and straddled (figure 7.5).

Figure 7.3a, b, c, d

 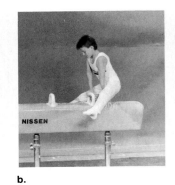 

a. b. c. d.

Figure 7.4a, b

a. b.

Figure 7.5a, b, c

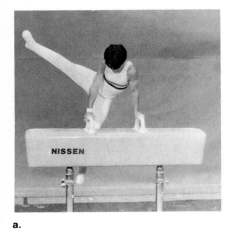  

a. b. c.

Figure 7.6a, b, c

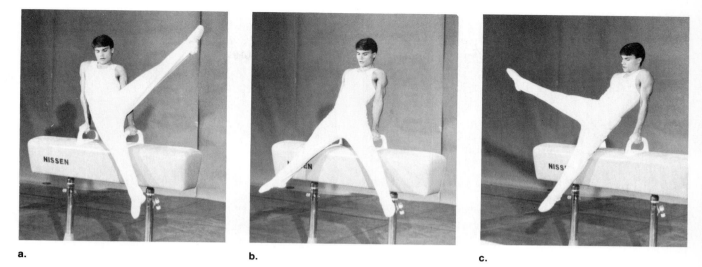

a.   b.   c.

Figure 7.7a, b, c

a.   b.   c.

Do the same in a rear support (figure 7.6). Try hard not to touch the horse with your legs by pushing back on the pommels.

Swing your body side to side in a stride support (figure 7.7). Be sure to straddle your legs as far sideways as possible. If you swing widely enough, you will be able to lift your nonsupport hand at the end of each swing. Note how much you have to lean opposite to your legs as you swing.

As a final exercise, get in a free (not touching) straight front support and squat your legs through (between) your arms to a free straight rear support, and go back the way you came. Repeat this many times. As you get better, see how far from the horse you can hold your straight body in both front and rear supports. Which is easier?

Figure 7.8a, b, c, d, e, f, g, h, i, j, k, l, m, n

Stephan loses his wide straddle in figure i, j, and l; otherwise these are fine.

a.   b.   c.   d.

e.   f.   g.   h.

Pendular Swings and Cuts

Single-leg Cut (Figure 7.8)

For the single-leg cut begin by straddling your legs and swinging side to side in a front support. As you swing up on the right, move your body forward a bit so that your right leg passes over the horse as you lift your hand off the right pommel. Regrasp the pommel as soon as possible. You will wind up in a stride support. In a like manner you can continue to cut one leg after another in an even, rhythmic fashion. You can do several different patterns, for instance right leg over, left leg over, right leg back, left leg back (illustrated here), or right leg over, right leg back, left leg over, left leg back, and so on. You can start with the other leg, and start in a position other than a front support. The important points to remember are maintain a wide straddle throughout the cuts, keep a

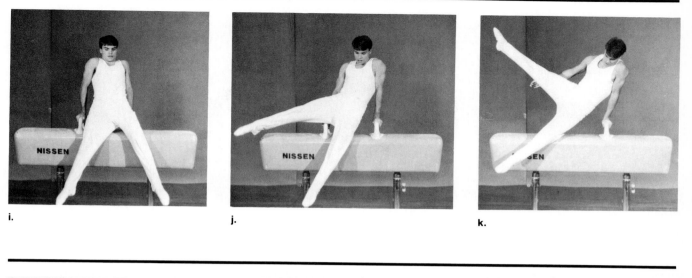

i.   j.   k.

l.   m.   n.

steady rhythm when doing sequences, make sure both legs swing to the side when you do a cut, push hard on the horse to get your body high to give you time in the air to do a pretty, flighty cut, and try not to pike during the cut. Also try to keep facing somewhat forward with your hips during your passage through a stride support. This will allow you to maintain a wide straddle with your legs close to the plane of the horse. When done well, you will get a bit of sideways play in your trunk that will allow your legs to whip through the bottom and help you to lift them. You will also get a bit of a dip in your shoulders through the bottom, which you will push out of on the way up to add to your height.

These single-leg cuts are also called overcuts because your top leg goes across the horse while your bottom leg stays on the same side as it was originally. (When swinging to the right, your right leg is your top leg and your left leg is your bottom leg.)

Common problems are piking, not being directly over the horse when doing the cut, letting your straddle change during the cut, having poor rhythm, and not leaning far enough to counterbalance.

Stephan has trouble maintaining a wide straddle in figures f, g, and i–m, but those two undercuts are harder to do than the other two.

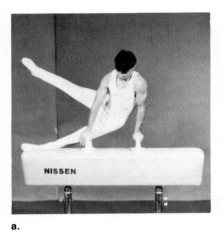

a.

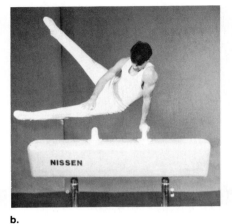

b.

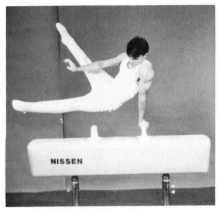

c.

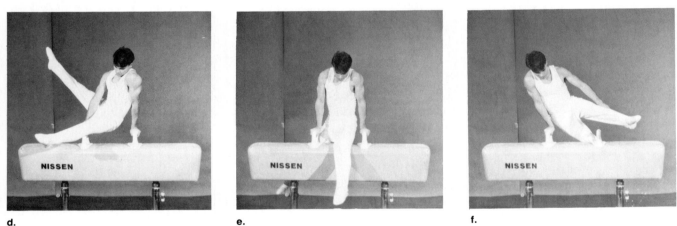

d.

e.

f.

Undercut (Figure 7.9)

These begin as the single leg cuts did, but the difference is that instead of your top leg passing over the horse, your bottom leg does, and your top leg stays on the same side of the horse as it originally was. These are more difficult to master than the cuts, as you must lift your body much higher to do an undercut than to do an overcut. Once you learn to do them singly, try to do them in sequence just as you did with the cuts. If you master all of the cuts and undercuts, you will have little trouble with future legwork.

Common problems are the same as for cuts.

g.

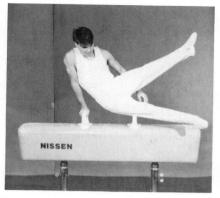

h.

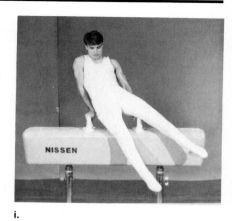

i.

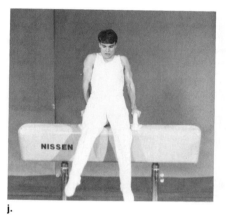

j.

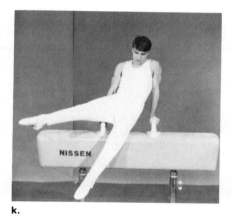

k.

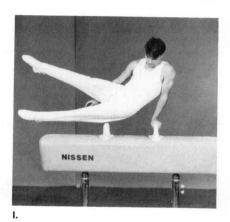

l.

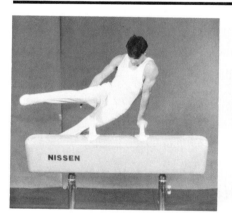

m.

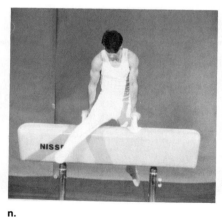

n.

o.

Figure 7.9 (continued)

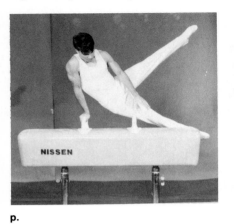

p.

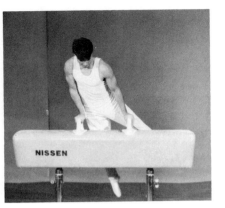

q.

Figure 7.10a, b, c, d, e, f, g
Stephan has a slight leg split in figures a, e, and g.

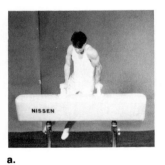

a.

b.

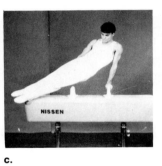

c.

d.

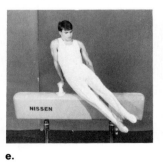

e.

f.

g.

Double-leg Cut (Figure 7.10)

Just as you did single-leg cuts in a straddle, you can join your legs and do double-leg pendular cuts to further build up your side support strength. Since your body is longer with your legs together than when you straddled, you will have to lean more when performing these cuts. These are a lead-up skill to double-leg circles. Do them over and back in rhythmic sequence, and try to touch the horse body as little as possible.

Scissor

Scissors are a combination requirement in a competitive routine, and often are the source of form deductions, so you must strive to learn them with good form. A scissor combines the cuts and undercuts that you have learned. Both legs cross over the horse. A forward (or front) scissor has the front of your body leading somewhat, and your back leg goes over your front leg. The backward (or back) scissor has the back of your body leading somewhat, and your front leg goes over your back leg. A scissor begins in a stride support (which you get to from a leg cut, an undercut, or another scissor) and ends in the opposite stride support.

Forward (Figure 7.11)

For the front scissor to the left, swing to the left through a stride support with your left leg in back. As your lower (right) leg swings up over the height of the horse to the left (your left hand is off the pommel now), roll your hips over a bit so that your left leg crosses over your right leg. Try not to pike. You will have to lean considerably to the right to allow your legs to go this high, and must push down hard on the pommel to keep up long enough to complete the skill. The faster you swing into the scissor, the higher you can go. Think of leaving your legs up as your hips descend, and reach in from behind with your left hand as soon as possible. You will finish in a stride support with your left leg in front, swinging to the right so that you can do a right front scissor. Doing series of scissors is a fine way to build up your swinging strength.

Backward (Figure 7.12)

To perform a left back scissor, swing through a stride support to the left with your left leg in front. As your lower (right) leg swings over the height of the horse to the left (your left hand is off the pommel now), roll your hips over a bit so that your left leg crosses over your right leg. Again, try not to pike. Try to stay up as long as you can. Finish in a stride support swinging to the right with your left leg in back, just where you want to be to do a right back scissor.

A good training drill for a scissor is to swing up as if you are going to do one, and put your lower foot on the end of the horse. You can then push up into a scissor position and see if your body is aligned well, if your legs are straddled wide, and if you are leaning enough on your opposite arm. Finish this drill by hopping your foot off the horse and completing the scissor motion.

Common problems are piking, not swinging hard enough, not straddling wide, not trying to hold your legs up—especially your top leg, and having slow hands.

You can help position your student during the drill if he can hold his body up in the scissor position with his foot on the horse.

■

Spotting

Figure 7.11a, b, c, d, e

a.

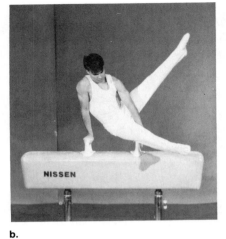

b.

c.

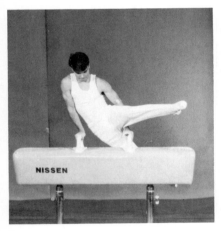

d.

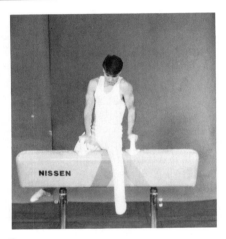

e.

Simple Travel (Figure 7.13)

(The term "simple" refers to a series of moves done with single-leg cuts that are the lead ups to moves done with double-leg circles.)

This move lets you travel from one part of the horse to another without changing the direction that you face. If you wish to travel from the right end to the middle, begin in a front support and do a right leg cut forward, then swing your left leg around as if you are going to do a leg cut, but do not let go with your left hand. Bring your left leg down and shift your weight over your left hand. As you cut your right leg back, move your right hand to the pommel where you will have a mixed grip. I prefer to have you put it behind your left hand as this will help you in a later pendular skill—the back scissor travel—although a travel sideways from a circle in front support (shown later) is usually

Figure 7.12a, b, c, d, e
Stephan should lift higher, and does not keep his straddle wide, especially in figures a and d.

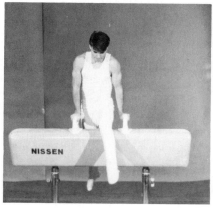

a.

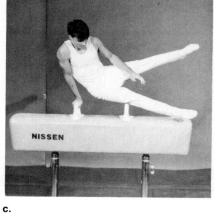

b.

c.

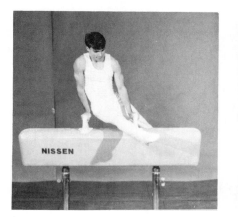

d.

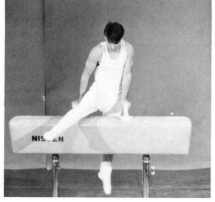

e.

performed by reaching in front. Finish the travel by swinging your left leg up and back, shifting to your left, and moving your left hand to the left pommel. You will finish in a front support, ready to do another travel, this time from the middle to the left end. You can also do the travels the opposite way, from left to right. The rhythm of this skill is the same as for the single-leg cuts, and you want to swing as high as you can.

To do a simple travel to a back scissor, as you push in (figure e) lift your bottom leg over the height of the horse and switch the positions of your legs, as described earlier.

Common problems are irregular rhythm, shifting your hands at the wrong time, and not lifting your legs enough.

Figure 7.13a, b, c, d, e, f

a.

b.

c.

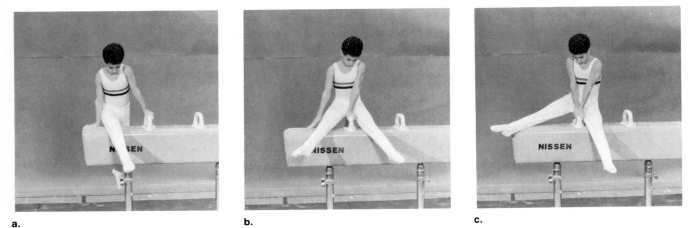

d.

e.

f.

Simple Reverse *Stöckli* (Figure 7.14)

For the simple reverse *Stöckli* (pronounced: shtehk'-lih) you will both travel on the horse and turn around. Your support hand gets twisted around (your forearm is supinated) so it may cause a bit of stress on a beginner's wrist. To perform a simple reverse *Stöckli* from the right end into the middle (if you move from the end to the middle it is also called a back-in, and the opposite motion is a back-out), cut your right leg over and swing your left leg around low, similar to the way the simple travel goes. Then cut your right leg back low, turn your body clockwise, and reach behind you for the empty pommel. As you put your right hand on the pommel, shift your weight over it and cut your left leg forward low to finish in a rear support. After the first cut, this skill is done in a circle plane—flat—rather than pendularly.

Common problems are poor rhythm and not reaching back hard enough for the pommel.

Figure 7.14a, b, c, d, e, f

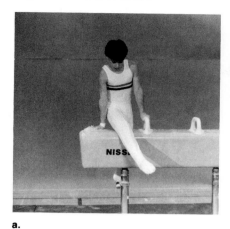

a.

b.

c.

d.

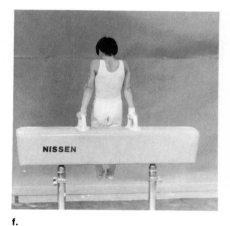

e.

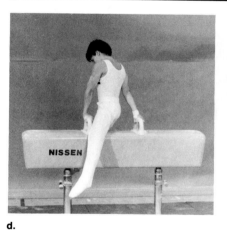

f.

Simple *Czechkehre* (Figures 7.15 and 7.16)

The simple *Czechkehre* (pronounced: chek'-kehr-eh; in the USA it is often [mis]pronounced: chek'-kehr) is also referred to as the simple Moore and means Czech turn. This move lets you change the direction that you face without changing the part of the horse that you are on. It is usually performed in the middle of the horse, and begins like the simple back-in/-out. Start with both hands on the front part of the pommels. To turn around clockwise, begin by doing a right leg cut, then swing your left leg around low but do not let go of the left pommel. Shift your weight over your left hand and cut your right leg back low, bringing your right hand to the left pommel next to your left hand with the same grip—you will have a double undergrip. At this point shift your weight to your right hand and reach for the empty pommel with your left hand.

Figure 7.15a, b, c, d, e

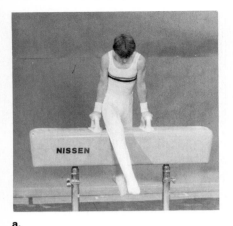

a.

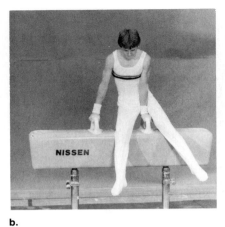

b.

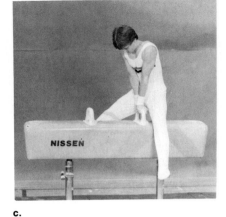

c.

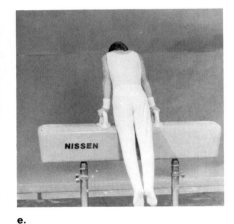

d.

e.

Your right leg continues around to join your left leg, and you finish in a front support facing the opposite direction from your starting position.

When you become stronger, you can finish this skill by bringing both legs around while you are in the double undergrip support and passing them over the empty pommel, then reaching for that pommel with your left hand, finishing in a rear support (figure 7.16). This finish is considerably tougher than finishing in a front support, and is a further step toward doing a *Czechkehre* (or Moore) while doing double-leg circles.

Common problems are poor rhythm, and putting your hands in an incorrect position on the pommel. For the second variety, the common problem is piking as you swing your legs over the horse.

Stephan's pike in figure e is a slight flaw.

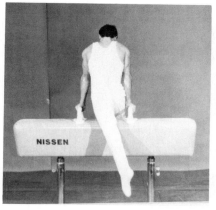

a.

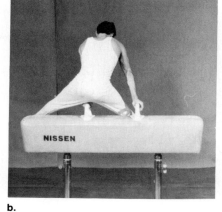

b.

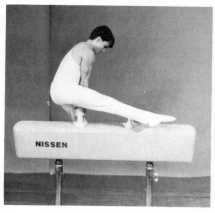

c.

d.

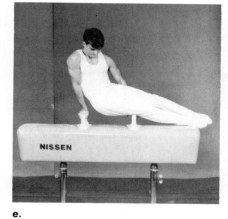

e.

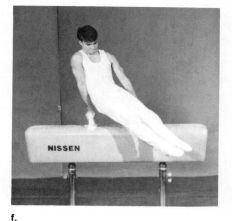

f.

Simple Swiss (Figure 7.17)

This move begins differently than the other simple moves described so far, and turns around without traveling as the simple *Czechkehre* did. When you learn it first you do not hop your hands, rather you walk them through their changes, but eventually you will be able to hop them around. This is a move that can be done from and to a circle as well. Begin in a front support. To turn clockwise, have your right hand at the back of the right pommel. Do a low left leg cut forward and reach for the right pommel with your left hand. Put it next to your right hand in a double overgrip. Leave your left leg trailing behind rather than pulling it ahead. Shift your weight to your left hand, reach back for the empty

Figure 7.17a, b, c, d, e, f
Lenny's leg cut in figure b is too high—this is a circular move—and his left leg is a bit too far around in figure c.

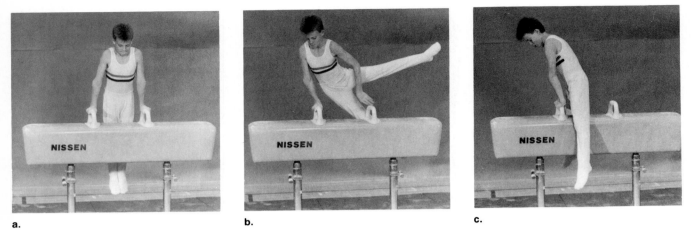

a.

b.

c.

d.

e.

f.

pommel with your right hand, then shift onto your right hand as your left leg continues to swing into a low cut forward under your left hand into a rear support. Your right leg has not gone anywhere, while your left leg has made a complete circle.

The most common problem is poor rhythm.

Pendular Swiss (Figure 7.18)

This is another step toward doing a circling Swiss (a definite hop), which is a skill beyond the scope of this book. To perform the pendular Swiss with legs together (it can be done straddled as well) in a clockwise fashion, begin in a front support with your right hand back, and swing your joined legs to the left

Figure 7.18a, b, c, d, e, f
Other than a slight form break, this is fine.

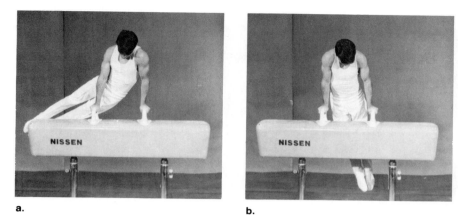

a.

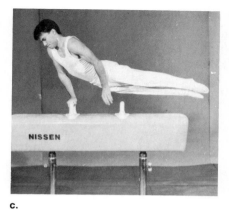

b.   c.

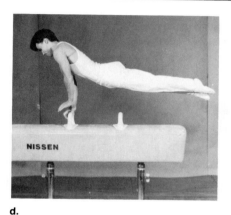

d.

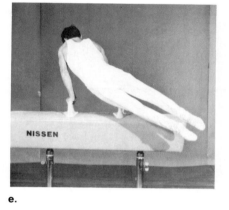

e.

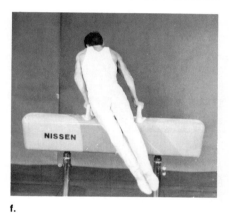

f.

and over the horse. As this happens, turn your shoulders to the right and reach for the right pommel with your left hand. Quickly exchange your right hand support for left hand support and reach for the empty pommel with your right hand, completing your body turn and finishing in a front support.

Common problems are not turning your shoulders hard enough, and not shifting your weight correctly.

Single-leg Circle (Figure 7.19)

As a lead up to double-leg circles, a single-leg circle may be learned. In this skill one leg goes around in a flat, circular pattern, while the other leg relatively stays put. The most useful single-leg circle for learning double-leg circles is the one that involves a low undercut back from a rear support, as this teaches you to turn your hips in during the undercut phase, which is a valuable lesson for a double-leg circle. To do this in a clockwise direction, begin in a stride support

Figure 7.19a, b, c, d, e, f
In figure d Stephan uses a leg kick to help
him turn in.

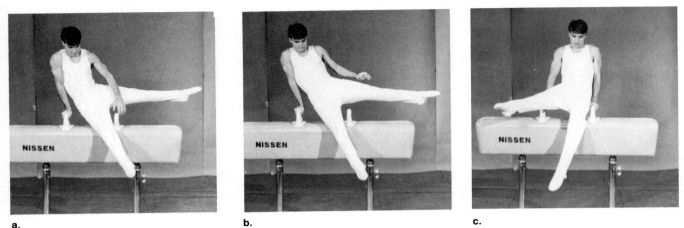

a. b. c.

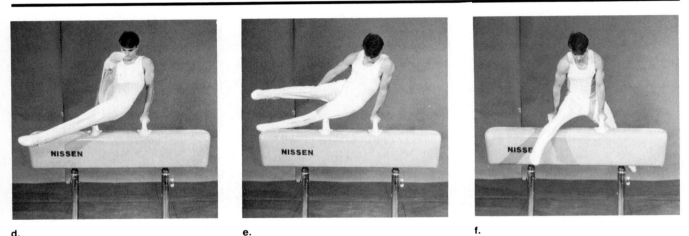

d. e. f.

with your right leg in front. Cut your left leg forward and low and shift your weight quickly to your left hand. Continue the circular motion of your left leg and undercut it back to the right, keeping your right leg low, too. Turn your hips to the left a bit to enable you to do the undercut. This is the turn in. You will finish in a stride support just as you started and should continue into another single-leg circle. Your left foot should follow a somewhat circular path about the height of the horse body.

Common problems are turning out during the undercut and not shifting your weight enough to do the undercut.

Double-leg Circle

Circles are the most important skill to learn on the pommel horse, and must be practiced throughout a gymnast's career. You want to avoid piking when doing this move, and you want to face in one direction with your whole body when

Figure 7.20a, b, c, d, e, f
Other than slight form breaks, Lenny's circle is pretty good on this very low mushroom.

a.

b.

c.

d.

e.

f.

swinging around. You will find that you will have to squeeze your seat to keep your body relatively straight. It is all right to have some bend in your upper body, that is, in your chest area. This will allow your body to swing in a wide circle from that point down. If you can eliminate any bend and swing from your shoulders, that is even better. Always swing in as wide a circle as you can.

There are many devices to aid in learning this skill. One of the most useful is the mushroom (figure 7.20). This device, which comes in various heights, allows the gymnast to keep his body straight as he learns to swing around the mushroom in a conical fashion that becomes flatter and flatter as the gymnast's strength increases or as the mushroom is lowered toward the mat. The mushroom is low so that it is easy to get into and out of skills. Begin by putting your hands about shoulder width on the mushroom. Jump your straight body around the left to a rear support. Notice how you have to shift your weight over your support (right) hand. If this is easy, continue the circle by shifting quickly to

Figure 7.21
A floor buck.

Figure 7.22
A specially made floor horse.

Figure 7.23
A floor horse without pommels.

the left side, turning in, and bringing your body back to a front support. Your eyes will be looking down and out so that you can see your body in front of you and the mushroom peripherally. Keep trying this until you can do circles continuously. As variations, put your hands close together and turn around either way while doing the circles. This is an opportunity to work on counterturning.

The same procedure is followed for circles on the buck (figure 7.21). This device does not force the same kind of conical path that the mushroom does, however. If you are working on a buck, try to do the circles both sideways and crossways (that is, with your shoulders aligned with or perpendicular to the long axis of the buck, respectively). Working on a low floor horse with pommels (figure 7.22) will force you to swing high, and training on a floor horse without pommels will help you to learn longitudinal circles (figure 7.23), which can be done on the end facing in and are called loops (described shortly), or can be done over the body of the horse (advanced skills), or on the other end of the horse facing out (advanced skills). If you work on a horse with pommels, in addition to doing them in the middle with your hands on the pommels (figures 7.24 and 7.25), you can do them on either end with one hand on a pommel and the other on the end. We call circles where your legs pass over the pommel from a front support first "uphill" circles, and those where your legs pass over the end of the horse from a front support first "downhill" circles.

Common problems are not shifting your weight quickly enough or pushing enough to maintain the circles, piking (figures 7.26 and 7.27), turning out, and touching your legs to the apparatus. If you are on a pommel horse, another problem is dipping in front and/or in back.

If you have become competent doing circles on the mushroom or on the other devices, or if you do not have access to these devices, then do circles on the horse. It is a bit more difficult to do circles on the horse (whether high or low) than on a high mushroom as you must lift your legs to clear the ends of the horse, yet you should not let them dip in front or in back of the horse during the circle. If you have trained on a low or floor mushroom or a floor horse you will know how to keep your feet circling in a flat plane. Try to keep your hands on the front part of the pommels.

Figure 7.24a, b, c, d, e, f, g
Oblique view of a circle.

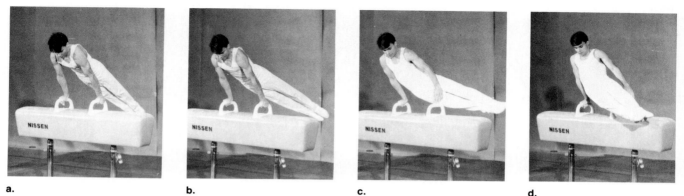

a.   b.   c.   d.

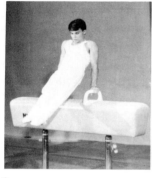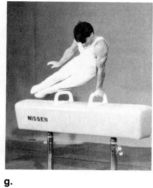

e.   f.   g.

Figure 7.25a, b, c, d
Side view of a circle—note Stephan's nicely
stretched body.

a.   b.   c.   d.

Figure 7.26
Avoid piking like this.

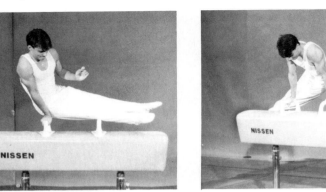

Figure 7.27
Avoid piking like this.

Figure 7.28a, b, c
Jumping into a circle.

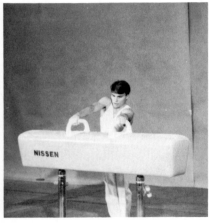
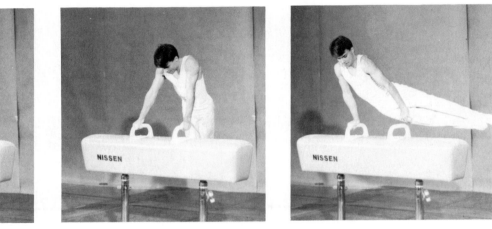

a.   b.   c.

You can begin a circle several ways. You can jump into one as you did on the mushroom or buck (figure 7.28), you can do a feint (figure 7.29)—swing one leg around your hand from a front support and swing it back to join your other leg with momentum to start the circle, or pick up a circle from a stride position by cutting one leg low across the horse to join your other with momentum (figures 7.30 and 7.31). In doing this your bottom leg pushes off the horse. Later on, try to begin from a front or rear support by using brute force to begin the circle—this may come in handy in future work.

You should keep your body as straight as possible, and swing your toes in as wide a circle as you can. The rhythm of your hands should be even. As you come back from the front, try to arch a bit. This will help keep you from piking, and it is OK to have a slight arch in the back of the circle, but not a pike. Generally, the faster you swing the easier it will be to do stretched circles, but as a variation you should try slow circles as well as fast circles.

Figure 7.29a, b, c
A feint into a circle.

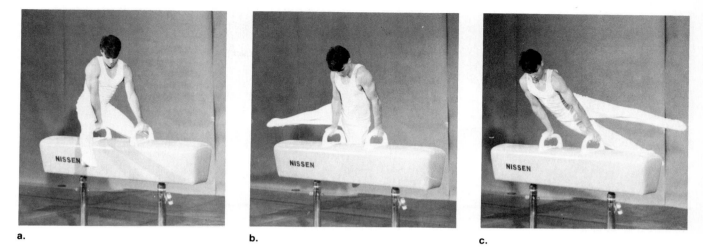

a.   b.   c.

Figure 7.30a, b, c, d
A leg cut backward into a circle.

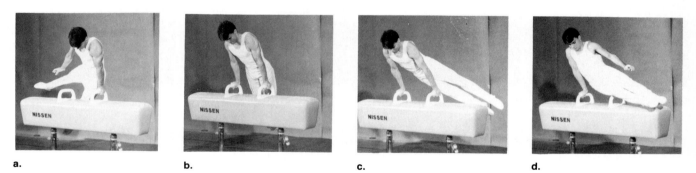

a.   b.   c.   d.

Figure 7.31a, b, c, d
A leg cut forward into a circle.

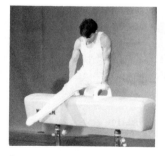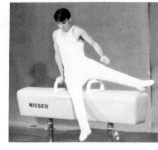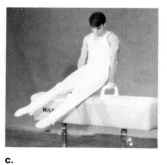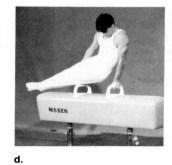

a.   b.   c.   d.

Figure 7.32a, b, c, d
Cutting out of circles in the front.

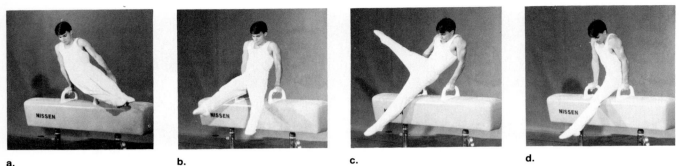

a.   b.   c.   d.

Figure 7.33a, b, c, d
Cutting out of circles in the back (the toe
hook is bad form).

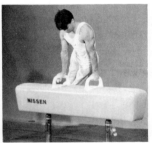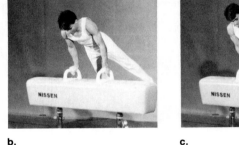

a.   b.   c.   d.

While you are working these on the horse, you should also learn them on the mat. This will force you to emphasize stretch and high swing and is an excellent training method. You can also use circles in your floor exercise routine. If you work on a floor mushroom, you are on your way to floor circles at the same time.

Getting Out of Circles into Leg Cuts

In order to perform pendular work such as scissors out of circle work, you will need to learn how to cut out of circles. If you want to do this in the front (figure 7.32), as your body passes over the left pommel, lift your right leg up in front of your face and push back with your right arm to stop your circle. As it stops, you will be in a straddled rear support tipped up to the right and can proceed into a cut backward. If you wish to cut from the back (figure 7.33), as your legs pass over the right pommel, push with your left arm to stop your circle, and begin to press upward as you lift your left leg up to the side. When your circle stops, you will be in position to cut forward.

Common problems are starting to lift your leg too late, not lifting it high, and not pushing enough to stop your circle, which often results in smacking your bottom leg into the horse.

Figure 7.34a, b, c, d, e, f
Stephan's loops are a bit tipped and are good for dismounts, but he will want to flatten out his circle plane for other work and extend more.

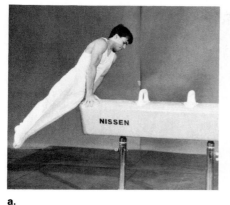

a.

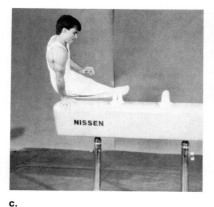

b.

c.

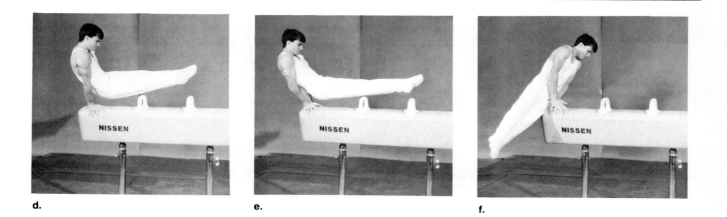

d.

e.

f.

Loop (Figure 7.34)

A loop is a circle crosswise on the end of the horse facing in. This circle is more difficult than one done in the middle on the pommels because your base of support is much smaller and you have to swing your legs over the pommel in front of you. It is often learned first on a horse without pommels (figure 7.23). Small boys may find this easier to do than circles on the pommels as their base of support is more comfortable—their small shoulders fit well over the width of the horse, but are too narrow for the pommels, which cannot be adjusted in far enough.

Loops can be done in two ways. If you want to continue into circle work, you will want to keep the plane of your loops rather flat. If you want to dismount, you will want to tip the plane up so that your feet are high over the horse as you pass over it, and your legs will point down in the back of the loops.

a. b. c.

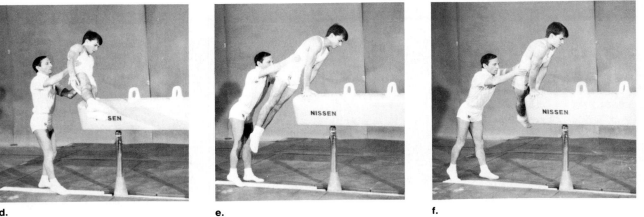

d. e. f.

You must lean over the horse quite a bit as your legs go behind you to keep from falling off, and you will find the sideways shift of your body that counterbalances your legs harder to do than for circles in the middle because of your small base of support. If you do these rapidly, this will help you to keep up your momentum. As with other circles, counterturning will help you to perform them well by getting your right hand back to the horse quickly so you can have support control.

Common problems are piking, turning out, not leaning enough, and going too slowly.

■

Spotting

You can spot this skill by standing behind your student and lifting at his waist to provide support and to help keep him on the horse (figure 7.35). You must be careful to avoid getting hit by his legs.

Figure 7.36a, b, c, d, e, f
Stephan could be less piked in figure e, and
could straddle wider in figure d.

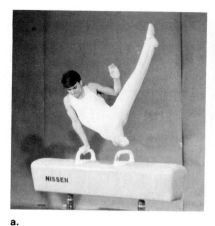

a.

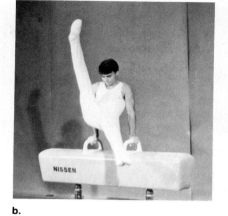

b.

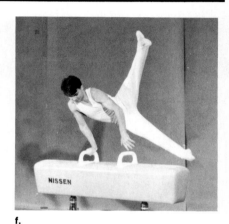

c.

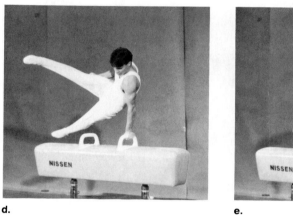

d.

e.

f.

Thomas Flair (Figure 7.36)

The Thomas Flair (also called an American straddled circle) was popularized
in the international arena by star USA gymnast Kurt Thomas, hence the name.
It is a circle with your legs straddled and swung high, giving the appearance of
a helicopter's rotors. It is often learned on the mushroom, but can be learned
on any of the circle-learning devices. Some feel that learning flaired loops helps
to teach loops as the flair helps learning the counterturning action. To get the
feeling of flair circles, do some circles with your legs apart a bit the whole way
around. Gradually increase the straddle of your circles until your legs are spread
as far apart as possible the entire time. You may feel like you are doing undercuts as you pass over the horse. When these are done well, each foot passes
over head height at some time during your circle. Stretch out with your hips as

Figure 7.37a, b, c, d, e, f, g, h
Aside from a slight pike in figures c and d,
this downhill travel is well done.

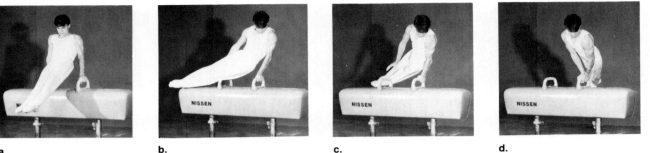

a. b. c. d.

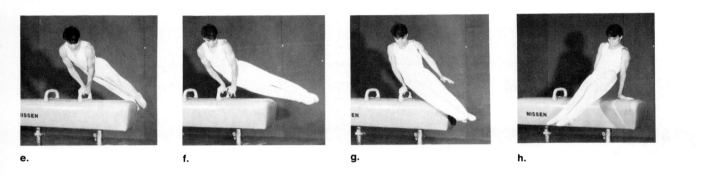

e. f. g. h.

far as you can as well. Try not to pike in the back or sides, although some pike is often seen. Ideally, your body would show no pike in the back and constant straddle width.

Common problems are not straddling enough, not maintaining a constant straddle width, piking excessively in the back, and swinging your legs and body too low in the back due to lifting into a pike too much in the front.

Side Travel Frontways (Figure 7.37)

This is the circular equivalent to the simple travel, except that your hand position on the pommel is usually different. Whereas during the simple travel you usually put your right hand behind your left hand, here you usually put your right hand in front of your left hand (so that you finish with your right hand in front of the pommel—better for the circle). It is a frontways travel since you travel in a front support (rearways is much harder). If you travel from the middle to the end, that is downhill. The opposite action is called uphill. The downhill travel is easier than the uphill travel (it is easier going downhill than going uphill on most anything), so I will describe that one first. The travel begins in a rear support with your left hand toward the back of the left pommel. Shift your weight more to the left than you would to continue circles in the middle. Look at the pommel and where you want to go as your legs come back over the right pommel. Put your right hand on the left pommel in front of your left hand. As your body continues around the back and to the left, continue shifting your

Figure 7.38a, b, c, d, e, f
Aside from the form break, this kehre-in from a downhill circle is good.

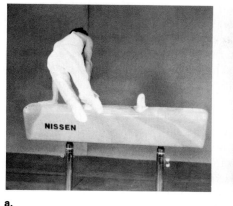

a.

b.

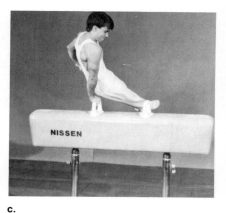

c.

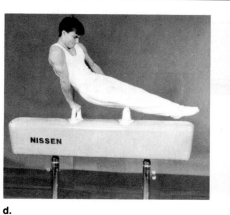

d.

e.

f.

weight toward the end, and reach for the end with your left hand as your legs pass over it. Finish in a rear support and continue circling. To help you go uphill, push your seat inside of and to the front of the pommel on the circle before you begin the uphill travel. I always found the travel easy if I wound up reaching for the pommel with my left hand directly behind my seat as I moved into the rear support just before the travel. You may also feel that you pull the pommel under you more than you do for a downhill travel, especially if you have not moved in enough. The rest of the action is the same as for a downhill travel.

Common problems are not shifting sideways enough, piking, having slow hands, and not pushing down hard enough.

Kreiskehre (Figure 7.38)

This skill is often tried as a mount before circles are mastered to get the feeling of turning on one arm. It is a move where you change both position on the horse and the direction in which you face. If done from the end to the middle, it is a *kehre*-in and from the opposite direction it is a *kehre*-out. The move can be described as a circling double rear vault and is pronounced: krice'-kehr-eh; (in the USA it is often referred to as a *kehre* and is [mis]pronounced: kehr.)

To do a *kehre*-in as a mount (figure 7.39), begin by standing in front of the left end of the horse with your right hand on the back (close) half of the pommel and your left hand on the end. Jump into a circle but lean into the middle of the horse more than for a downhill circle. Look into the middle and push down very hard with your right hand. Keep your right arm locked in place by your right side. As your legs come around, turn your body so that you ride into the middle pivoting on your right hand. Reach for the other pommel with your left hand as soon as you can. Finish the skill in a rear support and do a circle out of it.

To perform this from a downhill circle, the skill begins as you pass through a front support. Lean in by pushing on the end extra hard with your left hand and look where you are going. The rest is the same, although you will find you have more starting momentum from a circle.

As you found with the travel, a *kehre*-in (or uphill *kehre*) can be a bit tougher than a *kehre*-out because you have to go up.

Common problems are piking, not pushing in enough, not pushing down hard enough to provide good support, letting your support arm drift from a solid position by your side, and not being prepared to do a circle out of the *kehre*.

■

Spotting

You can spot the mount (when not done into circles) by standing by the middle of the horse on the same side as your student (figure 7.39). Grasp his upper right arm with your right hand, and lift his seat with your left hand as he goes for the move. If his leg hits you after the *kehre* it should not cause a problem, as it is not moving fast.

Czechkehre (Figure 7.40)

In the USA we call this move a Moore in honor of Roy E. Moore, an early pioneer. Remember the hand motions that you did for a simple Moore? Here is where you get to use them again. Like the *kehre*, this is often tried as a mount before circles are mastered. To perform the mount in the middle, stand in front of the pommels and put your hands on the front (far) half of the pommels. Jump to a front support on the horse while pushing your legs around to the left side, turning your body to the right, and shifting your weight over the left pommel. Move your right hand to the left pommel so that you are in a double undergrip. In the middle of this move you should be aligned with the horse lengthwise and will be facing it directly. Continue swinging your body around and shift your weight back into the middle, reaching for the open pommel with your left hand as soon as your weight leaves it and your legs pass over that pommel. Finish in a rear support and continue into circles.

This skill begins in a rear support when done from a circle. As your legs pass over the right pommel, shift to the left, turn your shoulders to the right, and reach for the left pommel with your right hand. The balance of the skill is the same as for the mount. You will find that the momentum you get from a circle may help you to do the skill.

Figure 7.39a, b, c, d, e, f

a.

b.

c.

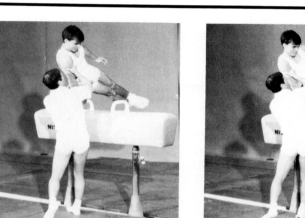

d.

e.

f.

Common problems are not turning enough or turning too much, piking, not balancing during the turn (leaning in or out too much), and taking your left hand off the pommel too soon.

When this skill is done on the end of the horse from a downhill circle (figure 7.41), so that your hands are on the end of the horse rather than on the pommels, it is called a loop around, or circle-loop-circle (*Schwabenflanke* is the [German] international term; pronounced: shvah'-ben-flahn-keh). It is important to maintain a flat circle plane if you intend to do a circle out of the loop.

Figure 7.40a, b, c, d, e, f

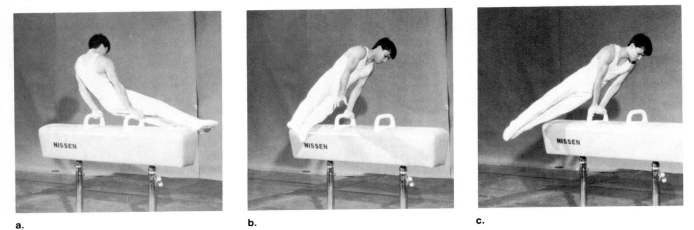

a.

b.

c.

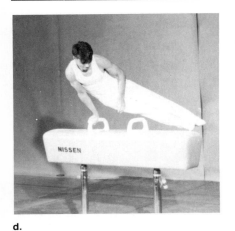

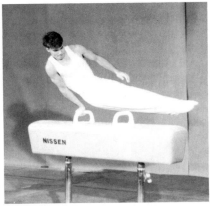

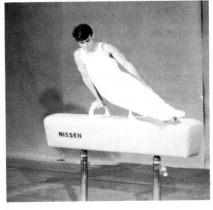

d.

e.

f.

Loop Dismounts

The loop dismount has several variations. It can be performed with or without a turn, and the kinds most often seen are the plain loop dismount, the loop with one-half turn inward, and the loop with one-half turn outward. For a long while the loop with one-half turn outward was everyone's standard dismount, but these days gymnasts are using handstand dismounts (which are advanced skills) as soon as they can perform them. Loop dismounts are done from loop circles, from a downhill circle that turns through a loop position, or a move that brings you directly to a loop position.

Figure 7.41a, b, c, d, e, f
Stephan dips around the end a bit too much if he intends to continue into circles, but if he wanted to dismount, the dip would be fine (note the slight form break in figure f).

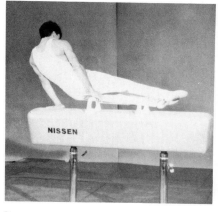

a.

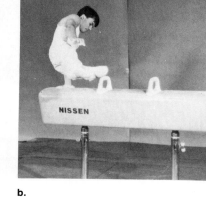

b.

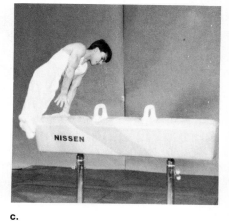

c.

d.

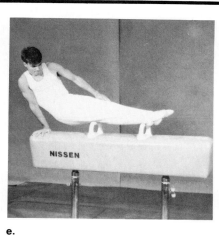

e.

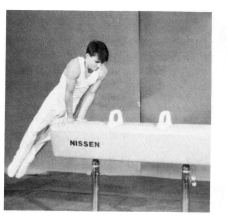

f.

When performing the plain loop dismount (figure 7.42), you drop your legs as they go around the end so that your plane is tilted up and so that you can lift your feet and get into a high pike as you come over the horse. To dismount, push off to the right side as your feet move to their highest point. Keep your left hand on the horse so that your feet will come down to the side of the end of the horse. You can get the feeling of this dismount by jumping into it from the mat.

Figure 7.42a, b, c, d, e, f, g

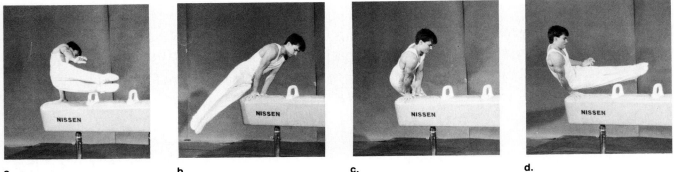

a.   b.   c.   d.

e.   f.   g.

The common problem is not lifting your legs forcefully enough to get flight over the horse.

To perform the loop with one-half turn inward (figure 7.43), start just as you would for a plain loop dismount. Just before you reach the peak of your upswing, counterturn and open from your pike into a stretched position. This will aid in performing the turn. Your right hand will replace your left hand on the horse prior to landing.

Common problems are starting the turn too late and not turning hard enough.

The loop with one-half turn outward (or *Schwabenwende:* means front vault; pronounced: shvah'-ben-ven-deh) is performed differently (figure 7.44). It is one of the few horse movements where you try to turn your shoulders well ahead of your lower body. As your legs come down and around the end of the horse, lean to the right, turn your shoulders hard to the right, and kick into an arch. You will be facing the horse if you have turned enough. This will put you in a position to push down on the horse to aid your legs in going up as they pass over the horse. Your arms will cross while your hands maintain support on the end. At the end of the skill your left hand comes off the horse to facilitate the landing.

Common problems are not lifting as you go over the horse, and piking instead of arching.

Figure 7.43a, b, c, d, e, f

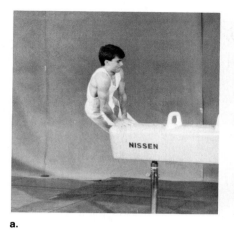

a.

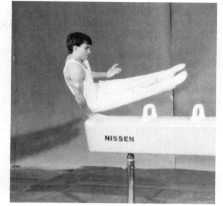

b.

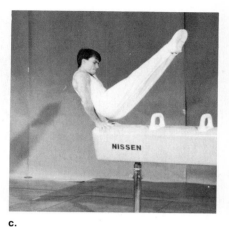

c.

d.

e.

f.

Sequences to Practice

1. Series of leg cuts in a row
2. Series of undercuts in a row
3. From the end, simple travel uphill, 4 leg cuts (over, over, back, back), simple downhill travel, pendular double-leg cut over and back with one-quarter turn in to a landing behind the horse
4. From the end, simple back in, cut back, cut back, cut forward, undercut back, cut forward to simple Moore, 4 leg cuts (over, over, back, back), cut forward, undercut back, simple Swiss
5. Series of 10 front or back scissors in a row
6. Work up to at least 20 circles on a mushroom, 20 loops on a horse without pommels, and 20 circles on a floor horse

Figure 7.44a, b, c, d, e, f, g
If Stephan turned his shoulders more in figures d and e, he would be in a better position to push down on the horse to lift his body.

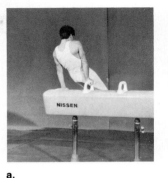

a.

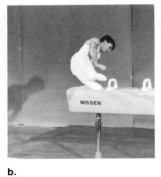

b.

c.

d.

e.

f.

g.

7. Five uphill circles, uphill side travel frontways, 5 circles on the pommels, downhill side travel frontways, 5 downhill circles, one-half loop around to 5 loops, turn in to uphill circles

8. Jump into 2 circles, cut forward into 2 front scissors, cut forward, cut backward, 2 back scissors, pick up circles in the back, 2½ circles, cut backward into 2 back scissors, cut back, cut forward, 2 front scissors, pick up circles in the front

9. From circles on the pommels, Moore, circle, side travel frontways, one-half loop around into 2 loops, loop dismount

10. From circles on the pommels, *kehre*-out, 1½ circles, *kehre*-in, 1 circle, Moore, 1½ circles, simple Swiss, 2 circles, side travel frontways, turn immediately into a loop dismount with one-half turn outward

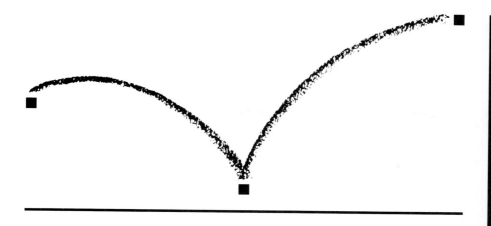

Balance beam is the most difficult event for most female gymnasts to master, and the reason is obvious—the margin for balance error is very small. The beam, although 5 meters long (over 16 feet), is only 10 centimeters wide, just less than 4 inches. If your center of gravity deviates a bit more than 2 inches from the midline plane, you will most likely fall off. A balance beam routine (as is women's floor exercise) is the longest routine performed in both men's and women's gymnastics, between 70 and 90 seconds. In competition, the performer must show dance, acrobatics, tumbling, and moves over and on the beam (in some cases moves under the beam are shown). No more than two hold moves are permitted, although other poses may be used. However, she must avoid unnecessary stops before and after skills. She will perform moves with forward, sideward, and backward movement in a variety of positions. There must be an acrobatic series (two or more tumbling elements), a gymnastic series (for example, two or more jumps or leaps or dance skills), a turn of at least 360°, a leap of great amplitude, and a dismount. There are minimum difficulty requirements for many of these skills.

Moves that are done on the beam should be learned on a line on the floor whenever practical. Do not be in a rush to do a move on the high beam if you have not mastered it down low. Another advantage of learning moves on the floor is that many students can practice them at the same time, whereas for most skills only one can be on the beam at one time. If you have enough mats, it is a good practice to stack them around your beam so that the mat level is even with the beam at the start, and to gradually remove them as you grow confident and competent. This way, the beam height stays constant, and the mat height changes gradually. If you do not have enough mats, a good progression of learning begins on the floor and proceeds to beams of increasing height. A floor beam is the logical next step after a move is learned on the floor. By the time a girl performs a move on the high beam, she will have practiced it many times at the lower heights and will be familiar with the move so that she will have little or no fear of performing it up high.

Skills that are practiced low are easily spotted. Tumbling skills are spotted often just as they are on the mat. Beam pads that wrap around the beam can be used to cushion rolls in the early stages. A spotting block or mat stack should be used to elevate a spotter to make the spotting task easier.

Learn moves going either way or starting with either leg—you will find which way you prefer. If a move is described one way in this chapter, you should also try it the other way.

Beginners, especially small children, may want to climb up onto the beam in a variety of ways and then crawl around on it to get used to its small width (for small children it is not nearly as narrow as for larger people). Beginners are encouraged to do such exploratory movements and to become familiar with the narrow surface on which they will have to be comfortable. Laying on their front, side, or back, crawling on the top of the beam, doing caterpillar walks (like an inchworm), doing crab walks (with their back toward the beam, walking on their hands and feet without letting their seat touch), and other such exercises not only promote familiarity with the beam but also strengthen their muscles and develop balance.

Terms Used in This Chapter

relevé   This is also called half-toe, and is pronounced: reh-leh-vay′. It means to raise up onto the balls of your feet. Other dance terms are explained where they are used in the text.

Organization of This Chapter

Walking

Running and Skipping

Dance Skills

Turns on the Feet

Poses

Transitions

Mounts

Dismounts

Handstand

Forward Roll With Hand Support

Jump to Forward Roll

Backward Roll

Cartwheel

Walkovers

Sequences to Practice

Walking

Walking on the beam is not quite like walking on the floor. Eventually you want to be able to walk on the balls of your feet (also called half-toe or *relevé*) with a slight turn-out. You will be comfortable enough to not have to hold your head down to see where the beam is—you learn how to look down with your eyes only and keep your head in line with your trunk. You can also look out to the end of the beam when you are far from it and your peripheral vision will tell you where the beam is below you. In addition, you learn how to feel comfortable when you look away at something else. Young children may have difficulty walking on the balls of their feet as they may not be strong enough to do that. This strength will come eventually.

Whenever your foot is off the beam, your toe should be pointed. If you get into this habit early, it will help you later on. As your foot swings alongside the beam between steps, keep it in light contact with the side of the beam. This will help you to know where the beam is—especially going backward. When you step, your big toe contacts the beam first, then the rest of your foot. When your foot is on the beam, all five toes are always pressing down on the beam—except during turns. To learn to not twist side to side when you walk (that is, to not look like a washing machine in action), it is helpful to walk with your hands on your waist or touching your shoulders and your elbows pointing sideways (figures 8.1 and 8.2). In this way you will clearly see and feel if you twist. The length of your step may affect your hips—too long and your hips twist.

Figure 8.1   **Figure 8.2**

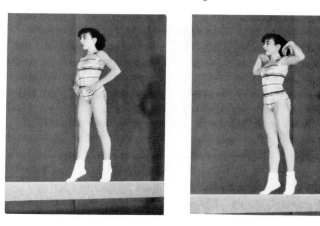

Try walking on one level with your legs straight, then walking with a dip—flex your supporting knee a bit to dip down and then extend it to rise up. Try different rhythms of stepping—slow, fast, mixed. You will find walking fast easier than walking slowly. Also try different arm positions as you walk—for example, hold them out to the side at shoulder height with a soft forward curve, swing them by your sides, hold them in front in different ballet poses. Relax your hands and keep your shoulders depressed so that you have a long-neck appearance. If your shoulders (and arms) tense up, it will affect the rest of your body and usually upset your balance. Some hints to keep in good alignment are: (1) Pretend that you have a metal rod from your head down to your pelvis and elongate along this rod; (2) try to touch your shoulder blades together to keep from hunching; and (3) keep your seat tucked under and your stomach in. At the end of each walking pass, practice various turns to become familiar with them (see later pages).

Forward (Figure 8.3)

When you first walk forward, just do it any old way to get used to the feel for walking on a narrow surface. (If you have spent time walking fences—not a recommended practice—you will have this feeling already.) After you have walked a few times, refine your movements—as you walk, keep your head in line with your trunk and keep your trunk upright, point your toe as your foot comes off the beam behind you and bring it alongside the beam to the front, and when you are strong enough, walk on the balls of your feet.

Backward (Figure 8.4)

The same procedure goes for walking backward. Once you have tried it, to refine it you learn to point your toe as it comes off the beam in front, bring it back alongside the beam, and feel for the beam behind you with your toe before putting weight on your back foot. Good alignment again is important, and since you cannot see behind you, learn to judge where the beam is by using your peripheral vision and feeling inner-thigh contact to give you cues.

Figure 8.3a, b, c, d, e, f, g
These are dip steps forward.

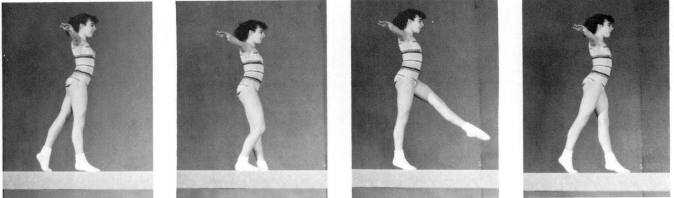

a.

b.

c.

d.

e.

f.

g.

Sideward (Figures 8.5 and 8.6)

There are several ways to walk sideways, and all are useful. Facing sideways, at first flat-footed and then on the balls of your feet, simply take side steps, moving one foot away from the other and then joining them by bringing your trailing foot to your leading foot. Remember, do not look down at the beam. Learn where it is by feel and repetition. If this is easy, try to cross your legs as you sidestep. For example, take your right leg and cross it over in front of your left leg so that the ball of your right foot steps on the beam to the left of your left foot. Transfer your weight to your right foot and move your left foot to the left of your right foot (back to a stand as in the way you started). You can repeat this action to the left, or go to the right, or you can cross one leg behind the other rather than in front of it. Keep your shoulders and hips in line with the beam as you do these side steps so that you will not twist from side to side like a washing machine.

Figure 8.4a, b, c, d, e, f, g
These are dip steps backward.

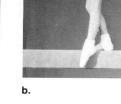

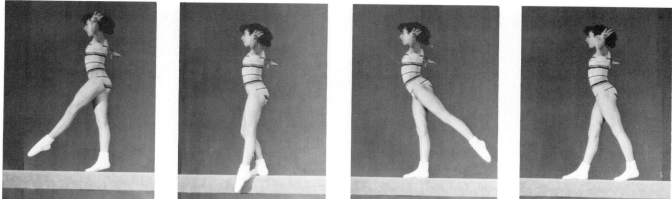

a.

b.

c.

d.

e.

f.

g.

Figure 8.5a, b, c, d
Side steps.

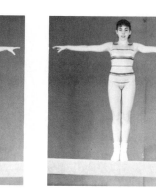

a.

b.

c.

d.

Figure 8.6a, b, c, d, e, f, g, h, i
Cross side steps.

a.

b.

c.

d.

e.

f.

g.

h.

i.

Figure 8.7a, b, c, d
Running.

a.   b.   c.   d.

Common flaws are holding your head down, hooking your toes when your feet are off the beam, twisting your hip girdle, and poor body alignment.

You can stand alongside of your student and provide touch support if needed.

Spotting

Running and Skipping (Figures 8.7 and 8.8)

Just as you can do these things on the floor, they can be done on the beam. Of course you will have to be careful where you put your feet! To build up to running (not full speed of course), which may look like fast walking and then light running, do just that—walk more and more quickly and add some bounce to your walk when you feel ready for it. Take long, low steps. Your foot should scrape the side of the beam as it swings forward. Skipping is done in the same fashion—start slowly and build up the speed when you feel comfortable. Each landing will be in a *demi plié*.

Common flaws are the same as for walking.

Stand by the beam and offer hand support if necessary.

Spotting

Dance Skills

These skills are also used on floor exercise and are only a few of the many dance skills used.

Chassé Forward (Figure 8.9)

A *chassé* (pronounced: shah-say') is often referred to as step-together-step. Step forward onto your right foot and jump forward a bit. As you leave the beam, bring your left leg forward to the back of your right leg, and then lift your right leg forward, landing on your left foot. You can do this sideward as well, by

Figure 8.8a, b, c, d, e, f
Skipping.

a.

b.

c.

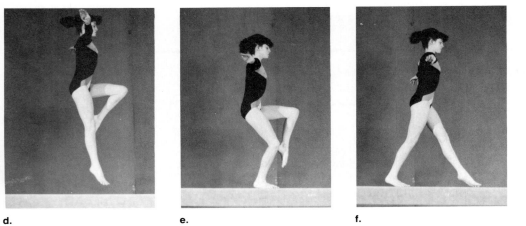

d.

e.

f.

Figure 8.9a, b, c, d, e

a.

b.

c.

d.

e.

a.　　　　　　　　b.　　　　　　　　c.　　　　　　　　d.

stepping sideward on your left foot, pushing into a small jump to your left, bringing your right leg to your left leg, and then stepping on your right foot as your left leg lifts sideward.

The most common problem is looking like a rocking horse as you do a *chassé*. You should keep your trunk upright during the move and not let it rock forward and backward, or side to side.

Straight Jump (Figure 8.10) and Tucked Jump (Figure 8.11)

Just as you do these on the floor, you can do them on the balance beam. Start these jumps in a *demi plié* or a *plié,* and remember to absorb your landings in a *demi plié*. When you jump from the beam, your toes leave just after the balls of your feet. When you land, the opposite sequence occurs.

Common problems are not pushing equally out of both legs, not completing extension of both legs, and taking off with your hips twisted or tilted. All of these will cause you to jump out of the vertical plane and probably fall off.

Stride Leap (Figure 8.12)

Step forward on your right foot, swing your left leg forward and up, and jump from your right foot to your left foot while maintaining a stride position in flight. When you land, hold your right leg up behind you. If you split your legs completely in flight, this becomes a split leap and is of higher value.

Common problems are not keeping your shoulders square (aligned perpendicular to the beam), not splitting your legs at least 90°, letting your trailing leg drop, looking down, and not jumping high.

Sissonne (Figure 8.13)

The *sissonne* (pronounced: see-sahn´) is a jump from two feet that finishes like a stride (or split) leap. From a two foot start, jump upward and forward, splitting your legs and lifting your back leg especially hard so that your front leg points down toward the beam. Hold your back leg up as you land in *demi plié*.

Common problems are the same as for a stride leap.

Figure 8.11a, b, c, d, e

Dawn's tuck should be tighter and her toes should be pointed in figure b.

a.   b.   c.   d.   e.

Figure 8.12a, b, c

a.   b.   c.

Figure 8.13a, b, c, d

a.   b.   c.   d.

Figure 8.14a, b, c, d, e, f

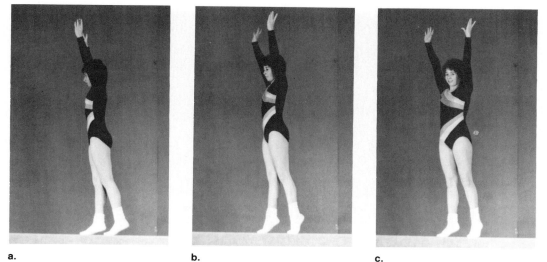

a.   b.   c.

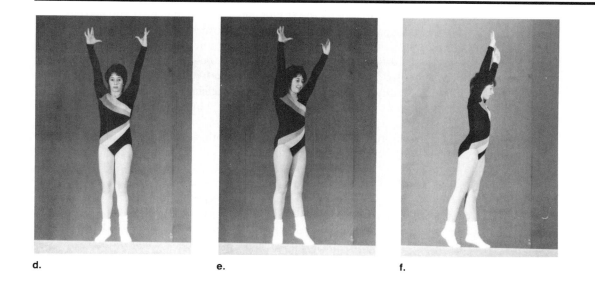

d.   e.   f.

Turns on the Feet

Although you may start in a flat-footed stance, all turns are done with your foot (feet) in *relevé,* as this position has the smallest contact area with the beam, and thus the least resistance to the turn.

Relevé (Figure 8.14)

The *relevé* turn (or pivot or two-foot toe turn) is done by simply turning around while in *relevé.* Begin in a staggered flat stance (for balance) with your right foot in front of your left. The heel of your right foot should be by the ball of your left foot. Your arms can be in a variety of positions, but for starters keep

Figure 8.15a, b, c, d, e

a. b. c. d. e.

them down by your sides. Raise up to *relevé,* keeping both legs slightly (and equally) turned out. Start and continue your turn to the left by moving your left heel forward. Once you have completed your turn, lower to a flat stance again. You will wind up facing in the opposite direction that you started, with your feet in opposite alignment. You can then turn back to the right and finish facing the same way as you began. Try to vary the position of your arms as you practice this turn. As you get better you may not need to start in a flat stance for balance. Keep your trunk erect during the turn, and be aware of your surroundings—you can watch everything at your eye level as you turn but focus on a finish point when your turn is completed. This will help to keep your head still in relation to your trunk.

Common problems are not turning smoothly and not keeping your trunk erect (usually bending at your waist).

Squat (Figure 8.15)

This is the most stable turn on the feet as you are the closest to the beam (your center of gravity is the lowest), and it is therefore relatively easy to balance during the turn. The turning action is the same as for the *relevé* turn. Begin just as you did with the *relevé* turn. Squat down deeply (but do not rest your thighs on your calves), keeping on the balls of your feet, and turn around to your left. Keep your weight equally distributed on your feet, maintain an equal leg bend, and do not let your knees drop forward during your turn. Finish in a squat, or stand up. You can then squat again and turn in the opposite direction. Try different arm positions.

Common problems are similar to the *relevé* turn.

Swing Forward (Figure 8.16)

This turn is done on one foot rather than two. The term *forward* refers to the direction that you swing your leg to initiate the turn. Step forward on your right foot, then swing your left leg forward and over the beam, passing close to the side of the beam. As your left leg nears the end of its swing forward, *relevé* on your right foot and turn to your right, but leave your left leg where it was before

Figure 8.16a, b, c, d, e, f, g
Dawn could hold her leg up more in figures
e, f, and g.

a.　　　　　b.　　　　　c.　　　　　d.

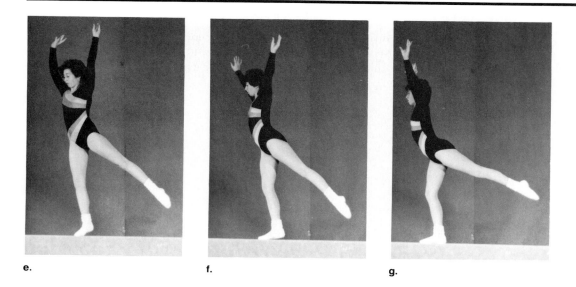

e.　　　　　f.　　　　　g.

you started to turn. It is as if you lifted your left leg and put it on a chair, then turned away from it. You will finish in an arabesque position with your left leg as high as your forward swing was. From this position you can do another swing turn. Try various arm positions.

Common problems are not turning sharply, swinging your leg around rather than along and then over the beam, letting your leg drop as you finish, and lifting your leg higher in the front than your finish position.

Figure 8.17a, b, c, d, e, f
Dawn turns too early in figures c and d—she
should face forward until her leg is as high
as it is in figure d.

a.

b.

c.

d.

e.

f.

Swing Backward (Figure 8.17)

This is done in a similar fashion to the swing forward, except that you swing your front leg rearward and turn toward it. Begin with your left leg up in front while standing on your right, then swing your left leg back by the beam and over the beam. As it goes up in back, turn to your left and keep it up where it was when you started to turn. Again, it is as if you put your leg on a chair behind you and turned toward it. Once you have completed the turn, you can do another.

Common problems are similar to the swing turn forward.

Figure 8.18a, b, c, d, e
Dawn could show more relevé in this half turn.

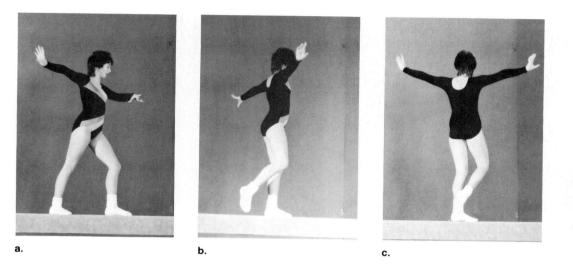

a.

b.

c.

d.

e.

Full Turn (1/1) on One Foot (Figure 8.19)

There are many types of full turns on one foot starting in a cross stand (facing along the beam) or a side stand (facing out from the beam), and many leg positions are used during these turns. Keeping your trunk and hips from changing position during a turn is the biggest key to turning. Another key is to turn more slowly than you might think necessary.

As a lead up to learn a full turn, it is useful to go at it stepwise, to learn to do two half turns in a row, then the full turn. Try this on the ground first, then on the beam. For a half turn, begin facing along the beam in a flat-footed

Figure 8.19a, b, c, d, e
Dawn's *retiré* position is not correct during this full turn—her hip should be turned out.

a.

b.

c.

d.

e.

lunge with your left foot in front. Bring your right leg to the back of your left leg and flex your right knee a bit. Figure 8.18 shows *coupé* position (pronounced: koo-pay′)—your right foot is by the bottom of your calf. At the same time, rise to *relevé* on your left foot. Bring your right arm to your left arm to start your turn and do a one-half turn to your left. Spot (look for) the end of the beam at the start of your turn, and spot the opposite end at the end of your turn. I suggest keeping your right leg low to promote stability in the learning phases, and to avoid tilting your hips, which will happen if you lift your right leg up to *retiré* (pronounced: reh-tih-ray′), the position shown in figure 8.19, without training in this position. If a half turn feels easy, then do a full turn in

Figure 8.20
A stand with extended leg lifted forward.

Figure 8.21
A stand with slightly bent leg lifted forward, called a front attitude.

Figure 8.22
A stand with extended leg lifted sideward.

Figure 8.23
A *retiré* position.

Figure 8.24
A stand with extended leg lifted backward = arabesque.

Figure 8.25
A V seat.

coupé position. You must turn a bit harder, but remember a smooth turn is the object. Spotting the same end of the beam as where you started will help you to turn. To stop the turn, lower to a flat foot. As you feel more comfortable with this turn, bring your right foot up to *retiré*. Be careful not to tilt your hips—keep them level. You can also try various arm positions.

Common problems are maintaining balance (low leg positions help you balance when you are learning), tilting your hips when you lift your leg (your hip line should be horizontal), and—when you do the turn in *retiré*—holding an incorrect *retiré* position.

Poses (Figures 8.20–8.32)

There are many of these. Here is a sample. Poses should be shown (up to a second), not held (more than a second). They all can be used on floor exercise as well.

Figure 8.26
A knee scale with hand support.

Figure 8.27a
A front scale facing along the beam (crossways).

Figure 8.27b
A Y scale facing out from the beam (sideways)—this is a kind of side scale.

Figure 8.28
A straddled split.

Figure 8.29
A stride split.

Figure 8.30a
A curtsey—head facing forward.

Figure 8.30b
A curtsey—head facing sideward.

Figure 8.31
A sideward lunge.

Figure 8.32
A forward lunge.

Figure 8.33a, b, c, d
Lowering to a seat on one leg—if you
reverse the figures, you will have a rise to a
stand on one leg (shown later in the section
on mounts).

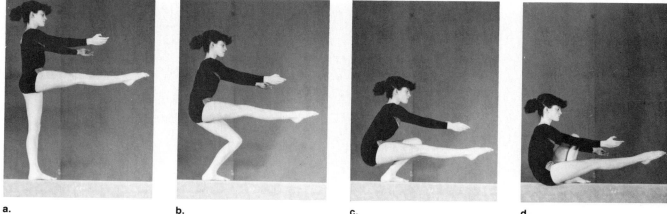

a.   b.   c.   d.

Transitions (Figures 8.33 and 8.34)

These are movements used to connect others, or to move from a stand to the beam and vice versa. They can be used on floor exercise as well. Here is a sample.

Mounts

From a Jump to a Front Support (Figures 8.35–8.40)

Figure 8.35: Begin next to the beam facing the beam. Put your hands on the beam and jump to a front support with your thighs resting against the side of the beam. Lift one leg to the side and swing it over the beam so that you are sitting on the beam in a narrow straddle with your hands on the beam in front of you. Once you are in this position, you can do many transitions to other moves. Figure 8.36: Swing both legs forward and backward and push down on the beam so that you can lift your body off the beam as your legs swing up behind you. When you are off the beam, bring your legs into a squat and put your feet on the beam under your body. Shift your weight to your feet and stand up. Figure 8.37: Another way to stand up is on one leg. Instead of squatting both legs under you, just bring one leg under you and leave the other behind. When you get into support on the one leg, stand up into an arabesque position. Figure 8.38: As a third variation, once you get into the straddled seat on the beam, lift your legs forward and upward into a V seat (you can pass through a tuck as shown, or lift your straight legs up), moving your hands to the beam behind you. From this V seat, or from the position in figure 8.38b, flex one knee and bring that foot down to the beam. Figure 8.39: Step forward so that both feet are on the beam and stand up. Figure 8.40: Transfer your weight only to that one foot and stand up on it. Reaching forward will help you shift your weight.

Figure 8.34a, b, c, d, e
Lowering to a *révérence* (pronounced; ray'-vay-rahns) kneel—if you reverse the figures, you will have a rise from the *révérence* position.

a.

b.

c.

d.

e.

Figure 8.35a, b, c, d
This mount leads to the following five transitions (at least).

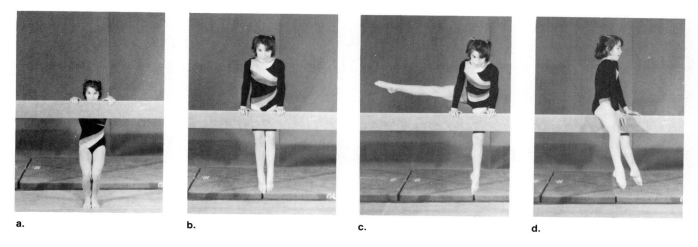

a. b. c. d.

Figure 8.36a, b, c, d
Swing up rearward to a squat stand.

a. b. c. d.

Figure 8.37a, b, c, d, e, f, g, h
Swing up rearward to one foot and stand
up.

a.　　　　　　　b.　　　　　　　c.　　　　　　　d.

e.　　　　　　　f.　　　　　　　g.　　　　　　　h.

Figure 8.38a, b, c, d, e
Lift forward through a tuck to a V seat (you
can omit the tuck if you want).

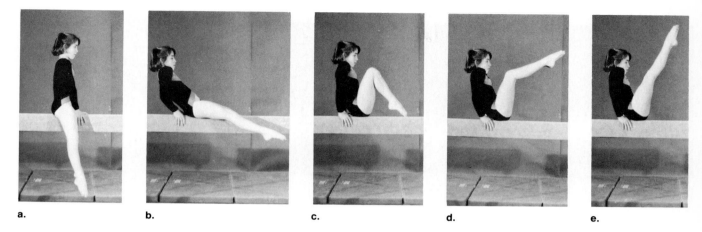

a.   b.   c.   d.   e.

Figure 8.39a, b, c
Picture this rise to a stand added after
figure 8.38b.

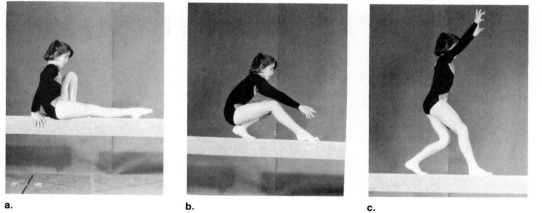

a.   b.   c.

Figure 8.40a, b, c, d, e
Picture this rise to a stand on one leg added after figure 8.38b—as you get better, your hands should be off the beam in figure a.

a.

b.

c.

d.

e.

■

Spotting

Stand nearby in case of a slip in balance. You can lift your student if needed.

Jump to a Squat (Figures 8.41 and 8.42)

From a stand facing the beam and by the side of the beam, put your hands about shoulder width on the beam. Jump up while pushing down on the beam to lift your seat up and squat so that your feet go on the beam between your hands. Using a vaulting board helps here.

Common problems are spreading your knees and/or feet so that your legs hit your arms, and hitting your shins on the beam due to a weak downward push.

Figure 8.41a, b, c, d
Spotting a squat mount from the back.

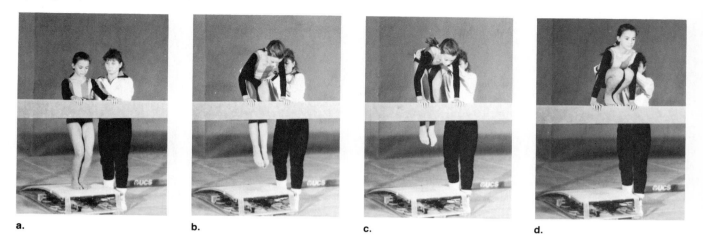

a.

b.

c.

d.

Figure 8.42a, b
Spotting a squat mount from the front.

a.

b.

Stand in front and a bit to the side of your student and hold her upper arms for stability, or if she cannot jump high enough, stand next to her behind the beam and lift her by the waist to help her get her feet on the beam.

Spotting

Jump to a Straddle (Figures 8.43 and 8.44)

In a similar fashion, instead of squatting your legs between your arms, you can keep your legs straight and straddle them when you jump, finishing in a straddled stand on the beam. A variation of this, called a wolf mount, finishes with one leg squatted in between your arms and your other leg straight out to the side like half a straddle (figure 8.45). You must lift your seat high to do this easily.

Figure 8.43a, b, c, d
Spotting a straddle on from the front.

a. b. c. d.

Figure 8.44
Spotting a straddle on from the back.

Figure 8.45a, b
The finish of a wolf mount.

 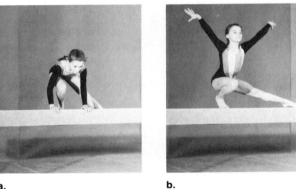

a. b.

The common problem is not lifting your seat high enough so that your feet or legs hit the beam.

■

Spotting

Stand opposite your student just as you do for the squat on, but for a student who cannot jump high enough, instead of standing by her side where you will get hit by a straddling leg, either reach over the beam and lift her abdomen (if your shoulder is well above the beam) or stand behind her and lift her by her waist.

Jump to a Squat-through (Figure 8.46)
This starts just like a squat on, but the difference is that you do not touch your feet to the beam, and you bring them through your arms so that you finish in a rear support.

160 Chapter 8

Figure 8.46a, b, c

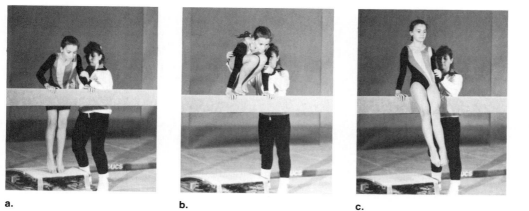

a.   b.   c.

Figure 8.47a, b, c, d
Note Tracey's hooked right foot in figure a—
it should point throughout this mount.

a.   b.   c.   d.

From behind the beam, hold your student's left upper arm with your left hand, and lift her seat, if necessary, with your right hand. From the front, hold on to her upper arms and be careful that she does not hit you with her knees as she brings her legs through. If she is doing well, you can hold just one arm.

■
Spotting

Scissors Leap to Stag Position (Figure 8.47)

This is a moving mount, one that comes from a walk or run. It is often done using a vaulting board as a takeoff surface. To do it from the left side of the beam, as you move parallel to the beam, your last step should be taken with your left foot. As you take this step, swing your right leg up and over the top

a.   b.   c.   d.

of the beam and jump off your left foot while pushing down on the beam with your right hand. As your right leg moves over and across the beam (just a bit, otherwise you will jump over and past the beam), bring your left leg after it while supporting yourself with your right hand. Your legs cross vertically in front, which is the scissors action (this is also called a hitchkick). Finish in a seated stag position with your left lower leg and your right leg on the side of the beam. Your left knee is flexed with your left thigh resting on the beam.

A common problem is jumping too far forward, which does not allow you to support your weight on your hand and can lead to a hard landing.

■

Spotting

Follow behind your student and lift her waist.

Step-on From the Side (Figures 8.48 and 8.49)
The step-on (or walk-on) is another moving mount that comes from a fast walk or run. The approach is the same as for a scissors mount. As you jump off your left foot, kick your bent right leg up and over the top of the beam. Put your right foot on the beam and, as your body gets on top of it, either bring your left foot to the beam in front of your right foot, or stand up on your right foot holding your left leg up in front of you. A variation is to punch the board with both feet, and jump up onto the beam with your right leg (this is a B-value skill).

Figure 8.49a, b
Spotting from the same side as your student.

a.   b.

You can stand on the opposite side of the beam and grasp your student's right hand or arm as she goes up, or if you are a bit concerned that she will not jump well, move with her to her left and hold her left hand as she goes up to provide stability and lift if needed.

Spotting

Step-on to the End (Figures 8.50 and 8.51)

From a run or fast walk, and using a vaulting board as a takeoff surface, lift your left foot while jumping from your right foot, and step onto the end of the beam with your left foot. Keep your eyes on the end of the beam where your left foot will land until it does so, then shift your focus to the far end of the beam for orientation. Be careful not to hit the end of the beam with your left foot on the way up. As a variation, jump from a two-footed punch to a one-footed landing (this is a B-value skill).

The common problem is moving too slowly to get up. Small students will have more of a problem learning this skill than larger ones.

You can run along with your student, holding her left hand with your right hand to provide lift and stability if needed, or stand by her landing point and offer her your raised hand to grab if she needs to.

Spotting

Figure 8.50a, b, c, d
A step-on to the end from one foot, with a
follow-along spot.

a.

b.

c.

d.

Figure 8.51a, b, c, d
A step-on to the end from a two-footed
punch, with a stationary spot.

a.

b.

c.

d.

Dismounts

Knee Scale Dismount (Figure 8.52)

From a knee scale position, swing your free leg forward and backward, jumping
off to either side as your leg reaches the top of its backward swing. Your bent
leg straightens as soon as it leaves the beam and joins your other leg by the time
you get to the high point of your dismount. Hold on to the beam with the hand
closest to it as you land until you are confident enough to push off with both
hands to a free landing.

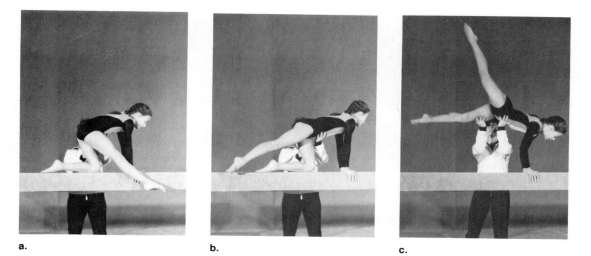

a. b. c.

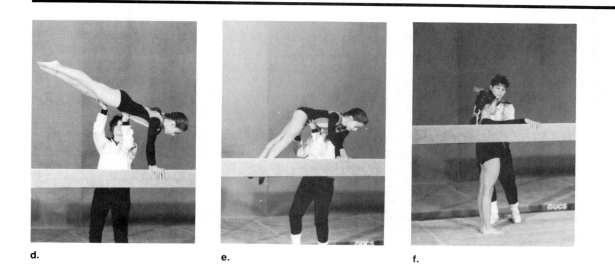

d. e. f.

Stand on the landing side by your student. Reach under her abdomen, providing lift and guidance if needed.

■

Spotting

Straddled Swing Off to the Side (Figure 8.53)
From a straddled seat on the beam with your hands on the beam in front of you, swing your legs forward and backward. As your legs swing above the beam in back, push down on the beam and push your body off to the side. Put your legs together and land next to where you were on the beam. Keep your arms straight during the support phase.

Figure 8.53a, b, c, d

a.   b.   c.   d.

■

Spotting

Do as you would for a knee scale dismount.

Jumps

All of the jumps you learned on the floor that land on two feet—straight (figure 8.54), tucked (figure 8.55), straddled (figure 8.56), split, toe touch, straight with a twist (figure 8.57)—can be done off the beam, either out from the end or out from the side. Since you will be coming down from a higher point than if you jumped from the ground, be sure to be ready to do a *demi plié* to absorb the momentum of your landing. Practice these jumps from gradually higher points until you feel comfortable doing them from the high beam. As you come down doing a one-half turn, look at the beam for orientation.

■

Spotting

Stay near the landing point to be sure your student is not rotating out of control as she comes to a landing.

Roundoff (Figure 8.58)

A roundoff can be done from the end of the beam to a landing relatively close to the beam. Do not do a cartwheel! (Cartwheels are outlawed because sideways landings from any height are dangerous due to the stress they put on the knees.) Stand back a bit from the end of the beam, step forward, and perform a roundoff somewhat as you would on the floor. Your hands go on the beam, with your second hand at the end of the beam, and you land on the mat. Be sure you do not go as hard, as you have extra time to rotate to your feet since you are dropping from the height of the beam. Most performers arch as they leave the beam, rather than snapping their legs down. You may have to do a practice lunge and reach to the end to see where you should stand to correctly place your hands on the beam.

The common problem is not going over the top.

Figure 8.54a, b, c
A straight jump dismount.

a.

b.

c.

Figure 8.55
A tucked jump dismount.

Figure 8.56
A straddled jump dismount.

For a left roundoff, stand just beyond the end of the beam to the left side and grasp your student's second (right) arm with your right hand. Your left hand reaches under her body to provide support on the way down if needed. As with a roundoff on the floor, it is a good idea to spot from the side that her back will face in case her legs do not go directly overhead.

■

Spotting

A jump with 1/2-turn dismount.

a.   b.   c.   d.

Figure 8.58a, b, c, d, e

a.

b.

c.

d.

e.

Figure 8.59a, b, c, d, e, f
Susan could arch a bit in figure d.

a.

b.

c.

d.

e.

f.

Forward Handspring (Figure 8.59)

Just as you learned to do a handspring on the floor from a stand, you can do the same thing from the beam. Start back a bit from the end of the beam and step forward into a lunge, putting your hands on the end of the beam. Do not go for it as hard as you would on the floor as you have a longer drop here. This skill presents what is called a blind landing: You do not see the ground behind you, but must judge where it is by your air sense and by cues from your surroundings, such as the wall ahead and your peripheral view of the floor way in front of you as you approach your landing. Watch the beam as you put your hands down on it, and watch them (they remain overhead) as you leave the beam. When your body gets close to horizontal, look forward to the wall for orientation. Be sure to land in a *demi plié*—locked knees must be avoided upon landing. This is the most difficult of the beginning dismounts presented here.

Common problems are kicking over too much or not enough at the start of learning this, pulling your head forward too soon, and landing stiff-legged.

Figure 8.60a, b, c, d
Kicking up to a side handstand.

a.   b.   c.   d.

Figure 8.61a, b, c, d
Quarter turn from a side handstand and
step-down.

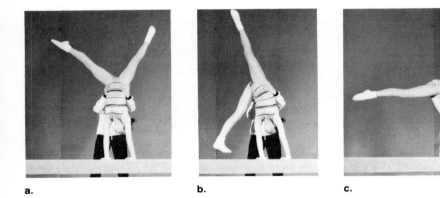

a.   b.   c.   d.

■

Spotting

Stand just as you would for a roundoff dismount. Grasp your student's left forearm with your right hand and reach under her lower back with your left hand to provide support if needed.

Handstand

Side Handstand

Just as you went through various steps to master a handstand on the ground, you can do several drills to get ready for a handstand on the beam. Practice stopping in the middle of a cartwheel on the floor and holding that handstand. Go to a low beam and, from a stand facing the side of the beam, kick up to a handstand with your palms on the top of the beam and your fingers partly over the edge and down the side of the beam (figure 8.60). If you go over, just pirouette off (figure 8.62). Next, get on the beam and do a half cartwheel into

Figure 8.62a, b, c, d
Pirouetting off.

a. b. c. d.

the handstand. Go slowly so that you do not go past it and do a full cartwheel. Once you can hold it, you can get out of it by finishing the cartwheel (figure 8.61), or by stepping down to the beam on one foot in between your hands, or by straddling down or stooping down to the beam. Also try various handstand positions—split, straddled, stag, and double stag.

Common problems are going too fast so that it is difficult to find your balance, closing your legs after your trunk gets vertical (going to a straddled handstand first), not pushing down hard enough with either arm, and kicking up to the half cartwheel outside of the vertical plane.

Just as you would on the ground. On the high beam, stand on the side that your student's back is facing, and provide support or balance help if needed. Be sure she knows how to pirouette off, and spot her through this a few times—reach under her as she comes down to slow her drop.

■
Spotting

A drill that will help you prepare for a press into a handstand is to stand next to the beam, put your hands on it, push to a front support, and push down on the beam to lift your seat overhead and thus lift your feet off the ground and onto the beam (figure 8.63). Keep your arms straight. See how high you can lift your feet in this way. Do this on beams of various heights.

A drill to prepare you for a jump to handstand mount is done in a similar fashion. Stand next to the low beam, put your hands on it, and jump up to a handstand (figure 8.64). You can do this in a tuck, straddled pike, or pike position. Try to do it on higher and higher beams, and keep your arms straight.

Figure 8.63a, b, c

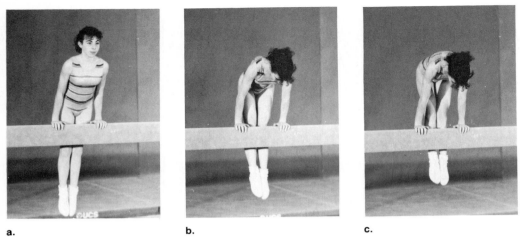

a.   b.   c.

Figure 8.64a, b, c, d, e, f

a.   b.   c.

d.   e.   f.

Figure 8.65a, b, c, d, e, f, g
Kicking into a cross handstand and then
stepping down from it.

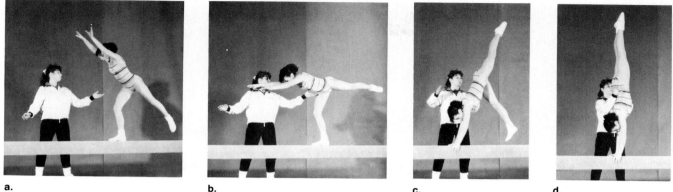

a.   b.   c.   d.

e.   f.   g.

As a variation, jump to your toes on the beam (a straddle-on mount) and jump up from there. If you go over, pirouette off.

Common problems and spotting are the same as for floor presses.

Cross Handstand (Figure 8.65)

Stand on the beam facing the length of the beam. Lunge forward and put your hands on the beam so that the heels of your palms are touching, your thumbs are pointing forward on top of the beam, and your fingers are pointing down the sides of the beam. Kick up toward a handstand and return to your lunge. You can also switch your legs in this exercise so that you kick up from a different foot each time. As you feel comfortable with this drill, kick all the way up to the handstand and try to hold it. Since this will be done first on a low beam, should you go past the handstand you can pirouette off. You can also do a forward roll, or a pirouette to a handstand sideways. Try various handstand positions, and work toward a press to this handstand, too.

Figure 8.66a, b, c, d
A drill for a press to a cross handstand.

a.   b.   c.   d.

A drill to start on the way to a press to a cross handstand is to get in a deeply piked stand, put your hands on the beam as described above, and push down to lift your feet off the beam (figure 8.66). Point your toes as you leave the beam, and bring your feet closer to your hands. Step down on your feet, lift your hands slightly to move them a bit forward, and repeat the drill. You can also stay in one place, just pushing down to lift your feet off the beam over and over until you can push your seat overhead and extend your hips to get your legs overhead. That is the press, which is a much harder skill.

Common problems are similar to the side handstand. The cross handstand has a smaller base of support and so is more difficult to master.

■

Spotting

For the low beam, do as you would on the ground. For a high beam, stand by the side of the beam facing your student's back and provide assistance if needed.

Forward Roll With Hand Support (Figures 8.67 and 8.68)

Before trying a roll on the beam you should be sure you can do one on a line on the floor. When doing this, get used to starting with your hands close together so that your thumbs touch, and push your seat up over your head so that you are able to practically put the back of your head down on the floor behind your hands, that is, on the side of your hands closest to your feet. The back of your head or neck can touch your thumbs. You will move through a tight pike position over the top. As you finish your roll, put your feet down in a staggered position—one foot in front of the other, rather than side by side. This is the action you will follow to do the forward roll on the beam. A small child with a proportionally large head may find this difficult to do, and will probably roll across the top of her head until her body proportions change.

Figure 8.67a, b, c, d, e, f, g, h
Forward roll from a lunge.

a.   b.   c.   d.

e.   f.   g.   h.

If you can do this on the floor, do it on the beam. You must be sure to roll directly over your hands and along the beam. Maintain a rounded back during the roll and come directly up to your feet finishing in a squat or a stand. As you go over, squeeze the beam with your hands, and keep your arms in by the sides of your head. As you gain confidence, you will be able to do this skill at various speeds and from a handstand. The handstand start will give you more momentum to begin with, so you want to be sure to roll straight or else you will be off the beam in no time. Lower from your handstand as you would on the floor, except remember to keep your elbows in so that your arms will be by the sides of your head as the back of your shoulders (instead of your head and neck) contacts the beam in front of your hands. (The contact point on the beam will not be behind your hands in this case, as you will not start behind your hands as you did from a lunge.) As a variation on the finish, instead of stepping onto your feet, straddle, reach for the beam between your legs, and swing backward and up to a stand behind your hands.

A lead-up drill that is useful for the finish of a forward roll and the start of a backward roll is: lay on your back on the beam with your hands on the beam just above your head, arms squeezing in to your head; bring your legs overhead and touch your pointed toes to the beam, then return to a rear-lying position or roll up to your feet. This is similar to a drill you learned on the mat for rolls.

Figure 8.68a, b, c, d, e, f
Forward roll from a handstand.

a.

b.

c.

d.

e.

f.

Common problems starting from a lunge are not going directly over the top, putting your hands out too far in front of you, not lifting your seat high enough to start the roll, not ducking your head enough at the start of the roll, not grasping the beam tightly enough (as you get better you will be able to let up on this squeezing of the beam), and separating your legs too soon to get up. From a handstand, an additional problem is not pushing down equally with both hands at the start, which will push you off to one side.

Stand in front of and just to the side of your student. As she begins the roll and is ducking her head, reach for her waist to guide her over the top of the roll. As the roll continues, release her waist and shift around behind her to assist her in rolling up to her feet. Watch out for flailing arms here—ask her to reach forward as she finishes the roll. If she rolls off the beam, you will be close enough to grab her and help break her fall. If you keep her upper body up by holding an arm or her waist, her feet will go to the floor. For a handstand roll, stand by her side just to the front and guide her as she lowers to the beam, then shift around behind as you would for the other roll.

Jump to Forward Roll (Figure 8.69)

If you can do the forward roll quickly, then you are ready to do it as a mount on the end of the beam. This is usually done with the help of a vaulting board to start higher and jump from, but it can be done on a lowered beam as well. To start out, stand next to the beam, place your hands on the end of the beam in a roll position, jump your seat over your hands, and go directly into the roll. Your legs will be straight, and your body will be tightly piked until you finish the roll, when you will complete your roll as you did with other forward rolls. If you are worried about jumping into the roll, place your hands on the end of the beam and do a few piked jumps to get the feel of the start. With confidence, you will be able to jump farther and farther into this skill, and roll up to a stand smoothly. If you do it from a run and jump, watch your contact spot on the beam until you duck your head into the roll.

Common problems are similar to a forward roll from your feet, but of course you have to be able to jump straight from the board or mat to the beam.

Stand to the side of the beam's end and reach under your student's abdomen with your right hand as she begins her roll. Your left hand reaches for her lower back as she goes over to provide guidance if needed. You will have to move your left hand out of the way quickly as the roll progresses or you will hinder the roll. Then shift around back to help her up if needed.

Backward Roll (Figure 8.70)

Just as you did with the forward roll, when you want to try this skill, begin with a roll on a line on the floor. Start in a squat, and when you go backward put your hands side by side so that your thumbs touch behind the top of your head to simulate doing this on the beam. Keep your elbows in, and keep your chin tucked to your chest to avoid banging your head on the floor mat or beam. You can try to do the roll from a position lying on your back on the floor as well. The faster you do this roll, the easier it will be.

If you are ready for the beam, begin in a seated position with your legs together or with one bent as shown. Lay back and grasp the beam so that your thumbs are behind the top of your head, squeeze your elbows in, pike and pull

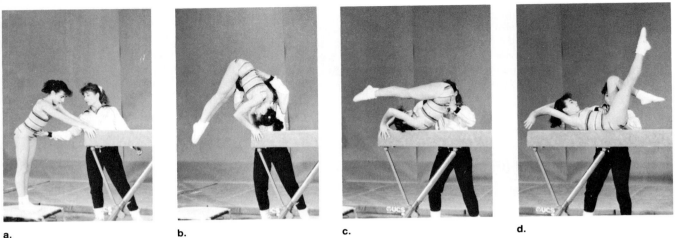

a.　　　　　b.　　　　　c.　　　　　d.

e.　　　　　f.

your legs over your head. Roll over, pushing down on the beam with your hands to take some pressure off your neck. Finish in a kneeling position at first. If you can do this easily, then do it from a squat or partial stand rather than a seat. Here you must be sure to roll straight backward. Put your hands in position behind your head at the start of the roll and be ready to grasp and push on the beam. A small child with a proportionally large head will find getting past her head difficult, and will have to be carried through it to get a feel for it until she grows and her proportions change. As another variation, when you feel confident enough, land in a squat with your feet either together or staggered slightly.

Common problems are not rolling straight, going too slow to complete the roll, opening from your pike, not pushing down on the beam with your hands to take pressure off your neck, and letting your elbows go out.

Figure 8.70a, b, c, d, e, f

 a.

 b.

 c.

 d.

 e.

f.

Stand next to your student facing in the direction that she will roll. Grasp her waist as she goes over, providing lift and stability if needed. As she finishes the skill, shift your grasp to her left arm if she appears unstable.

■

Spotting

Cartwheel (Figure 8.71)

Remember that you learned to do a cartwheel on a line to ensure good tumbling? It is especially important here, as you do not want to do a crooked cartwheel off the beam! If your cartwheel is straight, you should have little problem with it here. Do it just as if you were on the floor. Try several kinds—side-to-side, front-to-back, front-to-side, etc. (See the section on cartwheels in chapter 5 for these terms.) You will be able to keep your eyes on the beam for most of the time you are cartwheeling, and will have a good idea where the beam is so

Figure 8.71a, b, c, d, e, f, g, h, i
A front-to-back cartwheel.

a.   b.   c.

d.   e.   f.

g.   h.   i.

you can put your feet on it with relative ease. This series of figures looks like the side handstand series, doesn't it? When you practice one, you drill the other. Doing lunge drills—kicking up from and returning to a lunge—is further practice.

Common problems are the same as for tumbling.

On a low beam, or on a high beam while standing on a raised platform, spot just as you would on the floor. Stand on the back side of your student just ahead of her. For a right cartwheel (shown), reach up to the right side of her waist with your left hand and allow her to start the cartwheel. As she goes over the top, reach up with your right hand and grasp the left side of her waist. Guide her to a stand at the finish of the cartwheel if she needs it. Should she fall off the beam away from you, she will be able to see the ground, and you can help guide her down part of the way. If she comes over your side, hold her up and guide her to a safe landing.

■

Spotting

Walkovers (Figures 8.72 and 8.73)

These skills are done just as they are on the floor, with the exception that your hands are placed side by side so that your thumbs touch (unless you intentionally use a staggered hand placement). Be sure to practice these on the floor until you are confident of doing them on a line. A back walkover is more important to learn, and some students are not suited anatomically for front walkovers.

Common problems are the same as for the floor, with the obvious added problem of going out of the vertical plane.

On a low beam, or on a high beam while standing on a raised platform the height of the beam, spot just as you would on the floor. When spotting from below, a variation of the spot is often used. For the back walkover, this begins facing your student just behind her. Reach up and grasp her waist, left hand on her right side, right hand on her left side, as she begins the walkover. Guide her as she reaches for the beam, and continue guiding as she goes through her handstand. As she passes the handstand, shift your hands so your right one is on her abdomen and your left one is on her lower back, for guidance. If you and she have confidence, you may let her go as she is in a safe position to finish the move. If she is off center, she will fall off the beam to the side and land on her feet.

For the front walkover, since it is harder to do, spotting from a high platform is recommended so you can have control as you would on the floor. If you cannot stand that high, a variation is to start next to your student and help her up to a handstand if she needs it, then move quickly ahead of her, reach under her back with your right hand for the far side of her waist and for the near side of her waist with your left hand. This way you will have two arms under her in case of a problem. Guide her past the handstand onto a safe landing on her feet. If she goes crooked after passing the handstand, you will have hold of her and can put her on the beam or guide her to a safe landing on the ground. You can practice these techniques on the floor by getting on your knees to spot, or you can do them on a low beam as well to get used to them.

■

Spotting

Figure 8.72a, b, c, d, e, f, g, h, i
A backward walkover.

a.

b.

c.

d.

e.

f.

g.

h.

i.

Figure 8.73a, b, c, d, e, f, g, h
A forward walkover—Jaime's head comes
up too early in figure g.

a.   b.   c.   d.

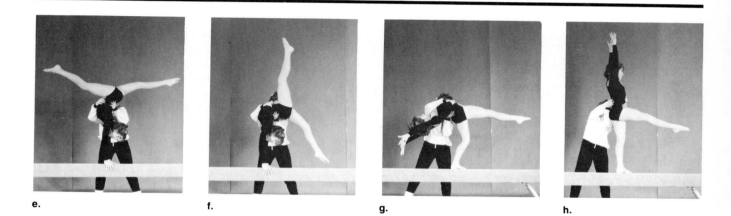

e.   f.   g.   h.

Sequences to Practice (Hold positions should last three seconds.)

1. Start at one end facing in and walk forward to the other end, *relevé* turn, squat turn, walk backward to the end, swing turn backward, one-half *relevé* turn, walk sideward using cross steps, straight jump dismount off to the side

2. Do a series of jumps in place—straight, squat, stride—and add a one-half turn to a plain jump or squat jump

3. Combine leaps and jumps: straight to *sissonne;* stride leap, step, stride leap; *chassé,* step, stride leap

4. *Chassé* (left foot forward), full turn to the left, *chassé* (right foot forward), full turn to the right

5. From a front support, swing a leg over to a straddled seat, bring your legs up forward to a V seat, swing your legs backward and rise to a squat, stand up with one-half turn, walk backward to the end, two backward swing turns, run to the other end, join your legs and plain jump in place, plain jump dismount from the end

6. Squat mount on end, stand with one-quarter turn to face along beam, run to the other end, swing turn forward, step forward to a lunge, kick up toward a handstand and return to a lunge, lift to a front scale (hold), lower and skip to the end of the beam, join your feet and tucked jump dismount

7. Jump to front support on the end, swing a leg over to a straddled seat facing in, swing your legs up behind to a single-leg stand up, *chassé*, tucked jump, step to a side lunge, cartwheel to a side stand, one-quarter turn and lower to a squat sit, straighten and straddle your legs, straddled swing dismount

8. Step-on mount from the side, stand up and kick to a cross handstand (hold), lower to a straddled seat and go directly into a backward roll to a kneel, step forward and stand up on that leg moving directly to a front scale (hold), kick directly to a side handstand and pirouette off

9. Step-on mount to the end, lunge to a forward roll, kick directly to a cross handstand (hold), lower through a lunge to a *révérence* kneel, stand up and step forward to a stride leap, swing turn forward, join your legs and fall forward to a bent-armed front support, bring one leg around to a low straddle or a straddled split, return to a straight-armed front support, squat up to a stand, step to the end and do a roundoff dismount

10. Forward roll mount on the end, straight jump, *sissonne*, step forward to a lunge and curtsey, kick to a side handstand (hold), one-quarter turn and step down to a forward lunge, full turn, kick through a cross handstand, forward roll coming up on one leg and holding the other up forward, slowly bring your raised leg around to the back and do a front scale (hold), lower to a stand, skip steps to the end, squat turn, *chassé*, stride leap, step to the end and handspring dismount off

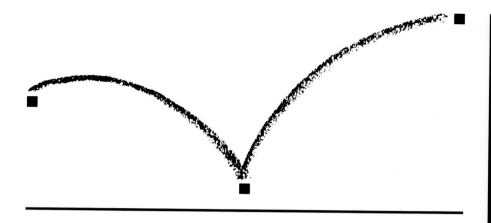

Rings is the event that is best known for moves showing brute strength such as an iron cross. However, to be a master of rings, a gymnast must be able to swing easily to and from a handstand as well as show strength positions. In fact, a handstand is the single most important move to learn on the rings because you are required to show at least two different kinds of handstands in your optional ring exercise—arriving at one through strength, and at the other through swing. (Most upper-level ring exercises contain more than two handstands, often three or four.) Another requirement is to show a strength hold plus another strength move that either is a hold or a slow, controlled movement. When starting out on the rings, you must learn basic positions and swing skills before tackling the swing to a handstand. You must also begin working toward a stable handstand as soon as you can.

Beginning gymnasts will have trouble with some of the strength demands that rings presents, but these will pass quickly with practice. One of the most instructive things to do with a beginning gymnast, to illustrate the strength necessary for this event, is to get him into a support position on the rings. Since the rings are made of wood, and are quite light, if a student has never been in a support, he will find it quite difficult to keep his arms from wobbling about because his muscles are not yet developed enough to keep him still above the rings.

Be sure to spend extra time warming up your shoulders when you work rings, as they will go through many motions and stresses during your ring training. Strength and flexibility are keys to ease of learning and injury prevention here, as they are in all events.

Terms Used in This Chapter

bail   This is a USA term, meaning a planned fall from a handstand into a swing below the rings.

Organization of This Chapter

Hand Care and Handguards

Rings will present a special problem to you in terms of wear and tear on your hands. Working on rings (as well as under the parallel bars, on uneven parallel bars, and on horizontal bar) brings a lot of friction wear to the hands, and this is often manifested in what we call "hot hands." This happens when friction causes your skin to become irritated. When your hands feel hot, it is time to stop and let them rest for the next day. If you do not stop, you may get a blister or rip. A gymnastics rip occurs when the skin on your palm, wrist, or finger tears off, usually in a small section. It is quite painful and must be treated as an open wound, because what you have done is torn your skin away and exposed the underlying layers to possible infection. (See chapter 15, **Medical Considerations,** for a brief discussion of rip care.) This does not happen much, but if you do rip, immediately go clean the wound and take care of it.

To prevent these rips or at least to prolong a workout, we often wear handguards (also called grips or palm straps) on any event that brings friction wear to our hands. Rings is a prime example. Handguards have evolved from simple pieces of leather or lampwick, which we used in the "old days," to a rather specialized leather handguard that differs from event to event. (Back in the 1960s when I competed, few wore handguards, so we usually worked bare-handed. Most young gymnasts these days are amazed that we could hold on!) A ring handguard has a dowel (usually made of leather, rubber, plastic, or a combination of these) in it that aids in holding on to the rings (figure 9.1).

Since dowel handguards allow you to hold on a little bit better, I think it is a good idea to use them after you have developed your grip strength somewhat. I do not think a beginning gymnast should wear handguards, but should strive to develop the callouses on his hands and the muscles of his forearms and later on start to use the handguards to prolong his workout. When the gymnast begins to swing well, he can then try dowel grips to help in holding on.

Grip and Hang Positions

Regular Grip (Figure 9.2) and Overgrip (Figure 9.3)

When you hang on the rings, you can hang with one of two grips: the regular grip, and the overgrip, which is also called the false grip. With the regular grip the bases of your fingers are on the top surface of the bottom part of the ring, and you are hanging straight down. With the overgrip, your wrist is flexed and part of the palm of your hand is on the top surface of this part. This is exactly

Figure 9.1
Dowel ring handguards.

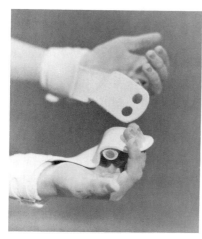

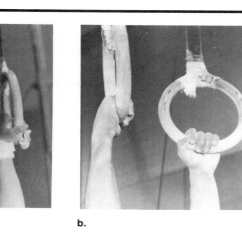

Figure 9.2a, b
Hanging with a regular grip.

a.   b.

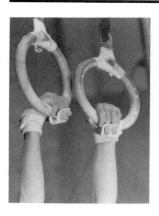

Figure 9.3a, b
Hanging with an overgrip = false grip.

a.   b.

the position your hand would be in if you started in a support, held on to the rings tightly, and lowered yourself down below the rings without slipping your grip around the ring. This grip is useful in doing nonswinging skills that wind up above the rings such as kipping skills or muscle-up skills.

When beginners learn to get this grip, it often gives them irritation and sometimes a rip on the insides of their wrists due to tenderness of the skin there, which is not used to rubbing against something, and because they try to get a false grip that is way too high, that is, too much on top of the rings so that the rings rub on their wrists. As a gymnast's forearm strength increases, he will have less and less problem getting this false grip and maintaining it throughout a skill.

Basic Hang Positions

There are several basic hang positions with which each beginner should become familiar. These are: hanging in an L position (figure 9.4), a piked inverted hang (figure 9.5), an inverted hang (figure 9.6), a hang rearways (figure 9.7), which is also called a "skin the cat," and a chin hang (figure 9.8). You can get to these positions by swinging to them, or by using muscle and moving slowly to them. I prefer to have my students move to them slowly because it helps them build up muscles that will be useful in later ring work.

Swinging in a Hang

Learning to swing well takes years. It takes a great deal of strength to swing efficiently so that you can go up to a handstand. But before you get to a handstand, there are many, many lower moves that must be learned, the first of which is just how to swing back and forth. For practically every move done on rings, the object of swinging is to learn how to turn over quickly (get your body upside down) from the bottom, be it swinging in the front or swinging in the back. (When you become more advanced and work on a front uprise, you will learn a hanging swing technique that does not turn over in front.) To get started from a hang, lift your legs up forward and backward and have your body swing from your shoulders. Then swing from your hands as you swing bigger (figure 9.9). You will have to lift your legs rapidly from the bottom going each way. In front, you will pike and then open your hips and shoulders. When swinging up in back, arch your back and point your feet up toward the ceiling, keeping your shoulders low, working to turn over. You probably have to do a partial inlocate to do this (the inlocate move will be discussed shortly). As your swing gets still bigger, you will find that you are able to start lifting your whole body up to ring level and above. Do this by piking your hips and shoulders quickly in the front, then as your legs become vertical, straighten your body quickly from your toes to your shoulders, turn the rings out (your forearms supinate), and pull down on the rings, which will cause your body to go up (figure 9.10). Have your legs pointing up rather than pointing out. In the back, as you pass through the bottom on the way back, lift your feet very hard into an arch, keep your shoulders down, and turn the rings out (your forearms pronate), causing you to inlocate (figure 9.11). This forearm turn is opposite from how you turned in the front. As you feel yourself going up in the back, press downward on the rings to the sides and straighten your body from your arch. During your entire forward swing it is helpful to be looking at your hands (you can see where you want your feet to kick as you pass under the rings). On your backswing, as you pass below the rings, look down at the mat and watch it all the way up. Once you stop going

Figure 9.4

Figure 9.5

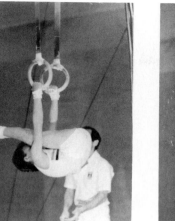

Figure 9.6

Figure 9.7

Figure 9.8

up, look again for the rings. This way you will have orientation points and will not have a wobbling head. As you pass through the bottom, you will learn to tap, which can help you lift your legs (for some gymnasts, this happens without having to think about it). Note in figures 9.9b, c, and d that Stephan approaches the bottom of his frontswing with a slight arch, and this rapidly changes to a pike as his legs whip through the bottom. The same thing happens in figures 9.9g, h, and i where he approaches the bottom on his backswing in a pike, which rapidly snaps into an arch as his legs whip through the bottom. This is called a beat or tap swing.

Figure 9.9a, b, c, d, e, f, g, h, i, j
Learning to swing back and forth—
Stephan's shoulders should be more open in
figure f.

a.

b.

c.

d.

e.

f.

g.

At the end of the lift on each end part of the swing, when you feel that you have stopped moving upward, stretch out to be as long as possible, and smoothly push the rings as far away from you as you can, so that you come down with a long body. The longer your body, the more swing you will pick up. As you approach the bottom moving forward you will have a slight arch that will whip into a pike as you pass bottom, and going backward you will have a slight hollow or pike that likewise will snap into an arch as you pass bottom. You want to be very careful not to have bent elbows, because this can present a big problem. If you hit the bottom of your swing with bent elbows or with an angle between your arms and your body, this will straighten out at the bottom and can cause

Chapter 9

h.   i.   j.

Figure 9.10a, b, c
Swinging above the rings in the front.

a.   b.   c.

excessive pressure on your hands, possibly causing you to rip off of the rings. This is not the way you want to learn the rings, flying through the air out of control. So always make sure that you stretch as far away as possible from the rings on all downswing work. This applies to advanced skills as well as beginning skills.

Common problems on the swing are bending your arms at some portion during the downswing, not turning your hands so that you can push downward as you go upward, not turning over fast enough on either side, and not stretching out as you come down.

Figure 9.11a, b
Swinging up in back and inlocating—
Stephan should be turned over more.

a.

b.

Figure 9.12a, b, c, d, e
A low dislocate from a piked inverted hang.

a.

b.

c.

d.

e.

Figure 9.13a, b, c, d, e, f, g
A high dislocate from a swing.

a.

b.

c.

d.

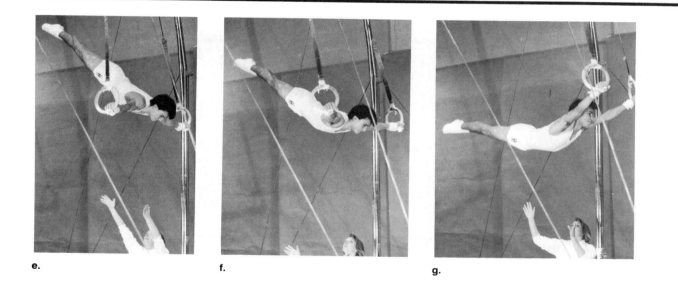

e.

f.

g.

Stand nearby to make sure that if your student comes flying off unexpectedly, you can catch him.

■
Spotting

Dislocate (Figures 9.12 and 9.13)

As soon as you have a feeling for swinging back and forth, you should go right away into some of the moves that utilize this swing. The first is a dislocate. Do this first from a piked inverted hang because it is pretty easy to spot this way, and later you can do the move from other positions.

Begin in a piked inverted hang, and look at a point that is about 45° up above horizontal. From a tight pike, shoot your legs in that direction, opening your body rapidly, and pull down and to the sides on the rings as you turn your thumbs out (supinate) so that you can push down on the rings. As your legs go up toward that point above the horizontal and your body straightens, you will find yourself being able to push down on the rings. Bring the rings around a bit, and when you feel you have stopped going up, bring them all the way in front of you, look at them, and make your body as long as possible so that you drop right into a swing.

When you start this move, you can also start in a plain hang. Lift to a piked inverted hang, and then begin the extension into the movement. Another starting point is an inverted hang. From an inverted hang, all you do is drop to a piked inverted hang and go directly for the dislocate.

If you feel comfortable enough with the dislocate and swing through the bottom pretty well, just lift your feet and do another one, and then another one. Doing series of dislocates is a fine way to learn how to control this type of swing on the rings. It will also allow you to go up higher and higher as each dislocate gives you more and more momentum to work with. Eventually you will go well above the rings and may reach a handstand (a more advanced skill). Doing series can be taxing on the hands, so be careful that you do not wear out your hands.

Common problems are shooting your feet too low, bending your arms during the dislocate, not pulling down on the rings, not stretching away, and arching way too much.

■

Spotting

For the low dislocate, stand to the side and just behind the rings. Reach up with your right hand, and put it underneath your student's legs. Your left hand reaches in so that it can support his abdomen as the move is started. Be careful not to stand next to the rings, otherwise you will get punched as he starts to dislocate. As he opens his body, lift upward on his legs and abdomen to help guide him through the movement. Make sure that he stretches completely before you allow him to drop so that he feels what the proper position is. As he gets more and more of the feeling, spot less and less; just be there in case a poor position causes a problem at the bottom of his swing. For the high dislocate, you can reach in and help him lift his legs if you are fast, and then watch to see that he is in a stretched position on the way down so that he swings smoothly through the bottom.

Inlocate (Figures 9.14, 9.15 and 9.16)

The counterpart move to the dislocate is the inlocate. This move is done on your backswing. For a low piked inlocate, as you drive your heels up behind you and begin to go up, turn your hands out (pronate) and lift your body into a pike, finishing in a piked inverted hang. This move can be tough on the shoulders, so it is important that you have a good swing to take the weight off your shoulders as you do it. Once you are in the pike, you can then just drop out into a swing, or learn to cast (covered shortly). Another way to finish the inlocate is in an inverted hang rather than a piked inverted hang. This requires more swing, as you must drive your heels up so hard that when you do the inlocating action your body stays slightly arched and winds up in an inverted hang. From the inverted hang, you can then drop into a swing and do another inlocate, which

Figure 9.14a, b, c, d, e, f, g
A piked low inlocate from a cast.

a. b. c. d.

e. f. g.

leads to series inlocates and is a fine way to build up this type of swing. You will find that just as with dislocates, as you do more and more inlocates and series they will go up higher and higher. As you develop your strength, and are able to kick your feet up very hard, you will push down hard on the rings during the movement and begin to lift over the top. The position of your head should be relatively neutral throughout most of the inlocate, although through the bottom if you look for the mat it will help keep your shoulders down and help you to turn over. It is important to not let your shoulders rise until you have turned over well in the back. If your shoulders go up before your legs, it means you are pushing down on the rings way too soon. The downward push occurs to the side of or behind your shoulders, not in front of them. For a high inlocate, as you lift over the top, straighten your body from an arch. As you descend

a.　　　　　　b.　　　　　　c.　　　　　　d.

e.　　　　　　f.

below ring height into a swing, round your back a bit. Do not allow your shoulders to drop forward until you are well past vertical, so that you maximize your drop and thus your swing power.

The way that you usually get into an inlocate is from a cast (figure 9.14 a-c), rather than just dropping from an inverted hang or taking a low swing into it. The cast begins in a piked inverted hang. Begin to open your body, and pull hard with bent arms on the rings, trying to pull the rings behind your head. As your body opens and you are pulling on the rings, you will find that it will roll forward a bit and move in front of the rings. When this happens, stretch out and push the rings behind you, getting as long as possible on the downswing. This will give you plenty of power and eventually will carry you way above the rings.

196

Figure 9.16a, b, c, d
The top part of a high inlocate—Stephan
should be more inverted in figures b and c,
his shoulders should not be so far forward in
figures c and d, and his knees should not
bend.

a. b. c. d.

Common problems are bending your arms during the inlocate, not driving
your heels (turning over) hard enough, not inlocating before pushing down on
the rings, not swinging hard enough to take weight off your shoulders, and having
tight shoulders. For the high inlocate, other common problems are letting your
shoulders drop before passing an inverted position (pulling your arms together
rather than keeping your arms out to the sides and pushing down), and arching
on your downswing.

Stand to the side a little bit behind the rings, and as your student's body passes
through the bottom, reach underneath his abdomen and legs to provide lift to aid in
the inlocating action. For the low inlocate, once this action has been accomplished,
your left hand can shift quickly to underneath his back or shoulder just in case any
further problem develops. Your right hand can continue to help lift up into a piked
inverted hang or an inverted hang. For the high inlocate, be ready to stop him if he
doesn't look like he will swing smoothly through the bottom.

Spotting

Dismounts

Flyaway Backward (Figures 9.17, 9.18 and 9.19)
This is the beginning of a long series of dismounts that will culminate in mul-
tiple somersaults and twists. To do the tucked flyaway backward (or back salto),
all you need do is swing up from the bottom, get into a tucked position, start
to turn over, let go of the rings, and land on your feet. If you feel a little bit
scared of the beginning, hold on a long time and turn over until you can see the
mat and you know your feet are pointed toward the mat. As you feel more and

Figure 9.17a, b, c, d
A tucked back flyaway.

a.   b.   c.   d.

more confident of your swing, you will find that you are able to let go on the way up. If you swing very big, you will be able to pull directly down on the rings on the way up, bending your arms, which will help you go up high. Think of kicking your toes over the rings, and then pull just before you release. Throw the rings out to the sides as you release them. If you pull back (over your head) on the rings just before you release, you may go up higher but you will rotate more slowly, so do not do this until you can rotate very well. If you rotate quickly, you will be able to extend out of your tuck well before you land, showing that you have good rotation and are in complete control. As you go into this flyaway and release the rings, you will probably look back for the mat so that you can see it early and spot for the landing. If you feel confident with your swing, you can do a flyaway in a pike or a layout. You will have to swing and kick much harder for the layout, as it is more difficult to start and to rotate with your body stretched than tucked or piked.

Common problems are holding on too long while you learn this skill, that is, turning around practically to a tucked hang rearways and then letting go, not swinging hard enough to go high, and not showing a good tuck, pike, or layout.

■

Spotting

Stand to the side, holding your student's left upper arm or shoulder with your right hand as he swings into the movement. Your left hand can help him swing up. As he demonstrates more and more competency, let go of his arm and just stand there watching to make sure that he has enough rotation to get to the mat with his feet. If he is not rotating, reach in underneath and turn him over. If he is overrotating, reach behind his shoulders or grab his arm to stop his rotation.

Figure 9.18a, b, c, d, e
A piked back flyaway.

a.

b.

c.

d.

e.

Backward Straddle (Figure 9.21)

When you do a straddle dismount, your legs pass outside of the rings. Once mastered, this dismount can be done quite spectacularly way above the rings. However, when you first learn to do it, you always do it below the rings.

Swing up in front and straddle your legs so that they go outside of your arms with the insides of your thighs touching your arms. If you do this hard enough, you will feel like you keep on turning over a little, enabling your feet to point toward the mat. In this position you can look back and see the mat. If you have turned over so that your feet are pointing toward the mat, you can let go. Since you are looking at the mat, are still rotating because you swung into the move and have not stopped, and your feet are pointing toward the mat, you

Figure 9.19a, b, c, d, e
A stretched (layout) back flyaway.

a.

b.

c.

d.

e.

Figure 9.20a, b, c
Giving the feeling for a backward straddle.

a.

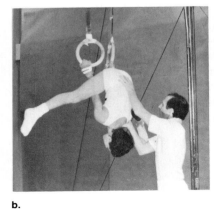

b.

c.

Figure 9.21a, b, c, d, e
A piked backward straddle dismount.

a.

b.

c.

d.

e.

will most likely land with your feet on the mat. You cannot do this move slowly—you must go very quickly to have enough rotation. As you feel better with this dismount and swing harder, pull on the rings to release higher, eventually pulling your seat well above the rings and in front of them (picture figure 9.19 done with a straddle). You will also open your body into a slight arch while in flight rather than stay piked. The higher you go, the more necessary it will be to throw the rings backward and together away from your legs, since if you do not do this, your legs may hit the rings on the way down.

Common problems are not swinging fast enough and letting go before you establish a good flight path.

■

Spotting

To give your student the feeling of this dismount (figure 9.20), have him turn upside down in a straddle with his legs pointed down to the mat as much as possible. Standing just in front of the rings, put one hand on his shoulder and the other on his seat or lower back. By pushing on his lower back and pulling a bit on his shoulder, you can get him to turn over so that his feet are pointed directly at the mat. At that point, tell him to let go. By keeping your hand on his shoulder you allow him to turn around that point while supporting him, and to land directly below the rings. Holding on to his shoulder and reaching behind him with your other hand will prevent overturning past a landing as well. For a free swinging performance, because this is a straddled movement, you will have difficulty spotting this from the side. The best idea for a beginning straddle is to have it done on rings just high enough for your student to swing freely. Stand to the left side and just in front of him with your right hand touching his shoulder. As his legs come up, step in quickly (watch out for his leg!) and reach under his back to help him go up and over, then shift your hands to steady him for the landing.

Forward Straddle (Figure 9.22)

This move is not often seen today, but it is useful because it is a relatively safe dismount, provides you with another way of getting off, and teaches you about a blind landing. To begin, start in a piked inverted hang. Straddle your legs as widely as possible, and for quite a while it is all right to bend your knees on this one. Rock forward so that your seat drops down a bit and your bent legs contact your arms with your lower legs on the outside of your arms. It is OK to bend your arms going forward. Your head is forward a bit so that you are looking between your legs. As you rock back and forth from the piked inverted hang to this position, you will feel that your trunk turns upright if you do it well. At this point, all you need do is let go of the rings, and if you are still moving a little, that is, if you have not stopped rotating forward before you let go, you should land on your feet. This dismount is usually done from an inlocate to a piked position, and it is done quickly, without the extra rocking back and forth.

Common problems are not rocking up hard enough and letting go after you stop moving.

■

Spotting

Stand behind your student. All you need do is put your right hand underneath his neck. Your left hand can be placed under his lower back for further support assistance. As he rocks forward, if you lift up on his neck or just support his neck when he lets go, he will land on his feet on the mat. This move is quite safe to miss, because if he does miss, usually he will land hitting his feet first and then his seat. It should be learned from low rings before it is done on high rings.

a.

b.

c.

d.

e.

Tucked Flyaway Forward (Figure 9.23)

This dismount is more difficult than the tucked flyaway backward because the end is a blind landing. It begins just like an inlocate. Swing hard through the bottom, kick your heels up behind you, and inlocate with your shoulders. At this point, pull your legs into a tuck. As you turn over toward an inverted position, let go of the rings. The end of this is just like a forward somersault on

a.   b.   c.   d.

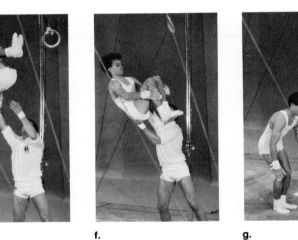

e.   f.   g.

the mat. If you swing up hard and do not push down in front of you, you will easily have enough rotation to turn over to your feet. Later on you can try this dismount in a pike or layout position. You will need to swing harder to turn over. Remember to look for the wall ahead for orientation as you finish your salto.

Common problems are not driving your heels up hard enough behind you, pushing down in front rather than inlocating hard, and kicking out before you turn over so that you do not have quite enough rotation for your landing.

Figure 9.24
An L support—Danny's rings are turned in just a bit, and his trunk is not quite vertical.

Figure 9.25
A straddled L support with a spotter's assistance—Lenny's legs are a bit low.

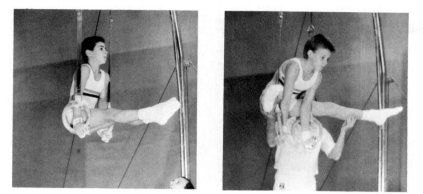

Stand just to the back and side. Hold on loosely to the front of your student's left shoulder with your left hand. I say loosely because his arm has to turn within your hand, yet you must be in contact with it in case he is in trouble so that you can lift him up. Also be aware that his hands and the rings are going to come to the sides, so do not get punched. Follow your student's shoulder as it goes through the inlocating motion. Reach under his body with your right hand to provide lift and rotation if needed. You can double tap him if you are quick, touching his legs or abdomen on the way up and supporting his back on the way down. As he becomes more competent, just reach under him to steady him for the landing, allowing him to inlocate and release without your influence.

■

Spotting

Support Positions

Get on a set of rings—low rings are better at first as you can jump to a support there—and get the feel of a straight support. You may find the rings hard to control if you are weak. If your support feels strong, you should know how to hold several support positions besides a straight support. The L support (figure 9.24) is used so often that it is a key position to learn. Just as you did on the mat, hold your legs horizontal while holding your trunk vertical with a flat back. The rings should be parallel. Keep your shoulders depressed (down) to keep your body high. A straddled L support (figure 9.25) is usually done with the rings turned out so that your palms are facing somewhat forward. This skill takes flexibility and hip flexor strength to do well. Your trunk will be hunched over forward in this skill.

Common problems are the same as for the skills done on the mat.

Muscle-up (Figures 9.26 and 9.27)

This is the first move that the young gymnast will learn utilizing a false grip. It is a beginning strength move that takes you from a hang to a support. Begin with an overgrip (false grip). Pull the rings down in front of your face and push them under your armpits. Then push up to a support. The difficult part of this

Figure 9.26a, b, c, d, e

a.

b.

c.

d.

e.

skill is pushing the rings down from in front of your face to under your armpits. That is where most gymnasts get stuck when they are learning how to do this skill. As you become stronger, this will become easier and easier. In fact, you will pull the rings down to the sides of your body when you do this well. If you cannot go up, do this movement in reverse, that is, start in a support and slowly lower down to a hang to build up strength.

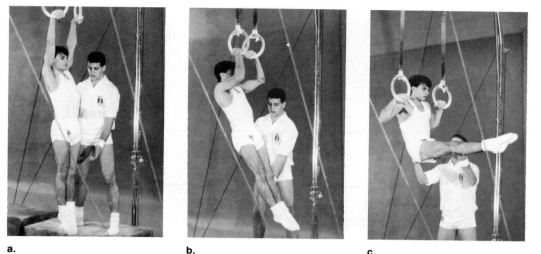

a.   b.   c.

d.   e.

If it is easy to do a muscle-up to a support, do it to an L support. Using a false grip, you can either hang in an L position and then muscle-up to an L support or start in a straight hang and lift your legs up as you go upward and finish in the L support. Do not dip your chest forward as you go up to the L support, and do not let your legs dip down below horizontal as you are going up above the rings. The rings should be pulled to the sides of your body here, just a bit in front of it. This skill requires many repetitions before you will be able to do it efficiently. Being able to do the muscle-up in an L position to an L support is one of the best drills there is for doing a kip to an L position. In fact, the strength required to do this type of muscle-up is very useful in all forward kipping actions, and muscle-up strength in general helps all skills that go above the rings to a support. Like the straight muscle-up, if you cannot go up, lower down slowly in an L position to build your strength.

Common problems for a straight muscle-up are letting the rings slip out to the sides (before you can handle this), pushing the rings below your armpits one at a time, and not being strong enough to push up to the support. When doing the move to an L support, common flaws are not maintaining a good L position (a 90° pike) and not keeping your trunk vertical (which makes your legs dip below horizontal, too).

■

Spotting

Assist your student simply by lifting him up when he gets in trouble.

Swinging in a Support (Figure 9.28)

This is an area that is not touched much by most gymnasts but is becoming more and more important, so it is useful to become strong in this position. All you need do is get in a support, be it on low rings or high rings, and swing back and forth just as if you were on parallel bars. The rings move a lot more easily than the parallel bars do, so you will find it much tougher to swing high, but if you can develop this swing to a good amplitude, that is, swing your body fairly high in the front (hips possibly as high as your elbows) and in the back (possibly going all the way up to a handstand), this will open up new vistas of ring work for you when you get to be a good gymnast. It is permissible to pike a bit in the front, but stretch in the back.

The common problems are bending your arms, letting the rings get away to the sides, and trying to swing a little bit higher than you are capable of controlling, which results in a fall below the rings. (The next skill covers going below the rings under control.)

■

Spotting

Stand by in case of a rotating fall below the rings. If your student can practice this on low rings where the rings are adjusted or the mats placed so that his feet are just above the mat, then no spot really is necessary. He just swings back and forth, small at first and then big later on, building up his strength.

Layaways From a Support to a Swing (Figures 9.29 and 9.30)

These skills are lead-up skills to a planned fall from a handstand and are useful connections. To do these, you simply get in a support, swing back and forth, and as you swing up on either end, push the rings away from your toes and make your body as long as possible. You will fall directly to a hang and swing through to whatever skill you want to do. When doing the forward layaway you

Figure 9.28a, b, c, d, e

a. b. c.

d. e.

will pike in front to lift your legs up high before stretching out and pushing the rings back. When you do the backward layaway, watch the rings as you push away and drop down.

Common problems are dropping down before getting sufficient lift above the rings, not pushing away enough, and not stretching well on the way down.

Watch to see that your student approaches and passes through the bottom well. Be ready to stop him in case of a problem.

■

Spotting

Figure 9.29a, b, c, d, e
Stephan drops too much between the rings
doing this forward layaway, and he needs to
stretch out more.

a.

b.

c.

d.

e.

Backward Uprise (Figure 9.31)

The backward (or back) uprise (also called *Stemme* [pronounced-stem'-meh] backward to support) is perhaps the easiest swinging skill to get you from a hang to a support above the rings, but it does require a good bit of strength. Being able to do a muscle-up and being able to do an inlocate action are very important prerequisites to being able to do the backward uprise well.

Figure 9.30a, b, c, d
Stephan is a bit too arched on the way down doing this backward layaway.

a.   b.   c.   d.

Begin just as if you were going to inlocate. Swing to the rear from a cast or out of a large swing. As your feet go up behind you, begin your inlocating action. Here is where the difference comes in. Instead of continuing to just turn over below the rings, push down on the rings very hard and lift your whole body above the rings. If you do this successfully and pull the rings behind your shoulders as you are pushing down, eventually you will be able to go up to a horizontal support position and, further on down the line, you will be able to go up to a handstand. Beginning gymnasts will find it necessary to bend their arms on the way up because they are just not strong enough to push down with straight arms, but eventually you will want to do it with straight arms. And eventually, as you go up above the rings and stop rising, you will want to try to keep your legs up behind you as long as possible. This will allow you to lower to a support in a slow and controlled manner and possibly to lift your legs to an L. A good beginner's back uprise finishes in a straight-armed support with the feet at ring level. I emphasize that you must bring the rings behind your shoulders as you begin the backward uprise. If the rings are in front of your shoulders, you will wind up pushing your feet down. If you think about inlocating and then pulling down hard on the rings to lift your body, your arms should move in the correct manner.

Common problems are not swinging hard enough to get above the rings, not inlocating, not pulling the rings behind you as you push down, and not straightening your arms at the end of your uprise before your legs start to drop.

Stand to the side of your student, just a bit behind him. Reach in and lift up on his abdomen and legs as he goes for the skill. Try to keep his legs up as high as possible at the end of the backward uprise so that a support is established with his body up fairly high. This way he will have a feel of where his body should be at the end of the uprise. If you are spotting on low rings, watch out for the rings, which will come out to the sides.

■

Spotting

Figure 9.31a, b, c, d, e, f, g, h
Stephan could inlocate a bit more in figures
c and d.

a.

b.

c.

d.

e.

f.

g.

h.

Shoulderstand (Figure 9.32)

This move is the precursor to the handstand on rings and gives you an idea what
it is like to be upside down and have to fight for balance, manipulating the light
rings. When you first try this, it is probably easiest to press up with bent arms
in a tuck from a support. Later on, you will learn a bent-armed press with your
legs straight, piked at your hips (legs straddled or together), or with your body
straight (called a hollowback). To do a tucked press, begin in a support and
slowly push your seat over your head, bending your arms so that your shoulders
come down close to your hands. As your seat goes overhead, slowly extend your
legs up so that your body is straight or has a slight arch and is generally vertical.
For balance, do not keep your bent arms very close to your body, but do not let
them spread very wide, either. A medium position is best for balance because

Figure 9.32a, b, c, d

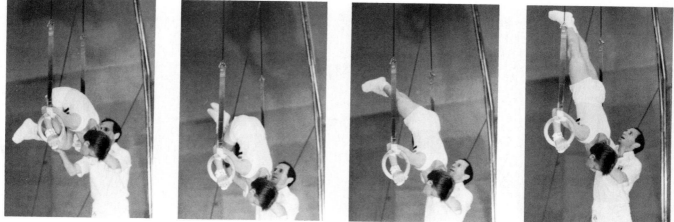

a.　　　　　　　b.　　　　　　　c.　　　　　　　d.

then you can open your arms or bring them closer to your body to control balance. Look out of the tops of your eyes directly down at the mat with your head in line with your trunk. Your shoulders should be settled well into the rings, not on top of the rings. If you have trouble balancing, it is very easy to spread your legs and put them on the cables or straps that suspend the rings. Keep your feet on the straps until you feel confident of the balance and then slowly bring your feet together. You can just barely touch the insides of the cables with the outsides of your feet as you get used to the balance or you can wrap your feet around the cables if you are unsure.

Should you fall over toward your back, just hold on tight to the rings and let your arms straighten out so that you can swing out of the fall. If you fall toward your stomach, you have two alternatives. One is to lower down to a support; the other is to push away on the rings and just go into a swing. These falls from a shoulderstand, forward and backward, are referred to as baby bails, and are the precursors to falling into a swing from a handstand (they are the next moves described). When you first do these falls to a swing it is a good idea to get spotted, because if you are not stretched when you pass through the bottom you might rip off of the rings and go for an unexpected flight. If you can lower to a support easily from a shoulderstand, first tucked, then piked, and finally with your body straight, this will help you build strength for moves that will come in the future.

Common problems are spreading the rings too wide or keeping them too narrow, going up too fast, and holding the shoulder stand too high, that is, not settling into a proper position so that you waste strength holding it up high.

Assist just as if this were a handstand. Stand to the side of the low rings (or on a platform next to high rings) and help your student get up into the position. As he turns upside down, help him balance until you feel that he can do it by himself, then slowly move away. If you are confident of your student's ability to fall forward or backward out of the shoulderstand, you can let him do it on his own, preferably first on rings just high enough to swing on.

■

Spotting

Figure 9.33a, b, c, d, e
Stephan lets his shoulders drop too much in figures b and c doing this baby bail forward—he should be more stretched on the way down—and his head should be down in figures d and e.

a.

b.

c.

d.

e.

Baby Bails (Figures 9.33 and 9.34)

This is a step, along with the layaway, to doing a bail. To build up to this planned fall, you can first learn to drop from a shoulderstand (as I described in the shoulderstand section previously). If it feels good from a shoulderstand, then push up to the halfway position between a shoulderstand and a handstand and fall over. In both cases, as you fall over, push the rings away smoothly and stretch your body away from them, moving into a hanging swing directly. You want to

Figure 9.34a, b, c, d
This baby bail backward is well done except
for a bit too much arch in figure c.

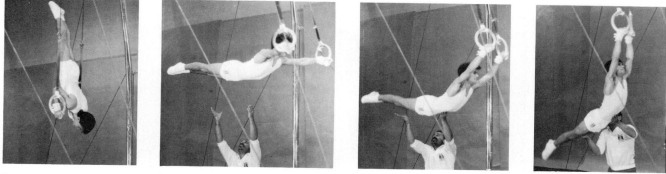

a. b. c. d.

be stretched by the time you pass ring height. When you fall over, your body must fall as a unit. You will have lots of swing to use for whatever skills you want to do, and you will be on your way to big swing. When you are learning it, make sure you have a spotter so that in case you do not get stretched on the way down, you do not come ripping off. Keep your head neutral as you begin your fall.

Common problems are not falling over enough, that is, leaving your feet up, coming down with your head or shoulders or hips leading rather than your whole body as a unit, not stretching enough, and pushing the rings to the sides rather than away from your toes.

Stand below as you do for a layaway and watch the approach to and passage through the bottom for potential problems. Keep one hand on each side of your student's body as he passes by you.

■

Spotting

Handstand

The handstand (figure 9.35) is the backbone move of all ring routines and may take the longest to learn well. To do it correctly, your arms should not touch the straps, you should have an extended body alignment, your head should be in line, and the rings should be turned parallel. Figures 9.36, 9.37 and 9.38 show problems often seen with ring handstands. Do not have your hands too high over the rings—you have to drop your wrists a bit (have your wrists slightly hyperextended) so that your thumb is not on top of the rings, but the middle of your palm is. This will enable you to do a free handstand without touching the straps with your arms. If you have a low set of rings that are just off the mat to practice on you will be able to kick up to handstands to get the feel of them. If you do not have access to a set of rings that low, usually you get to a handstand at first by doing a tucked press (figure 9.39), just as you did learning the shoulderstand. Begin in a support and bend your arms a bit as you push

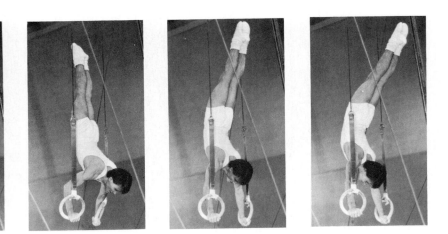

Figure 9.35
This position has small flaws—Stephan's elbows are flexed slightly, and his back is a bit arched.

Figure 9.36
An example of a problem—very bent arms.

Figure 9.37
An example of a problem—rings turned in and too much arch.

Figure 9.38
An example of a problem—way too much arch.

your seat up over your head with your legs tucked in. In this case, you do not bend your arms so much that your shoulders go down into the rings. Do not let your arms touch the straps throughout this move, if possible. As your seat goes up, slowly extend your arms and your legs so that your arms straighten out with your body extending upward. If you can do a tucked bent-armed press, try a straddled piked press (figure 9.40), and then a piked press. When you first work a handstand, you will most likely have to put your feet on the straps just to get a feeling of what it is like to be upside down on light rings, which move very easily (unlike the mat and the parallel bars), and to get a feeling for turning the rings out. Very often you will think that the rings are turned parallel when actually they are turned in, so you will need some feedback from a teacher to tell you whether your rings are turned out or not.

An exercise to develop this parallel ring position while in a ring handstand is to try to turn your palms out as far as you can, that is, supinate so that the sides of your hands by your little fingers are facing each other or at least are toward each other. This is difficult to do, but will develop the muscles needed to control a good parallel handstand. Experiment with your hand position. Keep your head in line and look out of the tops of your eyes right at the rings. You should be able to see the mat below the rings. It is helpful to be able to watch the mat because you will know whether you are swinging in the handstand or not. Push to make your body as straight as possible. Should you over balance or fall toward your back, lower toward a shoulderstand and do a baby bail—then you will be able to fall forward with less momentum than if you fell from the handstand. As you become stronger, you will be able to do a bail, which is described next. Should you fall toward your stomach, you can lower down to a support, do a baby bail, do a bail, or jump off (if you are on low rings). In fact, an excellent strengthening exercise is to lower slowly from a handstand with straight arms to a support. Another exercise that will help you down the road, once you learn a handstand, is to hold one while swinging. If you can hold a 30-

Figure 9.39a, b, c, d, e, f
A tucked bent-armed press to a handstand.

a.   b.   c.

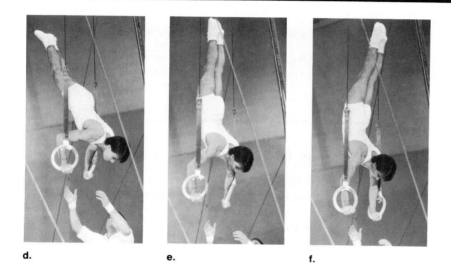

d.   e.   f.

second handstand on the rings, both still and swinging, you should not have any future troubles with it. When you master this handstand, you will make balance adjustments mostly with wrist movements.

Common problems are not trying nearly enough handstands to become strong enough to do one, lifting your head, arching your back excessively, planching (allowing a shoulder angle to develop), keeping the rings turned in rather than parallel, and flexing your elbows slightly during the handstand. You must not do a handstand with any amount of arm bend.

Figure 9.40a, b, c
The middle of a straddled piked bent-armed press—as you get stronger you should not touch the straps with your arms as Stephan does here.

a.

b.

c.

■

Spotting

If the rings are low, assist your student as you would on the mat. Another way to spot is to hold the rings steady—just keep the rings from moving and he will have much less trouble doing the handstand. If he is doing this on high rings, stand underneath the rings, and if he falls forward or backward, break his fall as he comes down.

Bails (Figures 9.41 and 9.42)

Once you are experienced on the rings and have developed your grip strength, you can learn a bail, which is a planned fall to a swing from a handstand. This is the start of a giant swing, which is a more advanced skill. You should have done a fall from a shoulderstand and partway up from a shoulderstand (baby bail) before trying to fall from your handstand. If you stretch away from the rings, falling either way, you will wind up with a great swing. Always try to be as long as possible during this fall. Do not bend your arms—bent arms are pretty sure to straighten out when you hit the bottom of the swing, and this can cause you to rip off of the rings. The same thing goes for your body. Do not shorten your body by tucking or piking or arching (except to set up a tap as you approach the bottom) because this will stretch out once you hit the bottom. Keep your eyes on the rings as you start the bail, but keep your head in line with your body. Eventually you will want your arms to be parallel or close to parallel during your fall, but in your early attempts you may spread them somewhat to pick up less momentum as you start (wider arms at the start means your body line is shorter, and so you generate less swing). Once you go below the rings you will be in familiar territory, since you have practiced swinging (although now you will be moving faster). From a bail you will have lots of swing to use.

Figure 9.41a, b, c, d, e
A forward bail—Stephan's shoulder angle should be open in figures b, c, and d, and his back should be straight in figure b and rounded in figures c and d.

a.

b.

c.

d.

e.

If you do a dislocate or inlocate from a bail, you should find it easy to do. You will be able to do dismounts from a bail as well, and the increased swing may make it possible for you to easily do layout dismounts rather than tucked dismounts, which you learned as a first stage.

Common problems are not stretching your body on the way down, spreading your arms excessively, bending your arms, and not keeping your head in a neutral position on the way down.

Figure 9.42a, b, c, d
A backward bail—Stephan should be
straight in figure c and a little less arched in
figure d.

a.
b.
c.
d.

Spotting

Stand below the rings just to the side as you do for a handstand. Watch your
student as he descends, and keep your hands below him as he comes down. If a
rip off occurs it will happen just past the bottom, so you should have your left hand
by his abdomen and your right one by his back as he passes this critical area.

Backward Roll (Figure 9.43) and Back Kip (Figure 9.44)

These strength moves utilize the muscles that you developed from doing muscle-
ups and from lowering slowly from a handstand to a support. Both can be done
from support to support or can be done from a hang below the rings up to a
support. The difference between these two movements is that for the backward
kip you open forcefully from a pike to an extended or arched position to go above
the rings, but doing the backward roll you do not open forcefully, and it is often
a slower movement. These moves resemble a backward pullover and hip circle
on the single bar, but are not as easy since the single bar does not move as the
rings can.

To do a backward roll (also called a *Felge* [pronounced: fell'-geh] backward) from a support, start to pike and lower yourself down by bending your
arms slightly. Squeeze the rings very tightly and pull your feet over your head.
Do not let your body drop all the way below the rings so that your arms
straighten. Keep your arms in close to your body, look at your toes going around,
and then as you pull above the rings, straighten your arms to a support. It is
tough to keep the rings in one position in relation to your body, that is, to keep
your arms in one position as you go around, but this is what you must do.

Figure 9.43a, b, c, d, e, f

a.

b.

c.

d.

e.

f.

Figure 9.44a, b, c, d, e

a.

b.

c.

d.

e.

To turn a backward roll into a backward kip, as you pass underneath the rings and start to come up, open your body forcefully so that you feel a bit of extra pull on the rings. At that point, as you open, yank down on the rings very hard, and get up to a position where your body is horizontal and stretched and your arms are straight before you drop into the support. It is very tough to do this until you become quite strong. As you become stronger you will be able to lower to a straight-arm piked hang and do the back kip from there, but a beginner should keep his arms bent under the rings to make it easier.

These skills can also be done from a hang. Using a false grip, lift your legs up while bending your arms, and proceed with the same finishing actions as you did when you started above the rings.

Common problems are letting the rings get out to the sides, dropping all the way down to a straight-armed piked inverted hang in the middle of the action before you are strong enough to do this, not straightening your arms above the rings before achieving a support, and, for the back kip, not pulling down hard enough as you open your body to produce lift.

■

Spotting

Stand to the side of the rings (preferably the low rings). Since the rings should not spread wide, you can stand close. As your gymnast turns upside down, reach in with your right hand underneath his legs and your left hand underneath his chest. As he attempts to go up on top of the rings, simply lift up on these two points and assist him doing so. Let him feel the finish position of the back kip when it is done. Hold him in that position, then slowly let his legs lower, and make sure he is fighting to keep his arms straight and his body up as high as possible all the way down.

Forward Roll (Figure 9.45)

The forward roll (also called a *Felge* forward) requires you to be strong enough to do a muscle-up and is done in a piked position at first. As you build up strength you can do it with your body straight, which is a B-level skill.

Begin in a support. Squeeze the rings tightly so that your grip does not slip below the rings as you go around on the roll. Bend forward by piking and as you feel yourself falling over forward, bend your arms and try to hold the rings in close to you. Your body will stay piked as you pass underneath the rings and go through a piked inverted hang but with bent arms. Continue rolling around and pull down on the rings very hard so that you can pull your shoulders up over the rings. Maintain your piked position until you get around on top of the rings. Then you can push down and straighten your body, finishing just as if you were doing a muscle-up, or keep piked and go to an L support.

Common problems are letting your arms straighten as you roll forward and underneath the rings, and letting the rings get away to the sides as you attempt to get back on top of the rings.

■

Spotting

Stand next to the rings and lift your student up as he attempts to get on top of the rings.

a.

b.

c.

d.

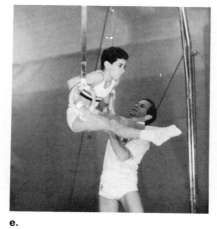

e.

f.

Forward Kip (Figures 9.46 and 9.47)

This is a quick move that requires muscle-up strength and takes you from a piked inverted hang below the rings to a support or an L support (called a kip L). It is easiest if you use a false grip, which can be a partial false grip or a full false grip. From a piked inverted hang with your arms straight, shoot your legs out at about a 45° angle above the horizontal in front of you, extending your hips from a pike to a practically straight body position. As you do that, yank downward on the rings very hard, but do not let them go too wide. You can bend your arms on this yank until you become very strong. Pull the rings down to your hips, lower your legs, and pull your chest up over the rings. If you are strong in a muscle-up, then pulling up over the rings should not be too much of a problem. To kip directly from your piked inverted hang to an L, pull the

Figure 9.46a, b, c, d, e, f
A kip to support—Danny is a bit weak
getting over the rings here.

a.   b.   c.

   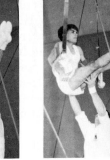 

d.   e.   f.

Figure 9.47a, b, c, d, e
A kip to L support—Stephan's shoulders are
pulled forward a bit in his L.

a.   b.   c.   d.   e.

Figure 9.48a, b, c
Jim's position in figure c is a bit high, very
slightly piked, and his feet are not side by
side.

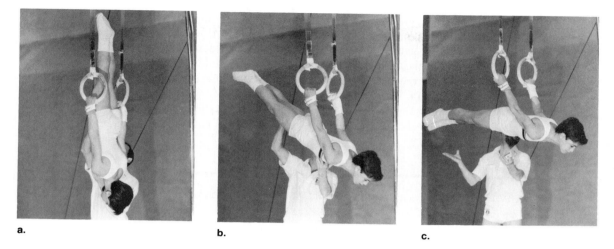

a.   b.   c.

rings down just in front of your hips, keep your chest up, and do not let your
legs drop below horizontal. If you can do this with straight arms, that is excellent. (Until recently, a kip L was rated as a B-level skill, but it has been
downgraded.)

Common problems are not pulling down hard enough, letting your arms
get too wide, not extending your hips fast enough, not extending your hips far
enough, and letting your trunk go forward as you come over the rings. For the
kip L, problems include pulling the rings too far back so that you tip forward,
and letting your legs dip below horizontal.

Stand next to your student, putting your right hand under his back and your left
hand on his seat or the back of his left thigh. As he initiates the skill, give a slight
push upward and help him achieve a support. Be ready in case he pulls his chest
so far forward that he falls forward. Sometimes this fall can be into a hang
rearways, which can be painful on his shoulders.

■

Spotting

Back Lever (Figure 9.48)

This is the first real strength hold that the beginning gymnast usually learns.
You hang below the rings with your body straight or barely arched, horizontal,
and your front facing the floor. There are several ways to get to this. I think
the best way to first try this is to start in an inverted hang and slowly lower
your body toward a horizontal position where your front is facing the mat. As
you start to lower your body down, turn your hands out (supinate) so that your
palms are facing back and toward the floor. Squeeze your arms into your sides
to help slow your lowering. Have someone tell you when you are horizontal.
Your eyes should be looking forward and down so that your head is in line with
your body. Do not look down too much, which will pull your head down so that

it is out of line. If you cannot stop in the horizontal position, that is OK; you will eventually become strong enough for it. Just keep trying, and strain all the way down to a hang rearways. Later you will be strong enough to stop and then pull back up to an inverted hang. Another way to get out of this move is to dislocate—just spread your rings and let your body drop into a swing.

A second way to get to a back lever is to begin in a hang rearways and lift up to it. This is tough for a weak beginner. It is not as easy to assume a correct body position doing it this way as when you lower down from an inverted hang. Yet, this is an excellent strength exercise and will help future ring work. From a hang rearways you should eventually be able to pull through a back lever right up to an inverted hang.

Common problems are letting your belly sag down so that your back is extremely arched, not being in a horizontal position, and having your head out of line.

Spotting

Reach in and hold your student in the proper position, giving him a feel for it.

Swing to Backward Roll/Kip (Figure 9.49)

Now we are going to combine some of the swing that you practiced earlier with the backward roll/kip that you learned. This will be a swinging move up to a support rather than a strength move up to a support. As you swing up in the front, pike and lift your feet very hard. Think of kicking your toes over the tops of the rings. At this point, open your body quickly, pull down on the rings with bent arms, and turn over to a support. Unless you are quite strong, you will not be able to get up and over the rings. The swing of your body has to be powerful, your downward pull has to be powerful, and if you do it well, you should wind up in a support with relatively few problems. This movement (also called a swinging *Felge*) is the lead up to a shoot to shoulderstand and later to a shoot to handstand, which is a B-value move. It is also a useful connection in an exercise. If you can do it easily, then perform it with straight arms throughout the movement.

Common problems are not kicking up hard enough or pulling down hard enough to attain the support, letting your arms go out to the sides once you are in the support (which will cause you to fall down), and not pulling your legs over enough so that you wind up going in front of the rings too much and cannot turn over to a support.

Spotting

Stand below the rings, making sure that if your student shoots up, he does not fall down in an awkward position below the rings if he cannot establish a good support. You can give him a boost on the way up if he needs it. He has to try this over and over again until he is strong enough to do it.

Chapter 9

a.   b.   c.   d.

e.   f.   g.   h.

Swing From a Hang to a Shoulderstand

Forward (Figure 9.50)

If you have learned how to do a swinging back roll/kip, the next step is to make it up to a shoulderstand. To do this move (called a shoot to shoulderstand or *Felge* to shoulderstand), you will have to kick up very hard but not over the rings this time. As your legs get about vertical, open your body forcefully upward and slightly in front of the rings and pull down on the rings with bent arms, going directly to a shoulderstand. Of course, you cannot do this with a small swing (until you are quite strong)—you have to have a sizable swing. You also need a very powerful leg lift and opening of your body coupled with a very strong pull downward on the rings to attain the shoulderstand. Once you get

a.   b.   c.

d.   e.   f.

the hang of it, it will be relatively easy and will put you well on your way toward learning to do a shoot to a handstand and dislocates at or above ring height.

Common problems are not directing your feet properly so that a good vertical shoulderstand is not attained, not pulling down hard enough to get over the rings, and opening into an excessive arch.

■

Spotting

If your student is having trouble getting up over the rings, give him a bit of a boost by pushing up on his body as he passes you on the way up to the shoulderstand. However, he will have to repeat this over and over again until he gets strong enough to do it. Be ready if he overturns or underturns the shoot, because then he is going to fall into a hang and you want to be careful that when he falls he does not rip off at the bottom if he has not stretched all the way down or if he is not strong enough to hold on.

Figure 9.51a, b, c, d, e, f
Stephan should inlocate and turn over on
the way up more.

a.   b.   c.

d.   e.   f.

Backward (Figure 9.51)

This is an extension of the back uprise described earlier (and is called a back uprise shoulderstand or *Stemme* backward to shoulderstand). If you develop enough power in your backswing to lift above the rings with enough rotation to get your legs well over your head, as you circle your arms around into position to push to a support, push to a shoulderstand instead. It takes a strong swing to get up this way, so do not try it until you are going above the rings easily doing a back uprise. This skill is also a step on the road to inlocates that are done at ring height and above, and to a back uprise to a handstand.

     Common problems are not enough power in your backswing, pushing down on the rings in front of your shoulders, and an unstable shoulderstand.

     Spotting hints are the same as for the shoot described above.

Sequences to Practice (Hold positions should last 3 seconds.)

1. From a hang, lift to an L hang (hold), lift to a piked inverted hang (hold), open to an inverted hang (hold), lower to a piked inverted hang (hold), lower to a hang rearways (hold), pull up through a piked inverted hang to a chin hang (hold)

2. From a piked inverted hang, dislocate, swing forward, swing backward, swing forward, swing backward to a piked inlocate, cast to several more swings

3. Do a series of dislocates, building height with each one

4. Do a series of stretched inlocates, building height and rotation speed with each one

5. Muscle-up to L (hold), piked press to shoulderstand (hold), lower to a support and swing forward and backward three times each, lift to straddled L (hold)

6. Back uprise to L support (hold), bent-armed straddled press to handstand (hold), lower to support and swing forward, backward, forward, and layaway forward to a stretched inlocate, back uprise to support, swing forward, backward, layaway backward to dislocate, tucked back flyaway

7. Back uprise to support, backward roll to straddled L (hold), lower your legs and hollowback (stretched body, bent arms), press to shoulderstand (hold), baby bail forward to tucked front flyaway

8. From an inverted hang, lower to back lever (hold), dislocate, high dislocate, shoot to shoulderstand (hold), baby bail backward to layout back flyaway

9. From an piked inverted hang, cast to a high inlocate, back uprise to shoulderstand (hold), baby bail forward to back uprise to shoulderstand (hold), lower to support and roll backward to a piked inverted hang, dislocate, layout back flyaway

10. From an inverted hang with a false grip, kip to L support (hold), bent-armed piked press to handstand (hold), bail to swinging backward roll to straddled L support (hold), bent-armed straddled piked press to handstand (hold), bail forward to a piked front flyaway

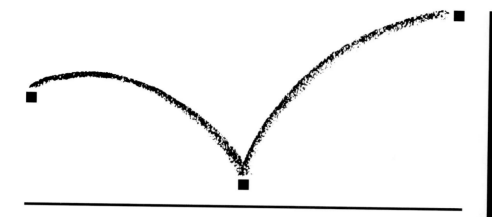

Vault is the fastest event in both men's and women's gymnastics. It begins with a running approach of no more than 25 meters. You run as fast as you can down a runway, hurdle onto both feet onto a vaulting board, then vault over the horse, touching it with your hands, and perform a movement in your flight from the board to the horse, or from the horse to the mat, or both, often involving a twist, a somersault, or a combination of these two. You finish by landing in a controlled stand, hopefully a good distance from the horse. For all vaults, your hands spend very little time on the horse. They must push off as fast as possible and in the correct direction to maximize your afterflight height, distance, and rotational needs. This is called *blocking* (this term is applied to takeoffs from your feet as well). The same thing goes for the hard vaults as for the easy vaults: The harder you push, the higher and farther you go.

Some advanced vaults feature somersaults or twists (more than one-half, one of which is covered here) done in the preflight. Advanced women frequently utilize a roundoff approach, where a roundoff is done onto the board and the vault proceeds from there, but that is a very advanced skill, and requires specialized training and equipment. Men have recently begun using this approach, although not nearly as often as women do.

Although older boys vault on a long horse, which is a horse turned lengthwise and raised up as high as 53 inches, younger boys, beginner boys, and girls vault on the side horse, which is a horse turned sideways and is lower (the height will depend on the ability of the vaulter during learning). This horse differs from the pommel horse in that it does not have the pommels (handles) on it, and no holes for pommel bolts. If a horse is utilized that used to be a pommel horse, the holes in the horse body where the pommels were bolted on should be filled so that a finger cannot get caught there.

The entire time of performance, from leaving the board to touching the horse to landing on your feet, takes less than 2 seconds. A vault is just one move, yet in competition the score for a vault is just as valuable as the score for any other routine (containing many more parts). So, if you compete, it is important to work on vault as hard as on the other events so that you can master it.

Terms Used in This Chapter

Afterflight   Also called post-flight or off-flight, this refers to the portion of the vault that occurs once hand contact with the horse has passed and up to the landing.

Preflight   Also called on-flight, this refers to the portion of the vault that occurs between leaving the vaulting board and making hand contact with the horse.

Organization of This Chapter

Board Drills

Jumping

Before jumping over the horse, the beginning student should get a feel for what it is like to jump on the board. There are quite a few different boards on the market today. Each one has its own characteristics. In the United States, we have a much greater variety of boards than is available in other parts of the world. So whenever you find a vaulting board that is new to you, jump on it and see where it is springiest. That is where you want to jump to when you are running down and hurdling onto the board for a vault. One word of caution: If the board feels springiest up at the far end, you do not want to jump all the way to the end of the board, because if you make a small mistake and jump a little too far, you will miss the board entirely and ram into the horse. So if the board feels springiest way up at the end, move your contact point back about a foot. Sometimes it is helpful to put a white line on the board so that you have something to look at and aim toward with your feet. You will learn to run down the runway looking at the spot on the board that you want to hit until you are very close to the board. Then you will shift your eyes from the board to the horse and look for the place where you want to contact the horse.

Newcomers to vaulting boards can practice jumping onto the board and springing onto a mat or an elevated surface, or doing dive rolls onto a mat, preferably a soft landing mat. If you have never been on a board, it may be very helpful just to bounce on the board a number of times as if it were a small trampoline. Your teacher can hold onto your hands as you bounce up and down just to make sure you do not bounce off (figure 10.1).

Next, start with very little run—actually just a few quick steps to get the feel of jumping onto the board. Your last step into your hurdle takes place before you reach the board (the distance will depend on the speed of your approach, so at first you will be fairly close to the board). Hurdle from your last step onto both feet (side by side) and punch the board (push down rapidly) with the balls of your feet. Rebound into a straight jump and land on a mat. Then place several boards in a row. Take a few steps, jump onto one, land past it on a mat, take a few steps, jump onto the next board, land past it on a mat, and so on as long as there are boards and mats.

As you feel more comfortable with the board, do something with your jump. For instance, put a pile of mats on the far side of the board, take a few steps, hurdle onto the board, and see if you can jump up as high as the pile of mats (figure 10.2). You can practice some of the jumps that you learned on the floor using the board. The height you will get from the board will give you more air time.

Figure 10.1a, b, c

a.   b.   c.

Figure 10.2a, b, c, d, e

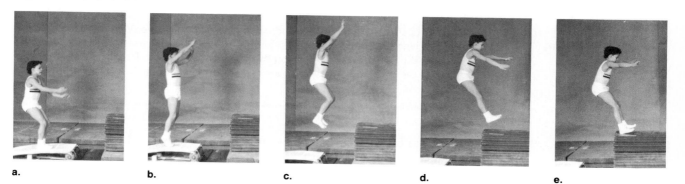

a.   b.   c.   d.   e.

Dive Roll (Figure 10.3)

Finally, it is a good idea to practice dive rolls onto a mat. Since most of the vaults involve turning your body over, this will help teach you how to turn your body over in a relatively safe fashion—if you know how to do a dive roll on the mat already. Remember that any head-under landing like this can be dangerous, so prepare for it by learning a dive roll and getting spotted when you first try it. Also remember the vaulting board will give you much more height, so even though it may make the flight part of the dive roll easier, it also means you come down from higher up so your landing will be a little more difficult to control.

Common problems with board contact are not hitting the correct spot on the board and not punching the board. When doing a dive roll, you will find

a. b. c. d.

that common problems are leaning back—this is overblocking, which results in height but little rotation—hitting the board with your body too straight (you must have a slight pike with your trunk leaning forward when you hit the board), reaching forward too slowly, and piking in the flight to the mat.

■ **Spotting**	Spot as if your student is doing a dive roll on the mat. This should be done first on a safety cushion, one that is soft for learning, and gradually you may be able to go onto a landing mat, which is only 4 or 5 inches thick, but is easier to roll up on. BEWARE: This head-under landing can be dangerous, so look out for your students, and be sure they are ready for this exercise.

You can devise contests to see who can do the longest dive roll, and see who can do the highest dive roll. These contests must be supervised and spotted to be run safely. The same thing can be done with jumps—who can jump the longest off the board, who can jump the highest off the board. Have some fun while your students get the feel of the vaulting board. Then it is time to move on.

Run and Hurdle

You cannot do a good vault unless you have a good, strong run to start with. The faster you run, the more momentum you will have when you hit the board and thus the more momentum you will have for your vault. So it is important for you to practice your run just as it is important to practice other gymnastic skills.

Find the length of run that is comfortable for you, but remember, you have a limit of 25 meters so it has to be somewhere within that distance. Find a distance that allows you to hit the board consistently. In this way, when you run down, you will always be able to hurdle to the correct place on the board and feel comfortable with your jump.

You can practice this run without the horse in front of you. Perhaps you can use the full run for a dive-roll drill. Make sure you have plenty of matting when you do this drill from a full run because the extra power that you get from a full run will make you fly high and far.

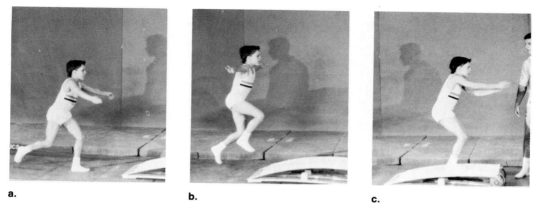

a. b. c.

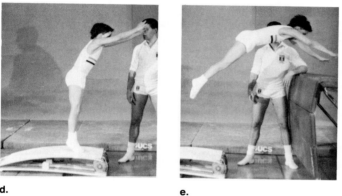

d. e.

During your hurdle, you want to move your arms into good takeoff position so that your hands contact the horse as quickly as possible. Two methods are generally used: figure 10.4 shows an underreach (also called an underarm reach or throw); and figure 10.5 shows an overreach (also called an overarm reach or throw). With the underreach, as you hurdle on to the board, you circle your arms around behind you and bring them forward quickly, passing your sides, and reach forward as you leave the board. An overreach does not have the circling action—as you hurdle, you bring your arms overhead and reach directly forward as you leave the board. Each method is useful. I found the underreach to feel better for me, and see it used more than the overreach, but some fine vaulters use an overreach as well. You can try both and see which feels best for you.

Board Position

Once you have put the horse on the far side of the board, you have to find out what position the board should be in for the particular vault you are doing. As a beginner, when you are first learning how to do a squat vault, you will not want the board too far away, because you have to become accustomed to how

Figure 10.5a, b, c, d
An overreach into a vault.

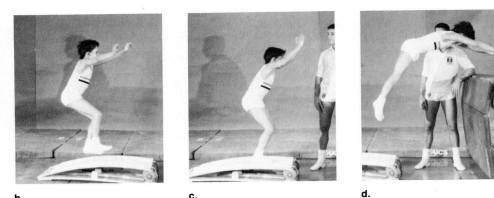

a.　　　　　　b.　　　　　　c.　　　　　　d.

it feels to go from the board over the horse. As you get to be a better vaulter, you will find that you will move the board farther and farther from the horse. This is to allow you enough time to make your body turn over to accomplish various vaults. Do not be in a hurry to move your board back, but when you feel confident of your jumping, move it back a bit at a time and make sure that you adjust your run as well (if you move the board a foot farther away from the horse you should move the starting point of your run back a foot).

Mat Drills

I mentioned earlier about doing dive rolls and jumps from a board onto a mat. When you become skilled enough to do a forward handspring vault, you may want to do another type of a drill. You can pile the mats up and practice doing handspring vaults before you even go over a horse. For instance, if you pile the mats up about 2 feet high in place of the horse, you can do a low handspring from the board to your hands and then to your back on a safety cushion that is as high as your mat pile (figure 10.6). You will not want to flip hard here.

Another drill that is very good for all vaulting and, in fact, for every dismount that there is in gymnastics, is practicing landings from an elevated surface (figure 10.7). The horse is a good bit off the ground, so if you stand on it and practice jumping to a landing mat and absorbing the landing by squatting partially (*demi plié*), and then vary this jump by doing a tuck jump, a straddle jump, a jump with a twist, and so on, you will get the idea of landing from a higher position than tumbling usually allows you to (more similar to jumping from a balance beam).

Before you ever do a handspring vault, you can get on a horse that is placed lengthwise, stand on one end, kick to a handstand on the opposite end, and fall over while you are being spotted (figure 10.8). This way you will see what it feels like to complete a handspring vault and fall all that way to the mat for a landing. The same sort of thing can be done with a roundoff for a roundoff vault. Do not go hard for these moves, or else you create the possibility of overturning due to the time your long drop gives you to turn over.

Figure 10.6a, b, c, d, e

a.

b.

c.

d.

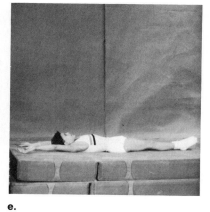

e.

Figure 10.7a, b, c, d

a.

b.

c.

d.

Vault   237

Figure 10.8a, b, c, d

a.　　　　　　b.　　　　　　c.　　　　　　d.

Figure 10.9a, b, c, d

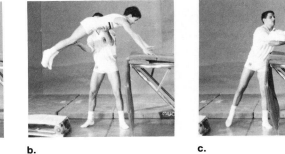

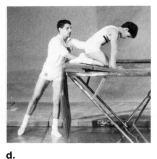

a.　　　　　　b.　　　　　　c.　　　　　　d.

Trampoline Drills

The trampoline is useful for teaching a number of gymnastic skills besides trampoline skills. Vaulting is one of the places where it can be used extensively. (NOTE: Trampoline is not found in most public schools; it is most often used in private clubs and universities.) Since the trampoline is about the same height as a beginner's vaulting horse, it can be used as a vaulting surface. By putting a mat on top of the trampoline you can jump onto the trampoline and get the feeling of running, jumping onto a vaulting board, and then flying in the air a bit (figure 10.9). It helps if you drape one end of the mat over the close end of the trampoline so that the mat does not slide back. The trampoline contact is softer than the horse because the trampoline bed gives a bit when you hit it whereas the vaulting horse does not.

You can use this method to lead up for many vaults. In fact, just about any vault can be done first onto a trampoline with this type of setup. Another advantage of the trampoline is that it has a much bigger surface for your hands to land on than the horse, so you can practice getting your hands in a certain place on the mat before you have to be very precise with your hand placement in vaulting.

The trampoline also allows afterflight practice. (See figures 10.22 and 10.24 for examples.) Bounce on the trampoline (around the middle), lean very far forward, and jump to your hands on a mat that is placed on the end of the trampoline, or on the horse itself, which is placed next to the trampoline. This simulates a vault. Then you can land on a mat that is placed on the floor next to the trampoline, which should be a safety cushion or landing mat. This way affords you many chances to practice your landings. Always get spotted when you are first learning to do this.

Do as you do for the vaults. For just about every case you can grasp your student's arm and help guide him/her through the air to the mat if needed (again, see figures 10.22 and 10.24).

■
Spotting

A third use for the trampoline is bouncing from your knees to your hands to get the feeling of jumping through the air, contacting something with your arms, and blocking (figure 10.10). Stand at the back part of the trampoline bed and do a knee drop that leans forward with your arms held straight up over your head. As you rebound, reach down to the trampoline with your upper body. This will cause you to travel forward, so it is not something you do from a big bounce. In fact, you should start from a stand without bouncing. When you land on your hands, you must push hard on the trampoline bed to push yourself back to where you bounced on your knees. To do this, you have to keep your arms in line with your trunk. If an angle develops between your arms and your trunk (a shoulder pike) you will not have as effective a block on the trampoline as you could. Later on in your training you will learn how to use a slight shoulder angle coupled with an arch to help push, but the purpose of this drill is to teach you to get into a very stiff position in the air and on contact with the trampoline bed. You will probably find that your shoulders depress (sink) a little bit when your hands contact the bed and then elevate (that is, you give in and then push up and out of your shoulders) as you leave the bed. This is good, because it is something you need for good vaulting.

Squat (Figure 10.13)

This is the first vault for most gymnasts, and there are several lead ups to make it easy to learn. When you begin to learn how to do a squat vault, do not worry about going over the horse. You just want to see what it feels like to jump from the board to the horse, landing in a kneeling position with your hands on the horse (figure 10.11). And you do not have the run up to the horse to do it. Put the board very close, put your hands on the horse, bounce a few times, and jump up to a kneeling position on the horse. If you can do this, you are well on your way. If it is difficult for you, perhaps if you are too small, then a run and jump onto the board should give you enough power to get up on top of the horse.

The next step is to jump to your feet in a squat position on the horse (figure 10.12). Again, you can start right from the board. Bounce up and down a few times. Then, as you jump up, push down hard on the horse with your hands and land on your feet. You can do the same thing from a run, which will make it

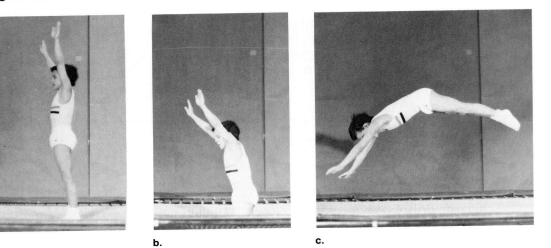

a.   b.   c.

d.   e.   f.

easier. From a run and hurdle onto the board, jump from the board to the horse, and once you land on the horse, jump off to a landing on the mat. The faster this goes, the more like a squat vault it will feel. If that is very easy for you, the next step is to do the whole squat vault. This you must do from a run rather than a stand, because if you do it from a stand, you will tend to keep your hands on the horse too long.

If you have done the drills, you are ready for the vault. Take a small run to start with, hurdle onto the board, then jump from the board to your hands on the horse, push down on the horse as hard as you can, and pull your knees through without touching your feet. You should become airborne very quickly and fly over the horse to your feet. Once you leave the horse, look for your landing area to orient yourself so that you can land on your feet and not move.

Figure 10.11a, b, c

a.

b.

c.

Figure 10.12a, b, c

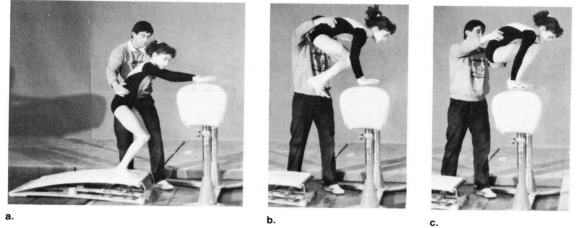

a.

b.

c.

Figure 10.13a, b, c, d

a.

b.

c.

d.

Figure 10.14a, b, c

a.

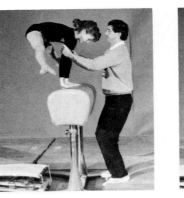

b.

c.

Common problems are not pushing off the board hard enough to get your feet over the horse, not tucking tightly, and not pushing down on the horse hard enough to lift your chest up as you fly over the horse (not blocking correctly). The extreme example of this last point is leaving your hands on the horse so long that your body is past the horse with your hands still on the horse. Your hands actually push off from the horse before your shoulders pass over the horse.

Spotting

You can stand on the approach side or the landing side of the horse depending on which lead-up drill your student is doing or the vault itself. For the lead ups I suggest that you stand on the approach side of the horse, because if she has trouble getting up onto the horse, you can assist by simply lifting at her waist so that her feet, knees, or shins can get on top of the horse.

Once she is good at doing this, then shift around to the landing side. From the landing side, you may be able to help someone who has trouble with the preflight, but certainly from the approach side you cannot help someone who has trouble with the afterflight. That is what you have to watch out for. Stand a bit to the side of her flight path as she jumps to the horse, and grab her left arm with both of your hands. Put your left hand down by her wrist and your right hand up on her upper arm. In doing so, you can actually lift her chest quite a bit if she is having any trouble or if she should happen to catch her foot on the horse as she flies over, which is a problem to watch out for. You can hold her up rather than allow her to fall flat on her face.

Straddle (Figure 10.15)

This vault is learned in a fashion similar to the squat vault. There are several lead ups that you do, and then you proceed to do the vault. If you cannot spread your legs very wide you are going to have to fly higher to get over. But if you have good straddle flexibility this vault should present no problem and may even be easier than the squat vault.

The first step is to stand close to the horse on a board, bounce a few times, and jump to a straddled stand (figure 10.14). Your hands will still be on the

Figure 10.15a, b, c, d

a.　　　　　　b.　　　　　　c.　　　　　　d.

horse as your feet touch in this first step. Next, jump up and push off with your hands, landing on the horse in a straddled stand. Be careful not to fall backward. Once you arrive at your straddled stand, it is very easy to jump forward. If you feel comfortable doing this, then just move back, take a run, hurdle onto the board, jump to a straddled stand, and immediately jump from the horse, landing on your feet.

Then, if this feels good, do not bother touching the horse with your feet. Take a run, hurdle onto the board, reach for the horse, push down as hard as you can, and straddle your legs wide. As you fly over, just remember to bring your legs back together so you can land.

Common problems are not straddling widely enough and not pushing down hard enough.

Stand on the landing side of the horse. Because your student's legs are straddled, if you stand on the approach side of the horse you will get kicked and you will be hurt as well as your student. You must avoid standing to the side on the landing mat as well, so you do not get hit with a leg. Stand right in front of her on the landing side of the horse, and as she jumps to the horse, grab her upper arms with your hands and move backward with her as she does the vault. In this fashion, if she should catch a foot, you are able to hold her chest up, and if she does not push down hard enough but does clear the horse and is nosediving, you can lift her chest. Once you see that she is going to land on her feet, let her go so she learns how to land. Once you have confidence in her, let her perform the vault without holding her arms, but stand on the landing mat and be ready to reach under her in case of a problem.

■

Spotting

Stoop (Figure 10.17)

Just like the preceding two vaults, this vault is learned in stages. It is tougher than the other two because you have to lift your seat up higher and then have to counterrotate (to change the direction of your rotation) much harder than on the preceding two vaults in order to land successfully. Here, you have to rotate your chest up quite a bit.

Figure 10.16a, b, c

a.   b.   c.

Figure 10.17a, b, c, d

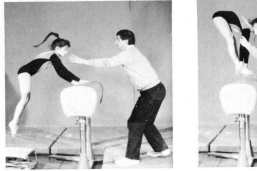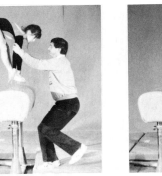

a.   b.   c.   d.

The first step is to bounce on a board with your hands on the horse and push up to a stoop position (figure 10.16). Keep your legs straight, push your seat high, and land on the horse with your feet while your hands are still on the horse.

The next step is to jump off the board, push down on the horse, then land on the horse with your feet but with your hands off the horse. As soon as you land, jump forward and land on the landing mat. Then do this step from a run.

If step two from a run goes well, then do the whole vault—go over without touching your feet. Remember you must push down very hard in order to be able to lift your chest at the end and land upright.

Common problems are not pushing down hard enough to get your chest up, not lifting your seat high enough to clear your feet, not being flexible enough to do a good stoop, and keeping your hands on the horse too long so that your shoulders move forward and cut the height of your afterflight.

Spot the preliminary steps just as you do for a squat. The vault itself is spotted on the landing side of the horse. This spot can be exactly the same as for the squat vault or the straddle vault. Be observant, because your student needs to have her seat much higher for the stoop vault than the squat. If she is not very good that way, she may hit her feet on the horse.

Layout Vaults

Once you have learned how to do the previous three vaults, then it is time to start increasing your preflight to the horse. To do this, you have to move the board back so that you cannot reach the horse easily while standing on the board. Very good vaulters have the board back quite far, so even though it may seem a long way, you will find when you run and hurdle on to the board with increased momentum, you get to the horse quite easily.

The term *layout vault* refers to getting your body straight or slightly arched, but at least horizontal, during your preflight for these particular vaults.

When you jump from the board, you do not want to go up high, at least not with your hands. Reach directly for the horse and rotate so that your heels come up behind you as you are flying from the board to the horse. At the moment of contact with the horse, shove down very hard (block) so that you can lift your chest in the afterflight. This push comes from your hands, arms, shoulders, and chest. Remember, you are dealing with much more momentum here because you are running and jumping from a farther position to reach the horse. You must go fast and have a very strong push on the horse to achieve good afterflight.

Common problems are piking in the preflight, overarching in the preflight, reaching too slowly, reaching too high or keeping your chest too high—not rotating enough—so that you have to reach down to the horse after you have completed your preflight (when done correctly you will feel as if you are jumping directly at the horse), and not putting the board back far enough to allow you to achieve good preflight.

Do as you do for the previous vaults (figure 10.18). Sometimes it is helpful to have two spotters, one for preflight and one for afterflight, so that your student can get an idea of what the layout preflight is like. However, if she has done plenty of board drills involving dive rolls, she should have a good idea what it feels like.

If you are confident of her afterflight abilities, you can spot the layout squat and the layout stoop on the approach side of the horse, assisting her to get up in the proper position for the preflight (figure 10.19). But you must make sure that she is going to clear the horse, because if you are on the near side and she hits her feet on the horse or does not push off from the horse well, you will not be able to get around to spot her afterflight. For those students that are good in afterflight and good with the push, it is no problem to spot the preflight. Do not lift too hard, otherwise you will hinder her downward push on the horse.

Figure 10.18a, b, c
Spotting the afterflight of a layout squat.

a.

b.

c.

Figure 10.19a, b
Spotting the preflight.

a.

b.

Handspring (Figures 10.20, 10.21 and 10.22)

If you are comfortable going over the horse and have no problem doing a good dive roll from the board to a soft mat and can rotate enough to land on your back on the soft mat without touching your hands, then you are certainly ready to try a handspring.

The object of this vault is to turn over completely once, that is, to jump from your feet on the board to your hands on the horse, usually contacting somewhere around a handstand position, and then continuing to rotate to your feet again. The angle at which you contact the horse is determined by the type of vault you want to do, whether you are going to flip extra after hand contact (advanced skills) or do a handspring with possibly some twists added on later (also advanced skills). But at first do not even worry about that. Just jump from the board to a handstand, or rather *through* a handstand, and then rotate over and land on your feet.

Figure 10.20a, b, c, d, e
Spotting the afterflight—Meggan should not be piked at contact in her preflight, her elbows flex a bit too much at contact, and her head ducks as she leaves the horse.

a.

b.

c.

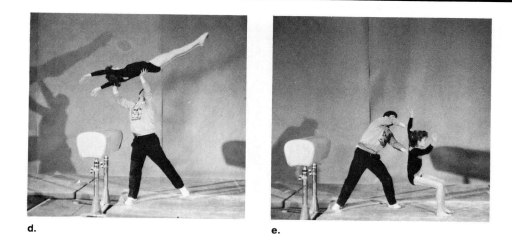

d.

e.

When you do this, as you come off the board, just as with the other vaults, you watch the horse—watch the spot your hands are going to hit. Rotate from the board so that your heels go over your head (with your chest low) to contact the horse near a handstand. The board should be back from the horse, as a close board will not allow enough time to rotate. You might try to put the board a body length away from the horse, and then see if you need to put it back even farther. When you do hit the horse with your hands, push on the horse as hard as you can (block), and keep watching the horse as you fly away from it. Your body should have a slight arch in the preflight and a slight arch in the afterflight. As you push off from the horse, you will feel the push coming from your hands and from your shoulders (actually you will probably bend your arms a bit and push out of your elbows, too, but do not think about this).

Figure 10.21a, b, c, d, e
Spotting the preflight—Melanie is a bit piked at contact, she ducks her head as she leaves the horse, and she is on the horse too long—she should be off of the horse in figure d.

a.

b.

c.

d.

e.

Once you are approaching horizontal in your afterflight and still looking back at the horse as you are flying away from it, pull your head forward and spot the wall, that is, look at a point on the wall in front of you for orientation. This will help you in landing—it will give you a cue as to where the mat is. You will probably see the floor peripherally as you are finishing the vault.

Common problems are piking in your preflight, not rotating enough to assure a good landing, bending your arms excessively or buckling (piking) in your shoulders on contact, piking in your afterflight, ducking your head (that is, pulling your chin toward your chest immediately) as you leave the horse, and being disoriented at the landing.

Chapter 10

Figure 10.22a, b, c, d, e
Using a trampoline to provide preflight when drilling the afterflight.

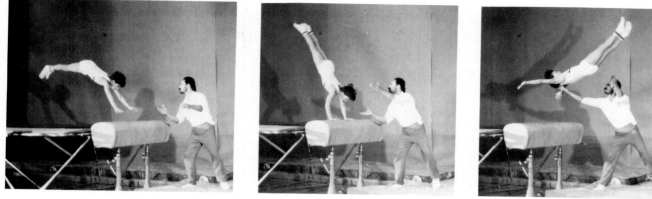

a.

b.

c.

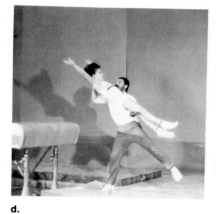

d.

e.

Stand on the far (landing) side of the horse, a bit to the side of the vault's flight path. As your student jumps to a handstand, your left hand reaches for her back, and your right hand reaches for her left arm. You will be able to hold her arm the whole way through her afterflight. The same spot is used when spotting afterflight from a trampoline approach.

If you are a single spotter and spot the afterflight, you have no one to help in the preflight. If your student is very good in the air and has no problem with orientation when turning over after the hand contact, you can spot the preflight instead. To do that, stand between the board and the horse a bit to the side, and as she jumps for the horse, reach underneath as you would for a dive roll.

■

Spotting

As you get stronger with your handspring, you can work toward two different types of handsprings; one that flips over extra in the afterflight, and one that goes up a little higher and farther than the first one because of the way you contact the horse and push.

The first kind is useful for later handspring-to-somersault vaults. The second kind is useful for a plain handspring, or a Yamashita, which is described next, or a twisting handspring. The push on the horse and contact angle are different for these two methods. If you are going to work on the first kind, the one that has extra rotation, I suggest piling up mats behind the horse so that you have a higher surface to land on. That way you will not flip past your feet and hurt yourself by falling on your chest or face. For this particular vault you should rotate your body as quickly as possible and contact with a body line that is close to vertical. When you push on the horse, push downward and a bit forward, which will push your heels over your head with more force. This should add to your rotation. Your contact position will be arched, and there will be an angle between your arms and your trunk. This will come out as you push into the handspring.

If you are going to work the second type of handspring, the single-flip type where you do just a half somersault between your hand contact and your landing, you contact the horse at a lower angle but with similarly fast rotation as you did on the first one, then push straight downward instead of downward and forward. Therefore your push is similar to the push for a layout stoop vault. If you come off the board rotating so quickly that you would otherwise flip past your feet instead of landing, this push will reduce your rotation and will add to your height and distance because of the way you are pushing on the horse. As you leave the horse, watch it go with your eyes. Keep your head back, let your arms spread, and arch slightly. This is the type of handspring that you will use eventually to do twisting handsprings (when you twist you will make some position changes).

Yamashita (Figures 10.23 and 10.24)

This vault was named after a Japanese World and Olympic vaulting champion, Haruhiro Yamashita. It looks like a handspring that pikes and then opens in the afterflight (this action is also called a jackknife). Piking your body makes you flip faster. So on this vault, you want to come in at a lower angle than for the handspring, and you want to push downward very hard on the horse. The push will help retard the rotation that you developed from the board (and give you extra height), but then in the afterflight, your piking action will speed up the rotation.

As with the handspring, keep your chest and hands low as you leave the board, but rotate rapidly. Your contact angle will probably be somewhere around 45° to 60° above horizontal when done well. (If you are not powerful, you will contact at a higher angle.) As you leave the horse, having pushed down, do not look back at the horse. Rather, as soon as your hands leave, you should move into the pike (you will see your legs) so that you can kick out well above horizontal or at least at horizontal. This will slow your rotation and make your landing easier.

Common problems are buckling forward (piking) at your shoulders upon contact, which reduces your blocking action, contacting the horse with your body angle too high, which may cause you to rotate over too much, not piking deeply enough, and not kicking out from your pike soon enough.

Figure 10.23a, b, c, d
Spotting the afterflight.

a.   b.   c.   d.

Figure 10.24a, b, c, d
The same spot using a trampoline to provide preflight.

a.   b.   c.   d.

Do this the same way as you spot a handspring. If you wish to help your student emphasize the opening out of the pike, and she is good at a handspring, put your hands under her back and hold her up in the air a bit, and allow her to feel where she should kick out.

■
Spotting

Roundoff (Figure 10.25)

The roundoff (or half-on) is a lead up to a number of different vaulting skills, so it useful to learn how to do one over the horse. You might think that before doing a roundoff you would try to do a cartwheel vault, which used to be done extensively many, many years back, but please **do not try to do a cartwheel vault.** It has been found that the landing is very dangerous for your knees because it is a sideways landing, and your knees are not made to take landings this way. A cartwheel vault **is not allowed** in competition.

Figure 10.25a, b, c, d, e, f, g, h

a.

b.

c.

d.

e.

f.

g.

h.

To do the roundoff vault, you do a half twist on to the horse and then push off from the horse to a landing facing the horse. Some vaults are done not from a complete half turn on, but from a quarter turn on or a third turn on. You can try all these vaults just as long as you make sure you turn to face the horse as you leave it, so that when you land you can absorb your landing in a safe fashion rather than a sideways fashion.

To learn the preflight twist, you can work at it bit by bit, doing a quarter turn, then a third turn, then a half turn, but the key is, as you leave the board, one shoulder lifts up (pulls back). Usually you twist your upper body the same way as you do for your tumbling roundoff (note that a left-hand-first roundoff utilizes a right twist). Keep your eyes on the horse, and you will see your hands twist ahead of you as your shoulders twist into the turn from the board. Your feet will be trailing a bit. When you contact the horse on its near upper surface, push down on it as hard as you can, fly through the air facing the horse, and land. Looking at the horse allows you to see the mat peripherally.

Common problems are letting your legs split apart, which hinders your twist, not doing at least a quarter turn on to the horse, and not finishing your twist as you come off the horse so that you do not land in a square fashion (that is, facing the horse).

Done in a similar fashion as for a handspring with this change: Find out which way your student twists, and make sure you stand to the side of the mat where his back will turn toward you (this will keep you from getting kicked if he does not go over the top). For preflight, if he does a left roundoff, reach under him with your right hand and over him with your left hand. This way you can lift him and provide a twist if he is not twisting enough. For afterflight, reach in and take hold of his right arm with your right hand. Reach under him with your left hand, and assist him if necessary.

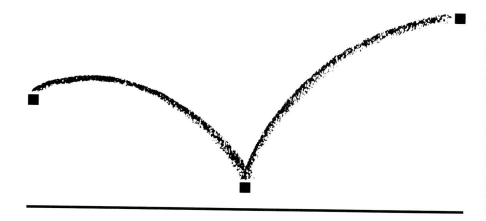

Parallel bars competition is in an exciting phase. Gymnasts are exploring the use of horizontal-bar-type movements on the parallel bars, and have opened up new areas of performance. While men have always competed on this event, women did so as well up to the early 1950s, when the uneven parallel bars event was introduced exclusively for women. So today, although both boys and girls can benefit from elementary skill work on the parallel bars, only boys train extensively on it as they may later compete on this event.

Skills are demonstrated above, on, under, and occasionally outside of the bars, and include moves that show swing, grip release and regrasp, a turn, and flight. Only three holds are allowed in an optional routine, so the routine is expected to flow mainly from skill to skill. As you get better, you will learn skills that are done on one bar only, as well as the bulk of skills that utilize two bars. This is mostly a support event as is pommel horse, so it is necessary to be quite strong in that area to perform well. Additionally, you will be spending much time in and through a handstand here also, so the more solid you become in a handstand, the better you will be at parallel bars (as well as at all events in gymnastics). When learning skills, the bars are often lowered.

Parallel bars is one of two events in men's gymnastics where adjustments in the dimensions of the equipment in competition are allowed (pommel horse is the other). Some height adjustment is permitted (for young boys especially), and you will see every performer make a width adjustment to set the bars at a width where he feels comfortable swinging. He must be able to swing in a support, an upper-arm support, and an underbar hang at one width. If the bars are wider, it may be easier to do a support swing, but it makes upper-arm support skills tougher, so a happy medium must be found. Each performer finds this measurement through experiment, and often uses his forearm and hand as the measuring device for setting the width. The distance is usually somewhere around the distance from the gymnast's fingertips to his elbow.

Supplementary learning devices are a set of low parallel bars that should be adjustable in width (figure 11.1); parallettes, which are short bars on some sort of stand that are easily movable and adjustable; and two stacks of mats set up to simulate parallel bars (figure 11.2). Cylindrical mats that wrap around the bars (called bar pads) are useful when doing skills that may result in striking a bar.

Figure 11.1   **Figure 11.2**

Young gymnasts often find that they have some irritation of the skin of their hands and underarms in the mid-upper-arm area due to friction on the bar. This will pass as training progresses and their bodies build up callouses to protect against the rubbing. Hands also become irritated in the early phases of underbar parallel bars training as they do with rings, horizontal bar, and uneven parallel bars. Refer to my brief discussions of hand care in chapter 9 (**Rings**) and chapter 15 (**Medical Considerations**).

NOTE FOR SPOTTING: It is extremely important that you are positioned so that if you reach over the bars to spot, the height of the bars is not around or above your shoulder height. You must not be able to reach over a bar so that if your student falls on your arm it will be pinned between his body and the bar, or so that it will be bent over the bar. When spotting skills above the bars, stand so that your shoulders are at least an arm's length above the rail. Often a spotting block or folded mat is used to provide a spotting platform. When spotting from below the bars, reach in from below and never put your arm or hand over the bar.

Terms Used in This Chapter

Inside Grip   When doing underbar skills, having your palms inside of the bars facing the inner surfaces of the bars, with your fingers overtop. Your thumb is also inside, held next to your index finger. You can start with this grip from a stand or drop to it.

Outside Grip   When doing beginning underbar skills from a stand, starting with your palms outside of the bars facing the outside surfaces of the bars with your fingers on top. Your thumb is also outside, held next to your index finger.

Underbar   Referring to any skill that passes through a long hang or a piked inverted hang.

Figure 11.3a, b, c

a.   b.   c.

Organization of This Chapter

Support Drills   *Streuli*
Balances   Forward Leg Cuts
Support Swing   Underbar Swing
Vault Dismounts   Drops
Handstand Dismounts   Kips
Presses   Baby Giant Swings
Upper-arm Support Swing Cast to Upper Arms
Forward Roll   Peach Basket
Backward Roll   *Stützkehre*
Backward Uprise   Somersault Dismounts
Forward Uprise   Sequences to Practice

Support Drills

All of these exercises should be done with the bars low enough so that if you fall from a support you will land on your feet with your shoulders well above the bars so that your arms cannot strike the bars on the way down. If the bars cannot be lowered enough, put mats under them to raise the floor.

Walking (Figure 11.3)

The first thing to try once you are able to get into a support on the parallel bars is to walk the length of the bars without bending your arms, both forward and backward. This can be done with several different tempos. At first, do it slowly to get the feel of shifting your weight from hand to hand, then increase the speed of the walk as you feel more sure of your movements.

Walking with Straddling (Figure 11.4)

This exercise introduces you to small swings. To go forward, begin in a support on the end of the bars, and swing your body up so that your legs go just over the bars. As this happens, straddle your legs and push off with your hands so that you are sitting on the bars, supported by your legs. Move your hands forward to the other side of your legs and shift your weight onto them so that you

Figure 11.4a, b, c, d, e, f
Keep good form—Lenny's knees should not flex in figure b. To go backward, reverse the order of the figures.

a.　　　　　　　　　b.　　　　　　　　　c.

d.　　　　　　　　　e.　　　　　　　　　f.

can lift your legs off the bars behind you. Swing them in front of your hands and repeat the sequence of movements that you just did. This will allow you to move forward from one end of the bars to the other. When you reach the end of the bars, reverse your actions and go backward (to visualize this, reverse the order of the figures). Try to minimize piking while doing this exercise.

Hopping (Figure 11.5)

Start in a support on the end of the bars and move to the other end by hopping both hands at the same time along the bars while keeping your body straight. This is accomplished by shrugging (elevating) your shoulders and then pushing them down (depressing) rapidly to produce the hop. Start with slow hopping and then build up to fast hopping. Do it both forward and backward.

Figure 11.5a, b, c

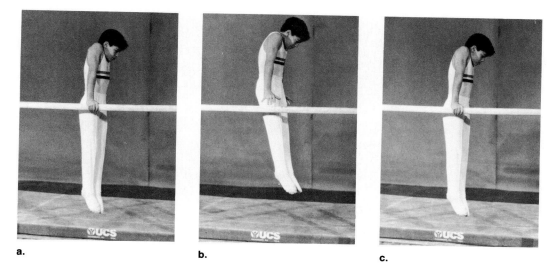

a.   b.   c.

Figure 11.6a, b, c, d, e
Keep form—don't split your legs.

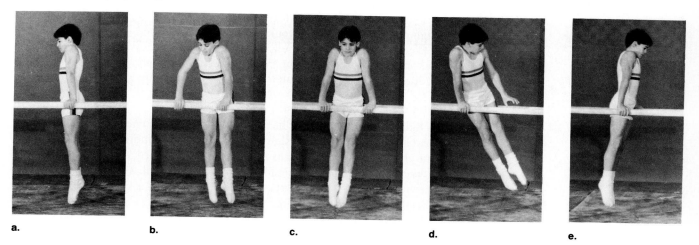

a.   b.   c.   d.   e.

Turning (Figure 11.6)

From a support, shift your weight to the left, turn around to your left, and reach for the left bar with your right hand. Shift your weight onto your right hand, continue turning, and reach back for the empty bar with your left hand. Finish in a support facing the opposite way that you began. Do this turning the other way as well.

Figure 11.7   **Figure 11.8**

Balances

L Support (Figure 11.7), Straddled L Support (Figure 11.8)

You may have already tried these balances on the floor or other events. You will find they are easier to do on the parallel bars than the floor because you have something to hold on to that gives you more control. If you are not strong enough or flexible enough to do these hold moves in proper position, you can easily see how far away you are from your goal of proper performance. The narrower the bars are, the easier the straddled L will be, but the bars must be wide enough to allow you to swing through them if you are going to perform any types of swinging skills after you do your straddled L.

Common problems for the L are hunching your back and having your legs above or below horizontal. For the straddled L the common problem is having your legs below horizontal due to poor flexibility and/or strength.

Shoulderstand (Figure 11.9)

This balance is similar to the headstand that you have tried on the floor. It can be reached by pressing to it slowly in a tucked, a straddled piked, a piked, or a straight body position. You can begin it in a straddled seat on the bars or in a support. This can be done on low parallel bars as well as high ones. You can also swing to it from a support, which is a lead up to a swing to a handstand and a swing to a forward roll.

To press to a shoulderstand from a straddled seat, place your hands on the bars a short distance in front of your legs. Lean forward and bend your arms, keeping your elbows pointing outward, so that your upper arms contact the bars just below your deltoid (shoulder) muscles. At this point you will have a six-point support on the bars—your upper arms, your hands, and your legs. Push down on the bars with your hands to lift your seat overhead, and lift your legs off the bars. Pike tightly, as this will make it easier to lift your seat. If you cannot lift your legs off the bars, put your feet on the bars and walk your feet along the bars toward your hands until your seat is up sufficiently to allow you to push your feet off the bars. Slowly proceed up toward an inverted position by straightening your body, finishing in a slight arch or a straight body, and balancing on your hands and upper arms. Narrow bars help in the performance of this skill, but you should learn to do it with the bars at the width that you swing at (as discussed earlier). Look at the mat below you throughout the press with your head in line with your trunk.

Figure 11.9a, b, c, d, e
A straddled piked press to a shoulderstand
from a straddled seat.

a. b. c.

d. e.

Common problems are letting your elbows come in toward your body, which
will cause you to slip down through the bars, not being vertical, piking your
final position, going up too quickly to control the move, and pushing your seat
too far over, which will cause you to fall forward into a forward roll. If this
happens, keep your elbows out and you will come through it OK.

Do as you would for a headstand, if you are above the bars. If you are below, reach
up between the bars and support your student by his shoulder, the top of his head,
or with one hand on his abdomen and the other on his back.

Spotting

Handstand

Having the parallel bars to hold on to makes this skill easier to perform here than on the floor and certainly easier than on the rings, as the parallel bars do not move, and balance is easier to control with wrist movements here than on a mat or on rings. It should be first tried on low parallel bars or parallettes (see figure 11.1), as you can kick up to a handstand there many times. It will take a little while to become strong enough to swing up to a handstand on the parallel bars with control.

Common problems and spotting are the same as for the handstand performed on the floor.

■

Spotting

Swinging to a handstand is covered shortly. On low parallel bars, spot as you would for a floor handstand.

Forward Pirouette (Figure 11.10)

If you feel comfortable in a handstand, learn to turn around while there. You should practice this first on the floor as described in chapter 6. The obvious difference here is that you must put your hands in specific places—on the bars—when doing the pirouette. Low bars offer a place to learn this move safely. Turn quickly rather than slowly, and it will help you to complete the turn if you think of turning more than halfway in the first part. This way you will have less of a turn to complete when heading back to a two-bar handstand from your brief one-bar support. Your hands should be around a shoulder width apart during your one-bar support, but you will find other widths useful for certain maneuvers later on in your gymnastics career. If you feel confident of this pirouette from a still handstand and have mastered a swing to a handstand, do it from a swing. Think of swinging to a handstand, and when you get there, perform the pirouette. As you become stronger, you may begin to turn before reaching the handstand, but this is dependent on the amount of speed you have going into the move. Remember to push down on the bars throughout the turn to maintain good handstand alignment. You must finish the turn in a handstand. If you become proficient at this skill it will be much to your benefit, as I have seen more gymnasts fall off the parallel bars doing a pirouette than any other skill. (A backward pirouette is harder and is rated as a B-level skill on parallel bars, and is not covered here. It looks just like one done on the floor.)

Common problems are not pushing down hard enough, allowing your shoulders to buckle (pike), which lets your arms come out of alignment with your trunk and drops your chest, lifting your head, not shifting your weight over your support hand(s) during the turn, which often results in a fall from the bars to one side or the other, or a missed handstand at the end of the turn.

■

Spotting

Spot as a pirouette on the mat is spotted. If the move is performed on the high parallel bars, be sure to help guide your student to the mat in case of a miss. If you spot while standing on the floor (your student is in relatively good control at this point), just be sure that he is on his way to his feet in case of a fall. Remember, do not reach over the bars from the floor if they are around or above your shoulder height.

Chapter 11

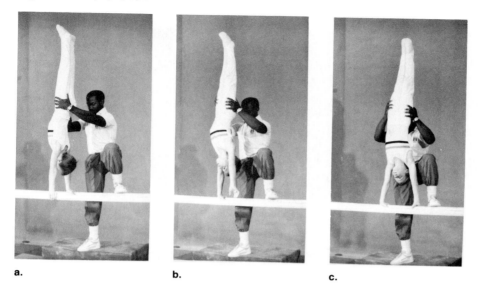

a.　　　　　　　　b.　　　　　　　　c.

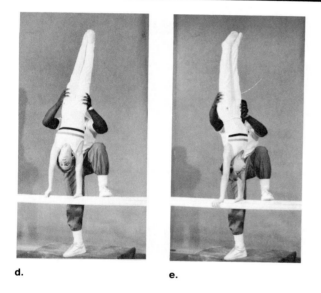

d.　　　　　　　　e.

Support Swing

Straight Arm (Figures 11.11 and 11.12)

You must spend a lot of time practicing this swing if you intend to advance on parallel bars, as so many skills use the strength developed by this exercise. Begin in a support on bars adjusted so that your feet are just off the mat with your shoulders relaxed so they are elevated (shrugged). Swing your body back and forth slightly, keeping it relatively straight and staying relaxed in your shoulders. You will get the hang of the shifts in balance necessary by starting small and working up to bigger swings. Look at the end of the bars for orientation.

Figure 11.11a, b, c, d, e, f, g, h
Swinging horizontal to horizontal.

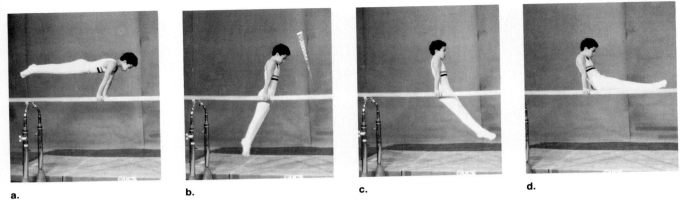

a.   b.   c.   d.

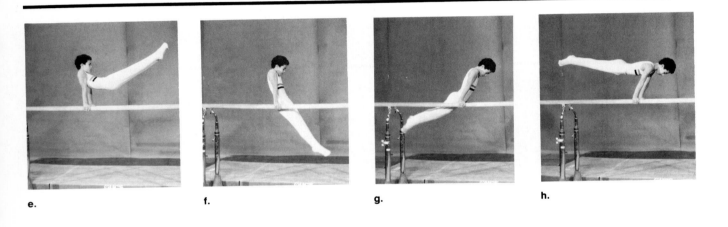

e.   f.   g.   h.

Figure 11.12a, b, c, d, e
Swinging to a handstand.

a.   b.   c.   d.   e.

When you are able to swing your feet higher than the bars at either end, push down on the bars to get out of your shoulder shrug and to lift your body up farther as it rises above the bars. This shoulder elevating and depressing action takes place on each swing and adds power to your swing. Note that there is a slight beating action (also called tap swing) going forward in figures 11.11a and b where your body goes from a slight arch to a slight pike, and the reverse happens on the way back in figures 11.11f and g. At first, do not think about this. Later on, you will learn to use this action to help perform different skills.

To get to a handstand, push forward very slightly as you begin your downswing in the front to get a bit more power. Be careful to do this only slightly, as overdoing it will result in a fall forward. As you swing up in the back, push down on the bars to aid you in getting to a handstand. Your gaze will shift to the mat below as you go up. In the beginning you will arch on the way up, but as you become stronger you will be able to hollow your chest to counteract the arch, and to swing quickly to the handstand and stop sharply, as well as swing slowly if you choose to.

If you want to get down to the mat from a support on high bars, you can do any of the simple dismounts that are described shortly, or you can get down safely by either pushing back with your body upright and your arms straight so that you drop to a stand behind your hands, or turn toward the left bar, move your right hand from the right bar to the left bar, and drop to a stand (of course, you can do the opposite actions as well). Do not drop straight down by bending your arms while holding on—you can hurt your shoulders and/or elbows this way.

Common problems are arching excessively in the backswing, piking excessively in the frontswing, bending your arms during the swing, not relaxing your shoulders as you swing through the bottom, lifting your head on the way up to your handstand, and leaning excessively (which kills some of the swing).

Stand next to the lowered bars and see that your student does not fall forward or backward. As he goes toward a handstand, you can help him to reach it by lifting his legs. You then help to stabilize his handstand just as if it were on the mat.

■
Spotting

Dip Swing (Figure 11.13)

A variation of the support swing is the dip swing, which is an excellent strength builder. Begin with small swings where your feet are just about bar high. As you begin to descend, dip down and pass through the bottom of the swing in a bent-armed support. Your elbows will face backward, and your shoulders will dip around the level of the bars. On the way up, push out to a straight-armed support and finish your upswing. Do the same on the return swing. As you build strength, you will be able to do this up to a handstand in the back, or will be able to hop off the bars at either end of the swing, or both. Be careful to start with a small swing until you are strong, as you will stress your shoulder muscles and joints quite a bit through the bottom. To visualize a backward dip swing, reverse the figures. As a variation you can dip going one way only, rather than both ways.

Figure 11.13a, b, c, d, e, f
A dip swing forward. To visualize a
backward dip swing, reverse the figures.

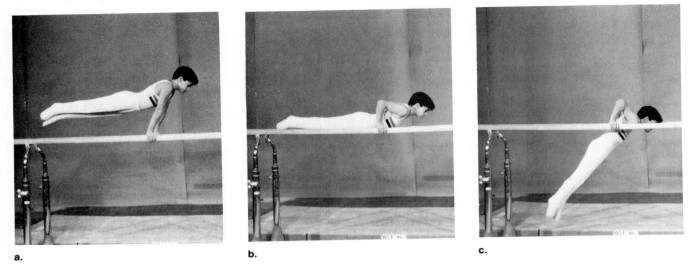

a.

b.

c.

d.

e.

f.

Vault Dismounts

Front (Figure 11.14)

As you swing to the rear, push your body to the side over the left bar and past
it. Shift your right hand to the left bar and move your left hand off. Your right
hand helps to guide you to a landing while your left arm is used for balance.
This is called a front vault because the front of your body faces the bar as you
pass over it. As you become strong in a support swing, you can do this up to a
handstand before landing on your feet. Do both sides and see if one is more
comfortable for you than the other.

Common problems are not pushing to the side enough and leaning too far
forward or backward so that your landing is not in line with your hands.

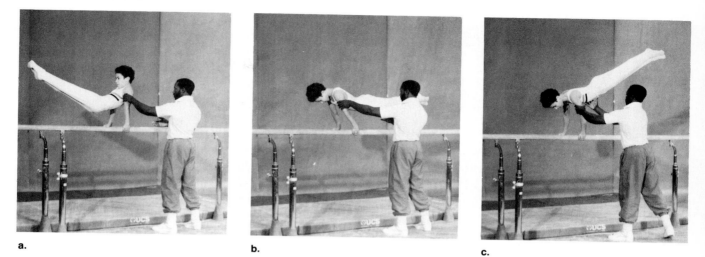

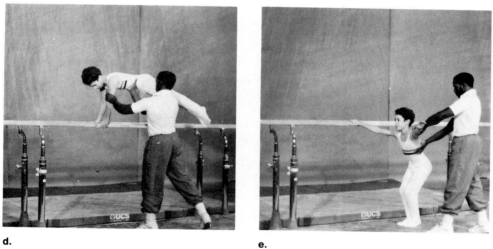

Stand to the left, hold your student's left arm, and guide him as he dismounts.

Rear (Figure 11.15)

Swing to the front and push your body to the side over the left bar and past it. You will shift your right hand to the left bar and move your left hand off. Your right hand helps support you and guide you to a landing. You will find it more difficult to push down on the bar in this behind-your-back position because we are much weaker in this range than we are in front of ourselves, and the range

Figure 11.15a, b, c, d, e

a.

b.

c.

d.

e.

of motion of our shoulder joint is not as great in back as it is in front. For this reason you will not be able to do this nearly as high as you can do a front vault. This is called a rear vault because the rear of your body faces the bar as you pass over it. Do both sides as mentioned above.

Common problems and spotting are the same as for the front vault.

Stützkehre (Figure 11.16)

The *Stützkehre* dismount (means support turn; pronounced: shtitz'-keh-reh) is an extension of the rear vault and is a lead-up skill to a turning release-recatch skill done on the front swing from support to support, which is described later in this chapter. The difference between the *Stützkehre* (often just called *Stütz*) and the rear vault is that this dismount is done with a one-half turn outward (away from the bars). As you swing up in the front, turn to the left as you push over the left bar and look down your left arm. You will not shift hands as with the previous two dismounts. Keep pushing down on the bar with your support

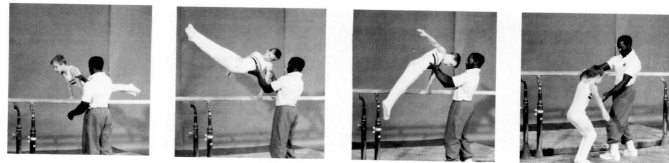

a.   b.   c.   d.

(left) hand as you complete your turn and flight to the outside of the bars. As you descend to the mat, your support hand helps to push your upper body up. Push off with this hand and either land without regrasping the bar or regrasp momentarily and then push off to land free of the bar. You will not be able to hang on because your left arm will be twisted around through the support turn phase (forearm fully pronated), and you will have a weak support grip as you come down.

Common problems are not turning enough and bending your support arm.

Stand on the left side and reach under your student to help in the landing. You can hold his support arm to pull him to the side if he does not move that way.

■

Spotting

Handstand Dismounts

Wende (Figure 11.17)

The *Wende* is a pirouette dismount; pronounced: ven′-deh. In the USA we often call it a windy. If you can swing to a handstand easily and have begun to work on a forward pirouette, this skill will be easy to learn. When done to the left, this dismount looks like a missed forward pirouette that swings through the turn phase on your left hand and then goes outside of the bars. This is exactly what you do. Begin the move just as you would a swinging forward pirouette. As you turn on your left arm, lean outside (to the left) of the bars more than if you wanted to complete a pirouette in a handstand. As you pass outside of the bars, keep pushing down on the bar with your support hand, and your body will continue to move past an inverted position toward a landing. The end of the skill is similar to the end of the *Stützkehre* dismount, except that it comes from a much higher position.

As lead-up drills, first do a pirouette on the floor in one step—begin with your support hand on a line and turned so that your fingers face sideways. As you finish your pirouette, lower to a front support on the other side of the line

Figure 11.17a, b, c, d, e

a.   b.   c.

d.   e.

from where you started. Then do the same thing on a set of low parallel bars. As you finish your pirouette, hop your support hand off the bar and land in a front support on the mat next to the bars.

Common problems are leaning too far forward at the start, not completing your swing through a vertical position, not completing your turn, and not pushing down long enough during the skill.

Figure 11.18a, b, c, d, e
Hooking your feet is a common flaw when
piking rapidly.

a. b. c. d. e.

■

Spotting

Stand by the left side of the bars just behind your student. Your right hand will reach under your student's body on the way up to insure that he goes through a handstand and leans outside of the bar, while your left hand can hold onto his near arm. As he passes over the bar and begins his descent, switch your right hand so that you can guide him to a landing and support him if he needs it. You can support his shoulders or hold the sides of his body. Stand clear of his head, and be prepared to move if necessary.

Handstand to Straddled Cut-off (Figure 11.18)

This dismount can be simulated on the mat or on low bars. Kick to a handstand, arch your upper back to move your feet over a bit, sag in your shoulders, then snap your legs down while straddling and land in a straddle stand. If you can land in front of where your hands were, then you can do the same motion off the parallel bars safely. To do it the first time on high bars, you can either do one-half of a front pirouette or stand on the bars and kick to a handstand on one bar. Once you are in the one-bar-handstand position, do the same actions, but lift your chest as you go down. You will land with your back facing the bars.

Common problems are not leaning over enough to clear the bar, not pushing off hard enough to lift your chest, and not straddling enough.

Done in a similar fashion to a straddle vault over the horse. Stand next to your student in his landing zone. Reach up and hold one or both of his upper arms. As he starts the dismount, guide him to an upright landing if needed. If you stand to the side as shown, watch out for his leg.

Spotting

Figure 11.19a, b, c, d, e
Danny goes a bit low in figure c—he was
relying on his spotter since he should be a
bit more forward.

a.

b.

c.

d.

e.

Presses

Bent-armed Straight Body Press to Shoulderstand (Figure 11.19)

The bent-arm straight body press (also called a hollowback) is easier to perform first on the parallel bars than on the rings, since the bars do not move. Usually you will start from an L support. Lower your legs into a straight body or slightly arched support position and continue rotating your whole body forward (with the same rhythm as when you lowered your legs) by flexing your elbows, keeping them in close to your sides. You must push down hard to keep from falling below the bars, and must lean forward a bit to accomplish the turnover. As you get close to vertical, put your elbows out so that the outsides of your upper arms rest on the bars and you are in a shoulderstand.

Common problems are not leaning forward enough and letting your elbows slip from your sides on the way up, which will lower your body and make it harder to finish the press.

Figure 11.20a, b, c, d, e

a.

b.

c.

d.

e.

Stand to the side and help your student to turn over and not fall through the bars if needed.

■

Spotting

Bent-armed Piked Press to Handstand (Figure 11.20)

Just as you learned to do this on the floor, you can perform it on the bars. You might find it easier to do here because you have the bars to hold on to, which gives you more control than palming the floor, although you will not be starting as high as you did on the floor. It is certainly easier to do it here and on the floor than on the rings.

This press can be done in several positions: a tuck (a lead up to the next two), a straddled pike, and a pike; and can be done from a support (all three positions), an L support (all three positions), or a straddled L support (usually just the straddled pike). Just as you may have done on the floor, you can do a frog stand to a press here, and can do half presses, lifting your toes to the level of the bars and returning to a support or seat as lead-up exercises.

To do a piked press from an L support, begin by pushing down on the bars and lifting your seat over your head while trying to pike deeply. Your elbows stay partly flexed during this phase of the movement. When your seat is overhead, slowly lift your legs out of your pike into a straight body position as you straighten your arms. Do this slowly and with an even rhythm. Keep your head in line with your trunk throughout the move, finishing with it in between your arms so that you can just see your hands out of the tops of your eyes.

Common problems are moving up too fast, being too weak to push and lift your seat overhead, opening from your pike before your seat is overhead, and bending your arms too deeply to allow you to straighten them out at the end of the press.

■

Spotting

Stand at your student's side (you can stand directly in front of your student if you stand on the bars or if you are teaching on parallettes), and help him through the move if necessary as though it were done on the floor. A variety of hand positions are used.

Upper-arm Support Swing (Figure 11.21)

You have to practice this swing just as you practice a support swing. Since many skills go through this position, you must build up your strength and the skin under your arms to be able to train the necessary skills effectively. The bars should not be so close that your armpits rest on the bars. If you have found a comfortable setting for support swing, it should also be comfortable for upper-arm swing. The bars should contact your underarms somewhere around the mid- to upper part of your upper arms. Your elbows should not be directly out from your shoulders, but rather somewhat forward of them. Your hands grasp the bars in front of your shoulders—the distance from your shoulders is dependent on the skill that you will do. Turn your hands so that your palms are partly on top of the bars and your thumbs are inside the bars.

As a starter, do this swing with your hands about one-half your arm's length from your shoulders. Keeping your body relatively straight, swing from your shoulders and lift your body to the height of the bars on both ends. You will find that you will hollow as you go up in front, and you will arch as you go up in back. Your shoulders will go up and down a bit as you swing in a fashion similar to the support swing. If you can swing above the bars, do so. If you are strong enough, try to stay at the extreme ends of your swing for a short time while holding on to the bars.

As you become more comfortable with the swing, you may introduce a slight beating action to the swing (with some gymnasts this happens naturally). To do this, on the way back, pull your hips through the bottom faster than your legs. If you are successful, you will find that your legs will snap your body into an arch and help speed you toward your upswing in the back. A similar action

Figure 11.21a, b, c, d, e, f, g, h, i, j

a. b. c. d. e.

f. g. h. i. j.

is done going forward. Push your hips through the bottom a bit ahead of your legs, and you will find that your legs will snap ahead of your hips once they have passed the bottom and help speed you toward your upswing. As you progress, you will find the timing of this beat differs according to the skill that you wish to perform.

Common problems are sagging in your shoulders too much, swinging with your elbows behind your shoulders, and piking or arching excessively on the upswing.

Stand by the side of the bars and be ready in case your student falls through due to upper body weakness.

■
Spotting

An exercise that will help you do rolls and finish a cast to upper arms (discussed later) is to swing up in front high enough to release your grasp, and balance there on your upper arms in a pike with your knees directly above your eyes (figure 11.22).

Figure 11.22

Forward Roll (Figure 11.23)

Learn this as a slow skill from a still position before introducing swing and speed to it. The slow roll may be performed from a support or a straddled seat on the bars. The swinging roll may be performed from a support or an upper-arm support. It may be finished in a straddled seat or an upper-arm support. The easiest way to do it is to start from a straddled seat and put your hands in front of your legs as you would to press to a shoulderstand. Begin the roll like a piked press—push on the bars and lift your seat over your head. Look at the mat below and keep your legs straddled. Continue to push your seat past your head, and when you feel your weight come off your hands, move them quickly to a position on top of the bars on the other side of your upper arms, and look for your knees. For good control, you must get your hands around before your body begins to descend. They will contact the bars just as you begin your descent. Keep your elbows pointing outward during the roll to keep from falling through the bars. As you complete the roll, push down on the bars with your hands and finish in a straddled seat. If this is easy, go from a support to an upper-arm support. The action is basically the same but it is a bit more demanding. As you feel more comfortable with this roll, swing into it with your body stretched rather than piked, but round your chest as you go over the top to help you regrasp early. It will be as if you swing through a hollowback press action (figure 11.19), and as you contact the bars you round (hollow) your chest and go through a shoulderstand into the roll.

Common problems are ducking your head, letting your elbows come in toward your body, which drops you between the bars, and reaching around late.

■

Spotting

Spot this from below the bars. If your student has trouble pushing into the skill, you can push on his abdomen or leg with your right hand to get him over while steadying his shoulders with your left hand. As he turns over, switch hands and support his shoulder blades and lower back with your hands. Be careful you do not get hit by a straddled leg.

Figure 11.23a, b, c, d, e

a.

b.

c.

d.

e.

Backward Roll (Figure 11.24)

As with the forward roll, I recommend learning this first slowly using strength, then learning to swing into it. This can be done from a straddled seat (this is not from a swing), a support, or an upper-arm support, and can finish in all three positions. It looks like a forward roll in reverse. To do one slowly from an upper-arm support to a support, pike and push your seat up and over your head while holding on to the bars. As your body goes overhead and you feel your weight coming off your hands, look back at the bars behind you, release your grasp and regrasp on top of the bars where you are looking, and continue to roll up into a support, straightening your arms. If you want to finish in an upper-arm support, do not regrasp, rather keep your hands to the outside of the bars and regrasp in front of your shoulders once you have turned over completely. As you become more adept at this skill, you will do it in a stretched position rather than a pike, and will be able to swing several rolls in a row without re-grasping the bars (this is tough on your upper arms so wear a long-sleeved shirt when you first try it!) or stop in a shoulderstand by regrasping the bars as you approach vertical, which is a lead up to a *Streuli* (discussed shortly).

Figure 11.24a, b, c, d, e, f
Bill's knees are a bit flexed here, and he reaches back too soon (figure c).

a.

b.

c.

d.

e.

f.

Common problems are looking back too soon, letting go too soon, not pushing your body over enough to take your hands off the bars, letting your elbows come in toward your body, which will drop you between the bars, and regrasping under rather than over the bars.

■

Spotting

Spot this from below the bars like the forward roll. As your student goes into the roll, support his lower back and shoulder blades with your hands. As he passes over the top, shift your hands to his shoulder and leg or abdomen. Be careful not to get hit by a straddled leg.

Figure 11.25a, b, c, d

a. b. c. d.

Figure 11.26a, b, c
A cast into a backward swing.

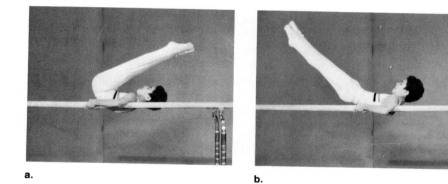

a. b. c.

Backward Uprise (Figure 11.25)

Since you have learned to swing in an upper-arm support position, you can now learn some useful skills that utilize this position. The backward (or back) uprise is a good starting point and is a way to get from an upper-arm support to a support. It is called a back uprise because you go up on the backswing. Later on you will learn to add other skills on to the end of this uprise to perform more difficult movements.

Begin with a strong swing to the rear and with your hands somewhat close to your shoulders. As your feet reach bar height, push down hard on the bars and rise up to a support. Do not slide your hands. The higher you can go, the better. To develop more swing power, you can cast into the swing (figure 11.26) from an inverted piked upper-arm position (often called a flex position). This is the position that you pass through going into a backward roll or finishing a forward roll. From this piked position, which you can get to by lifting your body

Figure 11.27
Another starting position for learning a back uprise—a forearm support.

up from a hang with your hands somewhat far from your shoulders, quickly extend your body out forward along the bars and pull your shoulders closer to your hands. This puts you in a swing that has the power to give you a high back uprise.

Common problems are swinging too slowly to get up, sliding your hands, dropping your hips during the cast before you extend your body, and not straightening your arms before you begin to descend after the uprise.

■

Spotting

Stand next to the bars and spot from below. As your student begins his ascent, reach under him and support his chest and legs if needed. See that he finishes his uprise with straight arms before he swings down, or else he may collapse and fall on or through the bars as he swings down out of it.

A student who has a lot of trouble going up can get a feel for the back uprise by swinging up high enough to hook his feet on the bars in the back and then doing a pushup (his feet help to support his weight). As an alternative, he can do the uprise from a forearm support as a drill (figure 11.27).

Forward Uprise (Figure 11.28)

The forward (or front) uprise is more difficult than the back uprise because the push down on the bars at the end of the skill is done behind you. This is a weaker push than pushing in front. I feel that not enough attention is given to this skill in training, since I often see it performed poorly.

Begin in an upper-arm support with your hands as far from your shoulders as you can comfortably manage. As you swing forward past the bottom, push down on the bars with your arms. At the same time, pull yourself forward past your hands and push up to a support. Keep your body fairly stretched. When done well, your body will be extended in a support swing position at the end of the uprise as if you just did a forward support swing. Your seat should be as

Figure 11.28a, b, c, d
Mike's elbows should be ahead of his shoulders and his hands further forward in his upper-arm hang for a front uprise, and eventually he will want to finish with his trunk horizontal (and not have a form break on the way up).

a. b. c. d.

Figure 11.29a, b, c
When he becomes stronger, Mike will push back more into his layaway.

a. b. c.

high as your shoulders to be considered a good performance (this takes considerable strength). If your seat gets that high, you can pike at the end of the uprise if you wish—kicking from a pike to a stretch can help generate more support swing once you have finished your front uprise.

To get more power into this skill, you can begin in a support and swing rearward to a layaway (figure 11.29), which brings you down to an upper-arm support. To perform a layaway, as your body swings up to the horizontal in back, push your shoulders back, bend your arms a bit, and push your upper arms down to the bars so that they contact the bars before your body passes

Figure 11.30a, b, c, d
One drill to help you learn a front uprise.

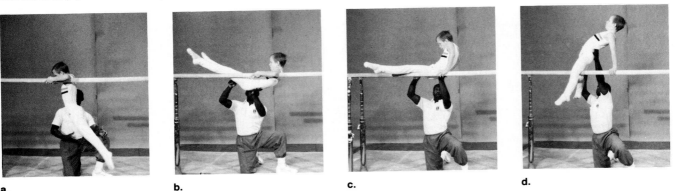

a. b. c. d.

below them. From this position, you proceed with the front uprise. Just remember that more power means a faster swing so you have to think and act more quickly. Eventually you will be able to do a layaway from a handstand, which requires much more strength. This should look as if you fell over from a handstand, and just before you pass the bars, you bend your arms a bit and push your upper arms to the bars. **NOTE**: Don't try this until you have experience doing layaways from progressively higher positions leading up to a handstand—if you are weak you could fall through the bars. To cut down on your swing into a handstand layaway, you can bend your arms early, but it should be performed with a late arm bend.

Common problems are piking excessively just past the bottom on the way up, not shoving down hard enough or soon enough, sliding your hands, not finishing your forward pull (which changes into a backward push as you pass your hands), and having your seat below your shoulders at the end of the uprise.

■

Spotting

Stand next to the bars and reach under the bars to support your student's seat and shoulders if needed.

For those who have trouble accomplishing this skill, here are several exercises to do: (1) Instead of keeping your legs together as you uprise, straddle them once your legs are past the bars, and go to a straddled seat as far in front of your hands as you can, finishing in an arch and pushing forward (figure 11.30); (2) do the uprise from a forearm support; (3) from a small forward swing, push up to a support from an upper-arm support (this is tough).

Streuli (Figure 11.31)

As your strength improves and your upper-arm swing becomes easier, you may try to do this skill, which is a swinging back roll that has so much power that it lifts off the bars up to a handstand. It is a hard beginning skill—if you hold a handstand at the end you will elevate the difficulty to B-level.

Figure 11.31a, b, c, d, e, f
Danny will open more aggressively in figures
c, d, and e as he becomes stronger.

a.   b.   c.   d.

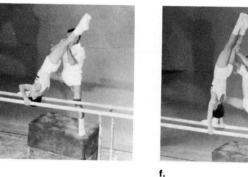

e.   f.

You should be able to do a swinging backward roll to a support consistently before trying a *Streuli* (pronounced: shtroy'-lih; in the USA we often [mis]pronounce it stray'-lee). The next step is to do a swinging back roll and reach back fast enough to stop in a shoulderstand. If you can do this, then roll to the shoulderstand, shift your weight to your hands so that your upper arms are no longer on the bars, and press up to a handstand. This requires more pressing strength than the *Streuli* will eventually require, but is a good exercise for both this move and your general strength.

To perform the *Streuli* well, it is necessary for you to shove downward on the bars with your upper arms as you swing up from the bottom. You will have a slight pike coming up, and when you are just past the bars you will open your body into an arch. A strong swing and opening coupled with the downward shove will lift you off the bars. Immediately reach back for the bars and push to a handstand, straightening your body as you get there. It is helpful to look for your feet to come above the bars before you vigorously open your chest—we often say "pop"—and push off the bars. As you pop, look back for the bars to see where to put your hands, although this is done partly by feel as well.

Common problems are swinging too far before popping, which causes you to overturn, not lifting enough to get to a handstand, not reaching aggressively for a handstand—stopping at a bent-armed handstand rather than pushing for a good handstand—and arching excessively at the end of the move.

Figure 11.32a, b, c
Hooking a foot is a common form break
when piking rapidly.

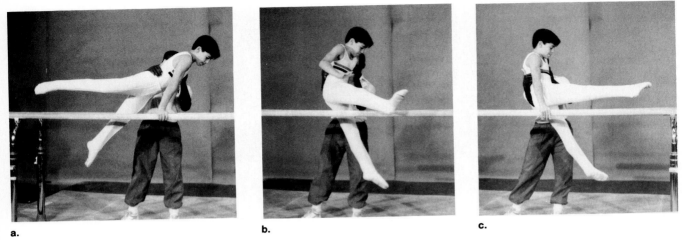

a. b. c.

■

Spotting

Spot this from above the bars and to the side. As your student initiates his pop, put your left hand under and your right hand over his legs and help him up to a handstand. This can be done with the fast-moving skill or the lead-up roll-to-a-press.

Forward Leg Cuts

Single-leg (Figure 11.32)

This is often the first release-regrasp skill to be learned on parallel bars. It begins with a small swing where your feet barely go above the bars on either end. Arch hard in your backswing and stay down in your shoulders. As your feet rise above the bars in the back, bring your right leg forward and outside of the bar quickly as you shift your weight to your left hand. This will allow you to cut your right leg over the bar, that is, to lift that hand and pass your leg over the right bar, bringing it to the front where it can rejoin your left leg as you regrasp the right bar. Do this with your left leg, too. Also do one after another in sequence.

Common problems are not swinging high enough in the back to clear the bar, piking your backswing, and not leaning enough to allow your leg to complete its cut over the bar.

■

Spotting

Hold your student's left arm with your left hand and put your right hand on his lower back. You can aid him in making the weight shift if needed, and hold him up in case he misses the regrasp.

Chapter 11

Figure 11.33a, b, c, d, e
Danny has several form problems here, and
he scrapes the bar as he brings his legs
inside the bars because he does not shift
his weight enough to the left.

a. b. c.

d. e.

Double-leg (Figure 11.33)

This is the same skill as described above but with both legs doing the cut. Because you will have your legs together, you will have to shift more to the side to counterbalance during the cut.

Common problems and spotting are the same.

Straddled Cut (Figure 11.34)

If you have learned the single bar cuts, you have an idea of how to do a straddled cut, which requires you to release the bars with both hands simultaneously and regrasp them. Before you try it, put stretch pants on so that if your legs scrape along the bars you will not suffer abrasions. Then go through the following lead-up exercises to get the feel of the move. Do a small swing rearward in a support with your shoulders shrugged, arch to lift your feet just above the bars, then

Figure 11.34a, b, c, d, e, f
Aside from a slight form break, this straddled cut to L is well done.

a.

b.

c.

d.

e.

f.

Figure 11.35a, b, c, d
A lead up to the straddled cut.

a.

b.

c.

d.

straddle your legs and pull them forward over the bars in a straddled pike position. When they reach your arms, sit briefly on the bars, let go and regrasp behind your legs, and finish by bringing your legs together in front. Next, stand at the end of the bars facing in with your hands on the bars and your teacher holding your waist (figure 11.35). As you jump up and straddle, your teacher will lift you to give you a little more time to cut both legs forward and regrasp. Try to catch this in an L support.

These two lead ups prepare you for the straddled cut in the middle. To do it, go through the same steps that you did first but as quickly as you can. As you snap your legs forward, push down hard on the bars to get airborne and to help your legs snap forward. Bring your legs together as they pass over the bars, and reach down for the bars. Try to catch in an L support—you must catch with your hands a bit in front of your hips to do this. As variations, you can do a support swing or a dip swing out of the cut.

Common problems are snapping your legs too slowly, not pushing down hard, not putting your legs together at the end of your cut, and swinging too high before starting your cut, which makes you cut down rather than across (that technique can be used later when you are strong enough to handle it, if you choose to do that style of cut).

Due to the straddling of your student's legs, you cannot hand spot this move in the middle of the bars (you can use an overhead belt). However, you can spot the jump to straddle cut on the end of the bars. As I described above, stand behind your student and provide lift and support by grasping his waist. Be careful at the end of this move after his recatch, because if he has weak hip flexors he will allow his legs to drop, and they may strike you. If you pad the bars, it will cut down on leg scrapes.

■

Spotting

Underbar Swing

Inverted Pike (Figure 11.36)

This is the third area of swing that you must learn. It is done most often in an inverted pike, although glide swings are upright for the first half, and some relatively newer skills are exploring a straight-body-flexed-knee hang swing (both are described next). You have a particular time period to your underbar swing—that is, it takes a certain time for you to swing from one end to the other. You must get used to this time so that you can learn when to make shape changes in your body to enhance the swing.

Hang upside down in a tight pike with an inside grip. Your knees should be directly over your eyes, and your back should be rounded so that you hang as low as possible. **NOTE:** Keep your thumbs inside of the bars along with your palms—if you put your thumbs outside of the bars, you risk injuring them on the forward swing. Begin with a small swing and feel when you reach each end of the swing. To build up your swing, just before you reach the end, open your pike a bit, and then close it as you hit the end. If you do this at the correct time, you will find that the size of your swing will increase. Doing it at the wrong time stops your swing quickly, so this is a self-instructive exercise. If you have trouble feeling both ends, open and close at one end only. The back end (your head leads) is probably the easiest to feel. Try not to let your shoulder angle

Figure 11.36a, b, c
You can picture this forward underbar swing in reverse (c-b-a) as well.

a.

b.

c.

change during this swing drill, as that will let your body tip one way or the other and is not correct. If you have a good feel for this swing, you may find that you go above the bars on either end. This is good, as many skills are now ready to be learned. If your hands are sore from training and you wish to practice this swing, you can do so with an outside grip, which puts less stress on your palms and may be easier to hold on with. This grip is not as useful as the inside grip, since any move that drops from a support to an underbar position uses an inside grip, and an outside grip is used only for some mounts (with only one exception that I know of to date, which is a D-level skill).

As a variation, you can do this swing in an open pike. Another way to try it is to stand between the bars with the bars about shoulder height. With an inside grip and thumbs inside, your arms extended, and pushing on the bars so that your trunk is as far from your hands as possible, jump up a little and bring your legs up quickly into a pike. As you drop between the bars, hold on tight and get into that balanced pike position that you swing in (see figure 11.42, which starts this way). You should be able to swing quite high on the front end.

Common problems are not maintaining a balanced position during the swing, and being off-time in the opening-closing action.

■

Spotting

Watch from below in case your student flips over while swinging, and give cues on the timing if needed. Check his hands, and ask him if they are sore or tired, and suggest that he stop if this is the case.

Long Hang (Figure 11.37)
There are two variations of a hang swing. First is one that became important in the 1980s as horizontal-bar-type skills were adapted to parallel bars. If you are a small person who cannot touch the floor with his feet when hanging below the bars, this swing resembles a long swing on the horizontal bar, but with your hands on the inside of the bars. If you can touch, but are not so big that your

Figure 11.37a, b, c

a.

b.

c.

knees hit the mat when you flex them at least 90°, then you do this swing with flexed knees, straightening them when you lift enough to allow this to happen. Your task is to swing back and forth so that you are at least bar high on each end of the swing. Just as you do on the horizontal bar, keep your body as long as you can for most of the swing, but as you pass the bottom going forward, lift your legs to generate more swing, and stretch out again as you reach the top. Practice two techniques: looking at your hands and looking at a point in front of but above you during your swing, as these two techniques will be useful down the road.

Glide Swing (Figure 11.38)

A second variation of a hang swing is a glide swing. You can first learn this from a stand, grasping the bars in front of you. Start in a piked stand with your hands, shoulders, and hips in line. Jump up and lift your toes so that they are just above the mat as you begin to swing forward. Look at your toes and keep them only a few inches off the mat throughout your swing. Keep your shoulder angle open. As you move forward, gradually open your pike so that at the end of your forward swing you are extended from your hands to your toes. As you swing back, pike gradually to keep your feet off the mat and return to a stand where you started.

The common problem with both of these swings is not being strong enough to put your body in the necessary shape. These swings will also cause wear on your hands, so be aware that you will get sore hands if you overdo your training. As your palm and finger callouses build up and toughen you will be able to train longer.

Watch the extreme ends of high swings to be sure your student does not lose his grip.

■

Spotting

Figure 11.38a, b, c, d
Note the slight form breaks.

a.   b.   c.   d.

Figure 11.39a, b, c, d

a.   b.   c.   d.

Drops

To get into an inverted underbar piked hang from a support there are several ways called drops. They generally fall into two categories: early and late drops. Each has its uses, as you can develop more power with the early drop, but the late drop gives you more time to set up for a following skill and can be quite spectacular. The difference is that when you swing from back to front, an early drop occurs before your hips pass your hands, and the late drop occurs after your hips have passed your hands. Some performers do a middle-of-the-road drop, kind of in between the two, but I will not cover that here except to mention it.

To do an early drop (figure 11.39), I suggest trying it first without a swing. Hold yourself in a support and push down and back a bit to get into a hollow position and to begin to drop. Look at the space between your hands and lift your shins to that space as you begin to drop, pulling into a tight pike. As you

Figure 11.40a, b, c, d

a.　　　　　　　　　　b.　　　　　　　　　　c.　　　　　　　　　　d.

pass below the bars you will be turning over so that you pass the bottom in the balance position that you learned doing underbar swings. You must be in a tight pike before you pass the bottom, for if you let your legs collapse into your upper body at the bottom, this will slow down your swing. Later on you will learn to control the amount of pike that you get into. If you feel comfortable with the drop from a still position, try it from a small support swing, beginning the push and drop when you stop at the back end of your small swing.

Common problems are turning over too much or too little to be balanced at the bottom, allowing your hips to come close to your hands during the drop, which reduces power, and letting your legs collapse into your upper body at the bottom rather than compressing before you pass the bottom.

To do a late drop (figure 11.40), swing forward, and when you pass your hands and begin to swing up, lean back and start to pike as you begin to drop. Push away from your hands (holding on tight) and get completely compressed in a deep pike before you pass the bottom, otherwise you will jerk and lose swing as your legs collapse into your upper body. As you become stronger, also learn to not compress completely on the way down and as you pass through the bottom (this is useful for an underbar cast to upper arms—which is covered later—in an open-piked position), and to swing up to a high angle as you lean back before dropping. Another style allows you to pike just as you pass your hands before dropping (shown), but I prefer a more open start to the drop on aesthetic grounds. (Picture a forward support swing that goes near or above horizontal as it is pushed back into a late drop. It is more spectacular.)

Common problems are not leaning back enough, which causes a small hitch in your swing (it looks like your body rocks forward a bit before dropping), having your hips close to your hands on the way down, and allowing your legs to collapse into your upper body at the bottom.

Spot from below to make sure that your student does not turn over too much and come off the bars. Also watch him through the bottom in case he jerks at the bottom due to an improper piking action and comes flying off.

■

Spotting

a.   b.   c.

d.   e.

Kips

Kip from Upper-arm Support (Figure 11.41)

This kip is also called a top kip. Begin in an upper-arm support and bring your legs up to an inverted pike position (also called a flex position). Put your hands somewhat far from your shoulders. Rapidly extend your hips so that your legs shoot out at about 45° above horizontal and push down on the bars. You should arrive at a straight-arm support and be able to swing backward, possibly to a handstand. As a variation, it is possible to begin in a support, lift your legs, drop back (called a layback) to an upper-arm support, and then do the kip back up to a support.

Common problems are opening too low, too much, or too slowly, and not pushing down hard enough to rise.

Spot from below, providing lift if needed. Watch to see that your student does not collapse forward in case of faulty execution. If he does a layback, watch that he does not overturn and panic, and that he puts his arms out to the sides to keep from falling between the bars.

Underbar Kip From a Stand (Figure 11.42) or Drop (Figure 11.43)

This is the start of a whole series of kipping movements that take you from underbar to support. You can do them on any section of the bars. From a stand, an underbar kip begins as you did when you jumped to an inverted piked underbar swing. After swinging forward (when your seat leads), as you approach the end of your backswing, open your body a bit (just like the swinging exercise) and push down on the bars with straight arms, keeping your legs and seat as high as you can. Ideally you should finish with your seat as high as your shoulders (just like a front uprise), but at first you may only get to an L support position. If you can go higher, open from the pike you had on the rise into a stretched swing and swing to a handstand. Some advanced gymnasts finish this move passing through what we in the USA call a Manna position (named after gymnast Bob Manna), which is a V support turned over backward 90° so that your seat is higher than your shoulders with your legs horizontal and pointing backward (this is quite difficult).

Once you know how to drop under the bars, and have done a kip from a swing, you can combine these two and do a kip from a drop. It does not matter what kind of drop you use, just as long as you can swing easily forward and backward from it. Simply drop below the bars, let your body swing forward and backward, and push down on the bars as you rise on the backswing to complete the kip as described in the previous paragraph.

Common problems are not having enough swing to get over the bars easily, not pushing down hard enough, bending your arms on the way up (you will do this only once and learn the hard way when your elbows hit the bars), and letting your seat drop on the way up.

Spot from below, lifting your student's seat and shoulders. You can emphasize a good finish position by holding him in one. Watch to see that he passes the bottom well in the first half, as that is where most falls occur.

Underbar Kip From a Glide (Figure 11.44)

The glide swing that you learned earlier is quite often used to begin a kipping action. This beginning is a little tougher to do a kip from as you need some strength to lift your legs up from the glide into the piked position of an underswing. Begin with a glide swing, and when you reach the front end of your swing, rapidly flex your hips to get into a pike for the backswing. Once there, the rest of the kip is the same as the other kips done on the upswing.

Figure 11.42a, b, c, d, e, f, g, h, i

a.

b.

c.

d.

e.

f.

g.

h.

i.

Chapter 11

Figure 11.43a, b, c, d, e, f, g, h

a. b. c. d.

e. f. g. h.

If this is easy for you, try three other ways of getting into a glide, all of which give you more power. The first is to jump into it—simply begin from a stand or a run outside of the bars and jump up before grasping the bars and proceeding to swing. The other two methods begin above the bars, and are drops into a glide swing. One starts in an upper-arm position (figure 11.45). As you swing back, straighten your arms, disengaging from the bars (this means bringing your elbows inside of the bars while retaining your grasp, which allows you to drop into an underbar swing), and proceed into a glide, piking when necessary so that you do not hit the mat as you swing forward. The other begins in a support (figure 11.46), and is similar in that you swing back and push back to fall below the bars. Be sure to pike when you get close to the mat or you will come to a startling halt if the bars are too low or you are too long.

The common problem with all glides is not being strong enough to lift your legs into a pike at the end of the front swing or keep your feet from hitting the ground in midswing.

Figure 11.44a, b, c, d, e
Mike could hold his legs up more at the end of this glide kip.

a.

b.

c.

d.

e.

Figure 11.45a, b, c
Disengaging from an upper-arm support to an underbar swing.

a.

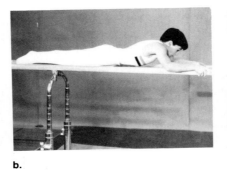

b.

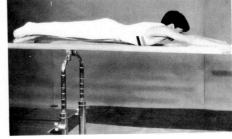

c.

Chapter 11

Figure 11.46a, b

Picture this drop into an underbar swing
coming from a backward support swing,
such as in figure 11.47a, b, and c.

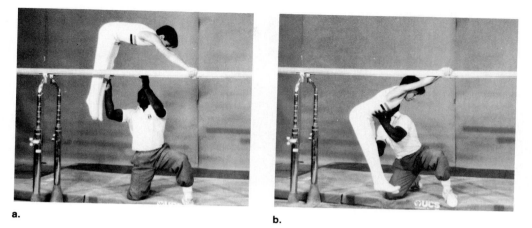

a.   b.

The same as with other kips on the upswing, and you can aid your student in piking
at the right time by reaching under his legs with your left hand during his glide and
lifting them into a pike if he cannot do it alone.

■

Spotting

Baby Giant Swings

Just as you learned to drop from above the bars into a glide on the previous
page, you can begin working toward a giant swing (a horizontal bar skill that
has been adapted to parallel bars) by combining the drop with an underbar long
hang swing (figure 11.47) and then with a few skills at the front end of the
swing. Begin these skills in either an upper-arm support or a support, as described for a drop to a glide. The difference here is that you proceed into a long
hang (your height will determine if you have to flex your knees to avoid hitting
the mat). These moves are called "baby" because they start with a low swing.
Eventually you will drop from a high swing or a handstand, but that is beyond
the scope of this book.

To Upper Arms Without Turning Over (Figure 11.48)

As you approach the front end of your swing you will rise above the bars. Pull
back on the bars, keeping your head forward, and land in a stretched upper-
arm support with your body extended forward. If you are still rotating as you
land, you can finish in an inverted pike position. In both cases, your hands release their grasp and you bring your arms forward, placing your upper arms on
the bars in front of your shoulders first. Push down with them to keep your body
up, and then regrasp in front of your upper-arm contact position.

Figure 11.47a, b, c, d
Dropping into a long hang swing from a
support swing.

a.

b.

c.

d.

Turning Over to Upper Arms or Support (Figure 11.49)

Here you begin heading toward a handstand, which is an advanced skill. As you pass the bottom, lift your legs so that you shorten your body (which increases your rotation) and then, when your legs are somewhat vertical, open your body and pull back on the bars to lift your shoulders above the bars. Hold on to the bars as long as you can, and look at your hands throughout. At this point, where you are turning over, are above the bars, and feel that your hands are coming off the bars, regrasp and finish in a shoulderstand or a support, or land on your upper arms and finish the end of a backward upper-arm roll. As you become familiar with this skill and gain strength, you will be able to catch in a high support heading toward a handstand.

Chapter 11

Figure 11.48a, b, c, d, e, f

a.   b.   c.

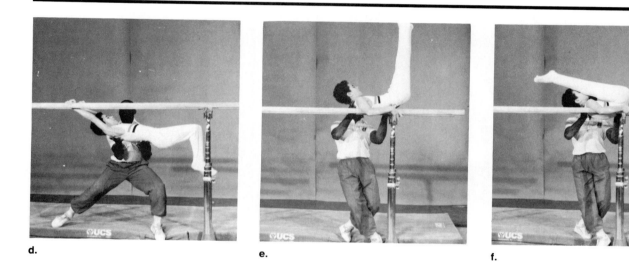

d.   e.   f.

Baby Flyaway (Figure 11.50)

Since you are doing a long hang swing, you should be able to relate it to the same swing done on the horizontal bar. A baby flyaway is a skill done on the end of a long hang swing, and parallel bar flyaways are coming into widespread use. You will learn this skill with your hands on the end of the bars, facing out. As you swing forward toward the bottom, look for a spot above the bars and in the distance. As you swing upward, when your knees (if you have bent legs) or feet (if you have straight legs) pass the spot you are looking at, release your grasp and somersault to a stand. Do not let your shoulder angle close (do not develop a shoulder pike) or you will come close to the bars. Do the flyaway in a tuck or pike, and later try a layout (see chapter 12 for flyaways from the horizontal bar).

Figure 11.49a, b, c, d, e, f, g

a.   b.   c.

d.   e.   f.   g.

Common problems with all of these skills are hitting the mat with your feet (while doing a flexed-knees swing) due to weak knee flexor muscles, letting go too soon, and not pulling back enough.

■

Spotting

The teacher spots from below, providing lift if needed. Be aware of the bottom of your student's swing—if it is not smooth, just past the bottom is where he will most likely fly off.

Figure 11.50a, b, c, d, e, f
Aside from a small form break, this is well done.

a.

b.

c.

d.

e.

f.

Cast to Upper Arms (Figure 11.51)

This skill utilizes a piked underbar swing and has its action occur on the front end, which is opposite to the kips. It can be done from a stand or a drop or just a large underbar swing. If you have practiced all of these, and have practiced the upper-arm support swing, especially the front end upper-arm inverted-pike support position, you will have all of the prerequisites that you need to do a cast to upper arms. From one of the starts just mentioned, as you swing forward, keep your knees over your eyes and pull back a bit on the bars to make your body rise above the bars. As this happens, release your grasp (it will be coming off anyhow), and bring your arms forward and down to the bars so that your upper arms contact the bars in front of your shoulders in that balance position that you have learned. Keep your back rounded, push down with your upper

Figure 11.51a, b, c, d, e, f

a. b. c.

d. e. f.

arms, and reach for the bars with your hands. You can then proceed into any upper-arm skill that begins from this position. As you get better at this cast, try to do it in an open pike, which is more the style these days. Dropping in an open pike will make your underbar swing go faster, and will allow you to wind up above the bars in a nice open position (figure d is an open pike—if the underbar swing and finish were in that position, it would be more impressive to me).

Common problems are not turning over enough to land upside down, opening rapidly (kicking open) from your pike while going up, putting your upper arms directly to the sides of your shoulders, which lets your seat drop right away, and pulling too hard on the way up, which results in a drop to the bars at the end of the skill, rather than a smooth transition from your swing to an upper-arm support. If you are one of the few who overturns backward, you finish in a backward roll, and then you are doing a lead up to the next skill, a "peach basket."

Place your hands on your student's lower and upper back, providing lift and rotation if needed. Usually I have to help my students rotate backward, as they most often do not have the feeling for this at first.

Peach Basket

This move got its USA name in the early part of this century. The shape of the swing and the position of the body below the bars reminded someone of a basket that peaches often came in, and the name stuck. (Inverted piked swings are sometimes called basket swings, probably since a peach basket passes through such a swing.) The peach basket is also referred to as an underbar salto or a *Felge* (pronounced: fell'-geh). The German word "*Felge*" indicates a circling action. This skill looks something like a cast that turns over and winds up in a support or upper-arm support, or drops into an underbar swing. There are several approaches to learning this move, and it can be learned from a stand or a drop, just as the cast was. This skill turns over more than the cast, and you have to start this turn-over early, on the way down from a drop or jump.

The first method of teaching the skill proceeds directly from a cast. As you finish your cast, if you have turned over more before you hit the bottom of the swing, you will land on the bars in such a way that you will do the end of a backward roll to a support. If you can turn over this much, then open your body from the bottom so that when you land on the bars you are in a stretched position rather than a pike. This is another difference between the cast and the peach basket: A peach opens hard from the bottom, while a cast to upper arms does not (a cast to support, an advanced skill, does). Look at figures 11.51a, b, c, and d, and tack figures 11.49f and g on to them. This is the action to which I refer. It is important to hold on to the bars as long as you can on the way up. If you pike completely on the way down, you will be in a position to open powerfully and create lift. It will help to think of opening on the way down before you pass the bottom, so that you actually do open on the way up just past the bottom.

Try to land in a hand support rather than on your upper arms as you become familiar with the peach (figure 11.52). Ideally your hands will regrasp in the same places as they were as you swung into the move.

The second method involves working at the peach from another angle for a different purpose—to teach a straight-arm regrasp (figure 11.53). It is being used more frequently now because we are encouraging straight-arm regrasps. To do this method you turn over past a horizontal finish position at first as this allows your chest to rise and makes a straight-arm regrasp more possible. As a starter, begin it with the bars a bit below shoulder height and with an inside grip. Jump up a bit and bring your legs into your body. As you drop, turn over and open your body rapidly from a pike to a stretched position past the bottom with your legs pointing down. Pull down on the bars and hold on as long as you can. As you rise up above the bars and feel your hands come off the bars, turn them around and regrasp, trying not to bend your arms. As you become familiar with this action, you will open from your pike earlier, so that your legs are pointing back rather than down (and then farther up), and you will find yourself regrasping at a higher and higher angle, heading toward horizontal and above.

Common problems are not turning over enough, letting go too soon, not opening soon enough, not pulling down hard, and not opening completely.

Figure 11.52a, b, c
Finishing the peach in a bent-armed support
ready for a layaway.

a.   b.   c.

Figure 11.53a, b, c, d, e, f, g

a.   b.   c.   d.

e.   f.   g.

Figure 11.54a, b, c, d, e
A first step to learning a front stütz.

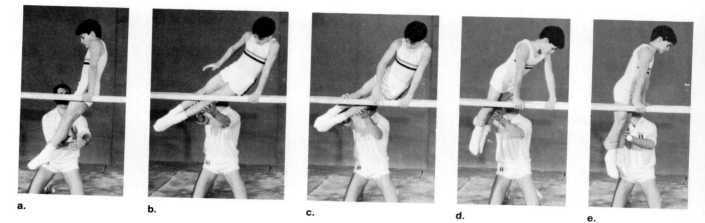

a.   b.   c.   d.   e.

Spot from below. For the first method, spot the first half as you would a cast, then shift your hands so that they are under your student's chest and legs to help achieve support. The second method is spotted mainly at the end of the movement, reaching under him to support his legs and chest if needed. You can supply lift as well by pushing up on his left shoulder or chest with your left hand once he passes the bottom. If you are sure he will make it over the bars, you may also assist him from above, grasping his legs as he opens and lifting him so he learns what direction to open toward.

■

Spotting

Stützkehre

Forward (Figure 11.55)

If you have learned the *Stütz* dismount, you have an idea of what the *Stützkehre* forward feels like. This means support turn and is pronounced: shtitz'-keh-reh. In the USA we often simply say front *Stütz*. Also, if you have turned around while in a support (figure 11.6), you have started toward this move. You should have an idea which way you like to turn when doing various skills, and should attempt to learn all turning skills in the same direction so that there will be a transfer of awareness between the various skills. **NOTE**: Learning this on stacks of mats or using bar pads often reduces any fear of hitting the bar or missing a regrasp.

Once you have done the stationary support turn, swing a bit and perform the turn on your front swing (figure 11.54). For a left turn, as you turn, maintain support on your left arm for a long time and look down your arm. Put your right hand close to your left. As you swing higher and higher, turn once you are past the bottom, and keep support on your left arm as long as you can. You will be swinging up sideways for a bit. The more power you have in your swing, the more you will lift off the bars during the release-regrasp phase, and you will find that although you release your hands one at a time, you will regrasp with both at the same time. Your hands should land in the same position along the bars that they started, but of course they have switched bars. Once you can do

Figure 11.55a, b, c, d, e, f

a.   b.   c.

d.   e.   f.

Figure 11.56a, b, c, d
An alternative spot—useful with a small
gymnast who is easy to manipulate.

a.   b.   c.   d.

this to a support, as a variation you can push back into a layaway after you regrasp. Eventually you can do this skill to a steep angle or to a handstand. Both are advanced skills.

Common problems are not turning enough, not turning soon enough, throwing your head back rather than looking down your left arm, not being on your left arm long enough, bending your left arm, arching, pushing forward, and leaning back too much. If you find that you hit the left bar, think of lifting your legs over the right bar.

■

Spotting

Spot this from above so that your student turns toward you—if he turns to his left (on his left arm), stand to his left. This way he will roll on to your lower arm. Place yourself about where his knees are on his front swing so that you will not be hit by an errant arm. As he swings up in front, reach under his legs with your right arm and over his legs with your left arm. This way you will have good control of him as he turns and releases. Help him to turn if necessary, and if he does the skill well just follow rather than lift. As he finishes his turn, if he is in a good support, let him swing down freely. As he goes above horizontal, you will find that you will switch your arms to be able to spot a higher body angle better, that is, you will reach under with your left arm and over with your right arm. You can walk a student through a *Stütz* motion on low bars if you can easily hold him up. With a smaller student you can spot slightly differently, starting with your right hand on his left shoulder and your left arm reaching under his legs (figure 11.56). In this way you have more control of his body but are nearer to his reaching right arm, so be careful—do not get hit. Also avoid getting your right arm caught across his neck as he turns (this is likely to happen if you are too close to his shoulder or if he reaches under your right arm with his right arm to regrasp).

Backward (Figure 11.57)

Although the backward (or back) *Stütz* is a B-value skill, I introduce it here in a low version, as you would do it to learn it (later you will do it with your feet above the bars). Like a front *Stütz*, it may be learned on stacks of mats or using bar pads to reduce fear of hitting a bar or missing a regrasp.

For a left turn, swing to the rear, lift into a slight arch, and turn as you pass the bottom. Look down at the left bar and reach for it with your right hand as you push your body back a bit. Put this hand in front of and next to your left hand. As you take your left hand off the bar, continue pushing your body back with your right hand and reach around for the open bar with your left hand. As you reach back, look to the left and see your stretched body finish its turn as you regrasp with your left hand. This move does not have a flight phase—you always have a hand on the bars. If you finish well, you will be able to swing easily out of your back *Stütz*. It will help you to think of driving your feet into the wall behind you as you swing into the move and turn. Similar to the front *Stütz*, this finishes in just about the same position on the bars as you start (you move forward about a hand's width) but with your hands switched.

Common problems are traveling forward due to insufficient backward push at the start, not turning early enough, not turning enough, reaching around late or not far enough with your left hand, and piking.

Figure 11.57a, b, c, d, e, f, g
Jim should push back and have his hands close together during his hand change.

a. b. c.

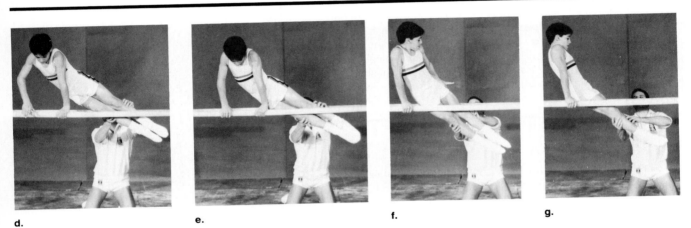

d. e. f. g.

■

Spotting

Since this is done low, it is easiest to spot from below the bars. Reach up and support your student's legs and/or hips as he does the turn. You can spot the low back *stütz* from either side, although I prefer to be on the same side as if I were spotting above the bars—I feel I can hold my student up better. When he gets better and is working on the B-value skill, spot from either below or above the bars. I prefer to spot from above the bars as I have more control that way. The spot from above the bars is similar to that for a front *Stütz*. Stand by where his knees will be on his backswing. For a left turn, stand on his right side so that he can roll onto your lower (right) arm. As he starts his turn, reach under his legs with your right arm, using your left hand to help turn him if he does not do it well. If he does not push back into his turn (and so will finish leaning back when he regrasps with his left hand), you can pull him a bit forward into a good regrasp position as he turns.

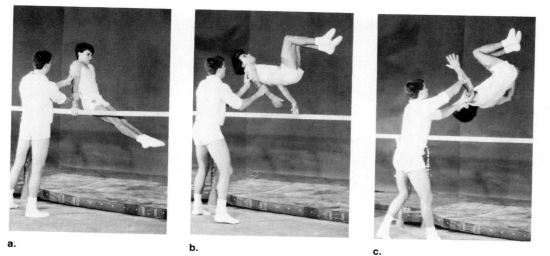

a.

b.

c.

d.

e.

f.

Somersault Dismounts

Somersault (or salto) dismounts are usually done to the side of the bars, and the sideways push is the same as you learned for the vaulting dismounts. Of course, since you will now be adding a somersault, the movement is much more complicated. Having experience with tumbling skills that turn over, including saltos, and/or having done saltos from other apparatus (it is usually a bit easier from rings or horizontal bar) is recommended. If you have access to an overhead belt system, training with that safety device can enhance learning.

Back-off (Figures 11.58, 11.59 and 11.60)

The backward somersault dismount, or back-off, requires a strong swing. It can be done in a tuck, pike, or layout. I will describe how to do a layout. To go right (shown in the figures), as you swing up in the front, lift your toes and begin to

Figure 11.59a, b, c, d, e
A piked back-off.

a. b. c. d. e.

Figure 11.60a, b, c, d, e
A back-off in layout position.

a. b. c. d. e.

push your body to the right side. As your feet get above bar height, open into an arch, continuing to push your body to the side over the bar. You can watch it move to the side. Push off the bars and look back for the floor. If you have swung through with enough power, you will turn over and land next to the bars after completing a layout somersault in line with where your hands were. Do not regrasp the bar to help you land; rather, learn to land free of the bar. Since the tuck and pike are easier to rotate, you may find learning them easier, although I prefer teaching a pike before a tuck to promote the toe lift, and I teach it first because it is quite a bit easier than a layout. A layout is the hardest to rotate, since your body is much longer than in a tuck or pike, but once you learn it, doing layouts is the best drill for increasing back-off power, which will help you later on with harder dismounts. You can always tuck or pike if you can do a layout, but the reverse is not true.

Common problems are not swinging hard enough to complete the somersault, leaning back too much, pushing forward, which makes you travel forward, and bending your arms going into the dismount.

This is usually done on low bars first. Hold your student's right arm with your left hand on his upper arm and your right hand on his forearm. (An alternative is to grasp his shirt rather than his upper arm.) This way you will be able to control him throughout the skill and can pull him off or support him if necessary. As he turns past vertical, release your grasp and reach under him or regrasp his arm for the landing. **NOTE**: If you use an overhead spotting rig, be sure that the ropes are in front of his arms and are set up to pull him to the side.

■

Spotting

Front-off (Figures 11.61 and 11.62)

Like the back-off, the front-off requires a strong swing. It can be done in a tuck, pike, or layout. I will describe how to do a piked front-off (to the right), which I prefer teaching since a layout is much harder to rotate, and you can always tuck if you can pike. As you swing backward past the bottom, drive your heels upward, causing you to arch, and begin shifting over the right bar. When your heels are as high as your shoulders, push into a pike, continuing to lift your seat, and push sideways to clear the right bar. You should be looking at that bar and watching it pass below you. You can push up through a position where (as seen from the side) you are in a piked handstand, that is, where your arms and trunk are in line while your legs are angled down (figure 11.63). If you swing to and through this position quickly, by opening your grip, your hands will come off the bars and you will rotate around to your feet. Since front saltos have a blind landing, to help you orient yourself, look for a point on the wall in front of you as you are finishing your somersault. Land without regrasping the bar, and land in line with where your hands were. If you rotate well enough you can open from your pike for a nice finishing effect, ideally at or before horizontal.

If you have mats that you can pile up to the height of the bars, you can get used to the sideways pushing action when swinging up toward a handstand by hopping from the bars to a handstand on the mats next to where your hands were. If you follow this with a forward roll, you will get used to the dismount action. The next step is to do the hop sideways and just before your hands touch the mat, duck under and land on your back. This is most of the dismount. All that is left to learn is how to land it. (This method cannot be used going backward, as it would be dangerous. You can see the mat and reach for it going forward, but not going backward.)

Common problems are leaning too far forward or pushing backward, not pushing down enough, ducking your head before completing your push, and swinging too slowly into the somersault to rotate to your feet.

Spot this from the side, preferably on low bars first, in a manner similar to the spot for a back-off. When spotting from the right, your right hand grasps your student's right upper arm, while your left hand grasps his forearm. (As an alternative, hold his shirt rather than his upper arm.) With this spot, you can pull him sideways or provide support if needed. If he turns over easily, reach under his back to provide landing support. **NOTE**: If you use an overhead spotting rig, be sure the ropes are behind his arms and are set to pull him to the side.

■

Spotting

Figure 11.61a, b, c, d, e, f
A tucked front-off.

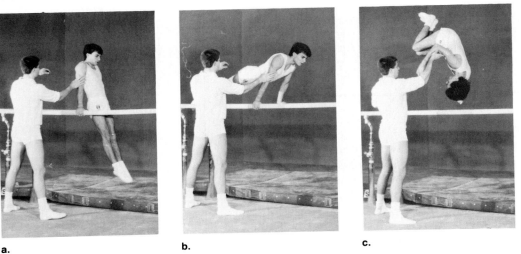

a.   b.   c.

d.   e.   f.

Sequences to Practice (Hold positions should last three seconds.)

1. Starting at one end facing in, straddled walk forward to the other end, put your legs together, swing in a support 3 times each way, stop and do one-half turn, hop to the other end, swing each way 3 times, straddled walk backward to other end, support swing backward, rear vault dismount on front swing

2. Underbar swing forward and backward 3 times, kip to support on last swing backward, support swing backward and forward 3 times, on next swing backward, layaway to upper-arm swing forward and backward 3 times, back uprise on last swing backward, swing forward, swing back to front vault dismount

Figure 11.62a, b, c, d, e, f
A piked front-off—Stephan should push
longer to go up better, as in figure 11.63.

a.   b.   c.

d.   e.   f.

3. Glide kip to L support (hold), piked press to shoulderstand (hold), release grasp and fall with your front leading into a stretched backward roll, swing up to a piked inverted support, top kip directly to a forward roll, back uprise, swing forward to a *Stütz* dismount

4. Front uprise, swing handstand (hold), lower to dip swing forward, swing rearward to a layaway, back roll to a shoulderstand (hold), lower with your front leading to a support swing forward, dip swing rearward, support swing forward and backward to *Wende* dismount

5. On the end facing in, glide kip to support, swing back to a layaway to an underbar swing, baby giant to upper arms without turning over, back uprise, lower to straddled L support (hold), bent armed straddled press to a handstand (hold)

Figure 11.63
A better release point than shown in figure
11.62b.

6. Front uprise, straddled cut to L (hold), bent-armed piked press to handstand (hold), front pirouette (hold), swing down and late drop to cast to upper arms, swing back and disengage to a baby giant that turns over to an upper-arm support, front uprise, swing backward and *Wende* dismount

7. Early drop to cast to upper arms, back uprise to support, *Stütz* forward, push back to layaway, front uprise, swing handstand and front pirouette (hold), piked back-off

8. Peach basket to support, late drop to cast to upper arms, back uprise to L (hold), piked bent-armed press to handstand (hold), *Stütz* to layaway, front uprise, double-leg cut over one bar, swing to handstand

9. Peach basket to layaway, *Streuli,* layaway to front uprise, straddled cut forward, swing rearward and up to handstand, front pirouette (hold), layout back-off

10. From a handstand, *Stütz* to support, early drop to peach basket to support, late drop to cast to upper arms, back uprise to straddled L (hold), bent-armed straddled press (hold), *Stütz* layaway, front uprise, piked front-off

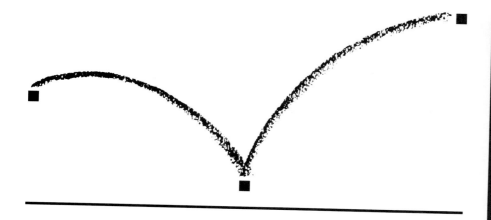

The beginning skills that you learn for both horizontal bar (often called high bar) and uneven parallel bars (often called uneven bars or just unevens) can be practiced, for the most part, on a single bar that is either a low horizontal bar, which is a spring steel bar just over an inch in diameter, or the low bar of the uneven parallel bars, which is more like the bar used for parallel bars (you can use one bar of a set of parallel bars as well; however, the bars for uneven parallel bars are being made more round now than those used for men's parallel bars, as women perform more and more horizontal-bar-type swinging skills on them, and a rounder bar is better for these moves). Once you begin long-hang-swing-skill training, you will need to raise the bar so that your feet do not drag on the mat. For skills requiring two bars, girls will have to adjust the bars so that they are fitted to their body proportions. Uneven bars are adjustable in width and somewhat in height. (In fact, the uneven bars have been modified several times in the past decade, getting wider each time to accommodate the larger swings that were being performed. This changed the nature of the routines considerably.) For beginners, both events should have variable heights to accommodate the various sizes of students. As you become more proficient, you will learn to train on equipment set at a prescribed height for your age group.

You may learn to use handguards here, as your swinging ability increases, to save your hands from excessive wear, and you will find that training on these events results in a protective layer of callous building up on your palms, wrists, and fingers. This will also help you to last longer in a training session here and on other events. Read about handguards in general in the introduction to chapter 9 (**Rings**). When I first began gymnastics in 1959, horizontal bar handguards were made of leather (or lampwick, which is not used anymore) and were worn with the finger holes at the bases of the fingers. Usually they were two-finger handguards, and fit around your middle and ring fingers. In the 1960s, gymnasts began wearing them up around the top joint of their fingers, finding that if they did that, the handguards would bend and form a pocket, which helped them to hold on (figure 12.1). Later on in the 1970s, a dowel was introduced that sat in the fold of the leather and increased the gripping strength of the handguard-plus-hand combination (figures 12.2 and 12.3). The dowel was mainly introduced to allow for easier performance of one-armed skills and regrasping the high-flying release-regrasp moves that were invented around that time. Women later adapted the dowel handguard to uneven parallel bars, as they began doing large swinging skills along with high-flying release-regrasp moves and had a tougher time holding on to the thicker bar that they used. Now, men often

Figure 12.1
Non-dowel two-finger horizontal bar
handguards.

Figure 12.2
Dowel three-finger horizontal bar
handguards.

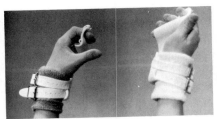

Figure 12.3
Dowel two-finger uneven parallel bar
handguards.

use three-finger handguards, which fit around their index, middle, and ring fingers. Often, a wrist wrap is used to cushion the pull of the handguard on the wrist area.

The use of a dowel puts much more stress on the leather than if it were not there, and has caused newer, stronger leathers to be developed. However, there is a cause for concern, too, as the extra stress sometimes causes the leather to stretch so much that the handguards become dangerous—either the leather gets too thin, or it gets too long and can wrap up around the bar causing potential hand, wrist, or arm injury. I do not see any reason for a beginning gymnast to use dowel handguards, if handguards are used at all. It is important to build up grip strength, and regular handguards will allow this to happen better. When you get beyond the beginning stages and are learning high-flying release-regrasp skills or one-armed skills, then you can learn to use dowel handguards. My suggestion is to use non-dowel handguards until that time.

Speaking of grip, there is a rule called the "rule of thumb" that governs most circling skills done on these events. This rule states that as you hold the bar with your fingers on one side and your thumb on the other side, you circle around the way that your thumb points. There are very few exceptions to this rule. The reason is simple: If you go the way that your thumb points, you will have four fingers holding on to the bar, and this is a strong grip. If you go the other way, only your thumb holds on, and you are likely to rip off and fall. You will learn some skills here that do not follow this rule, and later on you may learn a few more.

Another note concerning grip: Boys always keep their thumbs around the bar; however, because of the larger size of the uneven bars, very often girls keep their thumbs alongside their other fingers during rotating skills or pointing along the bar. This grip avoids tearing up the insides of the thumbs. During temporary supports, girls can have their thumbs around the bar for more gripping strength.

These events are perhaps the most spectacular to watch as performers are constantly moving through the space around the bar(s). For women, a competition routine must show moves outside, between, under, and over the bars, elements with turns and/or saltos, grip changes, several bar changes, and several directional changes. Only four skills may be performed in a row on one bar, and at least two skills must be performed on the low bar. For men, the routine must contain moves both close to the bar and away from the bar, but giant-swing-type skills are the main requirement. The routine must have a move with flight where the grip is released and regrasped, and a move where a type of giant swing is performed through the bottom with the hands rotated in an eagle-grip (explained shortly) or in a hang rearways (see chapter 9 for a picture on

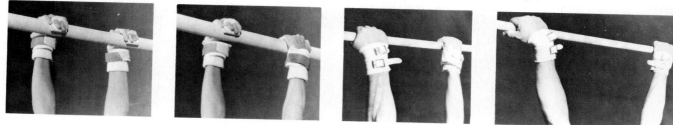

Figure 12.4
An overgrip.

Figure 12.5
A mixed grip (under and over).

Figure 12.6
An undergrip.

Figure 12.7
An eaglegrip (also called elgrip)—your hands are rotated 360° from an undergrip.

the rings). In both cases, the required moves must be of a certain difficulty, and stops are not allowed—the routine must flow from one skill to the next.

Where a skill I present is done only on the uneven bars (at this level), I designate it with **UPB**, and where a skill (at this level) is done only on the horizontal bar, I designate it with **HB.** Other than those moves, all others can be learned by both boys and girls.

A note for spotters: The danger point on most bar skills—where a student is likely to come flying off—is just past the bottom of a swing. This is where the forces are greatest on the performer's hands. So be careful to see that your student passes the bottom well. Be ready to hold him/her at this point to prevent or reduce a fall.

Terms Used in This Chapter

Various grip positions used on a bar—overgrip, mixed grip, undergrip, and eaglegrip—are shown in figures 12.4–12.7.

Organization of This Chapter

Backward Pullover
Casting
Backward Hip Circle
Undershoot Skills
Free Hip Circle Backward
Forward Hip Circle
Straddle-on to Backward Sole Circle Dismounts
Backward Sole Circle Shoot to One-half Turn
Squat-on and Squat-throughs
Single Knee Rise
Stride Circle
Long Hang Swings and Turns and Hops
Cast to Back Uprise—HB
Cast From a Front Support to Various Handstand Skills
Stem Rises—UPB
Kips and Combinations

Between-Bar Skills—UPB
Jumps Over the Low Bar to the High Bar—UPB
Sole Circles
Drop Back and Overshoot
Glide to Straddle-up to Rear Support—UPB
Stoop-in From a Hang and Overshoot
Cut-Catch
Seat Circles
Flyaway Dismounts—HB
Lead up to UPB Giant Swing
Giant Swing—HB
Pirouette From a Giant Swing—HB
Shoot to Handstand—HB
Stoop-in From a Front Giant to Seat Circle and Shoot to Dislocate—HB
Sequences to Practice

Figure 12.8a, b, c, d, e, f

a.   b.   c.   d.

e.   f.

Backward Pullover (Figure 12.8)

Perhaps the first skill that young students will be introduced to on the bar is a backward (or hip) pullover or a backward kickover. This is first done by standing at a bar that is approximately shoulder height, so that you start with your elbows flexed as in a pull-up position. Use an overgrip, although this can be done with an undergrip as well. Pike to lift your legs and pull your feet over the bar, watching your toes. Keep your eyes on your toes, and pull your hips over the bar and just past it. In doing so, you will find that you come around the bar and go on top of it, turning over backward. As you get on top, lift your head with your trunk and finish in a front support. I prefer having my students do this as a pullover rather than a kickover at first because it is a test of their body strength. To kickover, you start in the same position but put one leg back and then, to initiate the movement, instead of pulling both legs up, kick that leg up and over the bar. Your other leg as well as the rest of your body will follow. Finish in a front support. As you get better, you will pike less and less as you turn over.

Common problems are throwing your head back, which usually changes your body position, causing your body to fall away from the bar, and kicking

Figure 12.9a, b, c, d
To come back to the bar and repeat the
cast, just reverse the order of the figures.

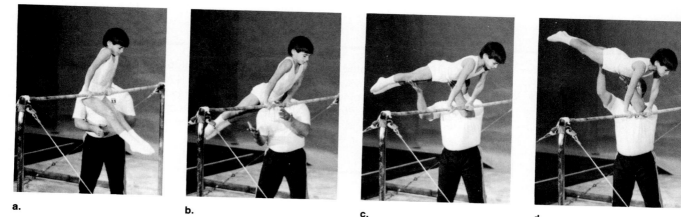

a.   b.   c.   d.

wildly with your legs. You have to learn to pull your body into a piked position
and hold the bar next to your waist. Then the turn-over is very easy to accomplish.

Stand next to your student just in front of the bar and reach underneath as he
begins the skill. Your left hand will lift his legs, while your right hand will go under
his back to help him lift and stay close to the bar if necessary. As he completes this
move, shift your right hand to the front of his legs to stop the action if he is going
past a support. You can also move your left hand to his left shoulder to stop him.

■

Spotting

Casting (Figure 12.9)

Once you have achieved a front support it is time to practice casting. This involves flexing and extending your hips, and pushing down on the bar, which
causes your body to leave the bar and move up a bit into space, eventually going
up to a handstand (covered later). Use either an overgrip, undergrip, or mixed
grip. Keep the bar right where your hips flex. You will have to shrug (elevate)
your shoulders to do this. When you flex and extend your hips you will find that
your body starts moving off the bar if you have done the extension forcefully.
You have to lean forward a bit during this entire action, otherwise you will fall
backward off the bar. This leaning will develop a bit of upper body strength.
Eventually you will be able to cast up, come back to the bar, and cast up again.
As you cast, you go into a slight arch and push down out of your shoulders. As
you become stronger and as your cast starts getting above horizontal, your body
can straighten out rather than maintain an arch. But your body does leave the
bar with a slight arch, and when it returns to the bar it should also have a slight
arch. If you contact the bar with a slight arch and then pike, the force at the
point of contact will be much less. Soon this cast will be done right up to a
handstand. Some of you are strong enough to do this right away but most of

you are not. It takes a while to achieve that strength and balance. At first your elbows may be flexed somewhat, but as you get stronger your arms will straighten.

Common problems are leaning back, extending your hips too slowly, bending your arms excessively, and not pushing down hard enough.

■

Spotting

Stand (on an elevated surface if you are not tall) next to your student behind the bar and either put your left hand on his shoulder while reaching under his legs with your right hand to provide lift, or use both hands to reach under his legs to provide lift. If you are confident that he will not injure himself coming back into the bar, then he can try this on his own over and over. If not, be there to reduce the shock of contact with the bar. A bar pad can help here.

Backward Hip Circle (Figure 12.10)

The cast and the backward pullover can be combined in sequence to produce a backward hip circle, or a backward hip circle can be done without a cast. It is done with an overgrip. To do this with a low cast, as you return to the bar, shift your weight backward slightly, so that your shoulders are pushed back a bit. Your head stays in and looks for your toes. As your feet come from under the bar, you'll see your toes as your shoulders start to go backward. You will find that if you hold the bar next to where your hips flex, you will circle around the bar and wind up in a front support again. Doing a series of back hip circles without a casting start will help you learn to initiate rotation, plus develop speed and muscle control. Eventually you will do this in a fairly stretched body position.

Common problems are the same as for the cast and backward pullover, plus dropping away from the bar as you begin the circle.

■

Spotting

Stand next to your student just in front of the bar. As he begins, it is a good idea to reach under the bar and around it so that your right hand goes over his lower back. Once the skill begins, the spot is identical to that for the backward pullover.

Undershoot Skills

Undershoot Dismount (Figure 12.11)

A good first dismount to learn is an undershoot dismount where you begin to do a backward hip circle. When you have gone between a third to a half of the way around, so that your legs are pointing upward, pull the bar back over your head to drive your legs (shoot) forward and upward and fly off forward. You have to be careful not to bend your arms when you pull, because you do not want to pull the bar right into your face. Look for the wall ahead of you for orientation as you fly to a landing. This can be done above the bar when it is well performed.

Common problems are bending your arms as you pull and dropping away from the bar as you pass below it. Be careful not to let your head whip back as you go under the bar—this may give you sore neck muscles.

Figure 12.10a, b, c, d, e, f, g

a.

b.

c.

d.

e.

f.

g.

Figure 12.11a, b, c

a.

b.

c.

Figure 12.12a, b, c, d, e
This is done with a free hip circle action rather than a hip circle action—note Courtney does not touch the bar with her body as she circles.

a. b. c.

d. e.

■

Spotting

Stand on the front side of the bar and put your hands underneath your student to provide support in the flight phase. Watch out for flailing arms as he comes off.

Undershoot to One-half Turn (Figure 12.12)

This begins as a backward hip circle, and eventually can be done up to a handstand when started as a free hip circle (covered next). As you get about a third to a half of the way around, start to shoot out as if you were doing an undershoot dismount. But do not open into an arch, and as you extend from the bar, turn your body over to the left. Once you pass the halfway point of your twist, you will have to change your grip, either regrasping with your right hand into a mixed grip with your right hand on the other side of your left, or switching both hands to a new overgrip. If you use the mixed-grip method, you will need to

Figure 12.13a, b, c, d

a.   b.   c.   d.

move your body over to the left by the amount of a shoulder width, so that you swing down straight. If you switch your hands, you will not need to move over, but you can if you want to.

Common problems are dropping your feet as you begin your turn, turning too little, and not moving over in the case of the mixed-grip regrasp.

Stand where you would for an undershoot dismount. Reach under your student to support her and help her turn. Be sure she is stretched as she descends. If you do this on a high bar, use a spotting block to get up near her.

■

Spotting

Free Hip Circle Backward

Once the backward hip circle has been accomplished, and you have done it with a fairly straight body (your first hundred may be very piked, but as you become stronger you will want to straighten your body and do more of the bend in your chest area rather than in your hip area), you can turn it into a free (or clear) hip circle where you go around the bar without touching it (figure 12.13). To do this you must learn how to keep your shoulders in a forward position (protracted) and to round your upper body, forming a hollow chest. Push on the bar as you come back toward the bar from a cast, and invert your body as quickly as possible, getting your shoulders underneath the bar. Keep your eyes on your toes to keep from pulling your head back and changing your body position. You push so hard on the bar that, when you invert, it will no longer be around your lower abdomen area, but it will be down around your lower thigh or knee area. You will come back to a free (not touching the bar) support and can continue into another free hip circle without casting—wait until you go just behind the bar to start the next one. A series of free hip circles can go around the bar several times without touching the bar. This helps develop the push on the bar, which will be useful for later skills. As a lead-up drill, stand behind a low bar and do a fast pullover without touching the bar, and land on the mat where you started. This will give you the feeling of doing a free hip circle.

Figure 12.14a, b, c, d, e
Danny should not bend his arms on the way up—he does this to help him shift his grip.

a.

b.

c.

d.   e.

The potential for developing power with this movement is great, and eventually it can be done up to a handstand. (This is rated a B-level skill for girls, but an A for boys.) To do this, as you pass under the bar and see your feet and the bottom half of your shins over it, yank on the bar to pull it overhead, directly to a handstand (figure 12.14). As lead ups, turn over more than I have described and shoot out flat (below a handstand) to get the feel of turning over and then pulling. It is important to think of pulling your wrists into hyperextension (pull back with your wrists) as you pull on the bar. This action will help you to shift your hands into a strong support position and to avoid bending your arms on the way up. In addition to the visual cue I have described, you will learn to feel the bottom of the free hip circle to cue you when to pull.

Figure 12.15a, b, c, d, e

a.   b.   c.   d.   e.

The most common flaw here, as with the back hip circle, is throwing your head back, causing your body to drop away from the bar. Other problems are not starting to drop far enough from the bar to develop power, not turning over enough, and not pulling with straight arms.

From the mat, spot the same as for the backward hip circle. This is a much faster move, so you have to move your hands more quickly if you are going to spot. For the free hip circle to a handstand, if you stand on an elevated surface, grasp your student's thighs as he lifts and guide him upward.

Spotting

Forward Hip Circle (Figure 12.15)

Remember that I said on most bar work there is a general "rule of thumb" to be followed for circling skills. There are some skills that do not follow that rule. This is one of them.

The forward hip circle is done with an overgrip, but you go around the bar the way your fingers are pointing. This involves a shifting of your grip, and there is a moment when your body is resting on the bar that allows you to move your hands rather than to hold on tightly. Start in a front support with an overgrip. Depress your shoulders as far as possible, and hollow your chest to push your body up. Fall over forward with your body straight (your chest moves forward and your feet move backward in unison). The bar will be somewhere around your midthighs. As you fall over, you pick up speed. When you are about horizontal (but not past it), flex your hips rapidly. At this moment, your thighs will be resting on the bar. Quickly shift your grip by flexing your wrists as far as possible, and pull your chest and shoulders around and on top of the bar. You must pull the bar to where your hips flex as well. If you do not move away from the bar, you will wind up in a stretched front support again, having passed through a piked front support.

As this skill is perfected, your body will bend less and less as you finish. Eventually, as you finish, you can cast out of it directly toward a handstand and do skills that are usually done from a kip (described later). A series of forward hip circles may be done as a drill.

The biggest problem here is allowing your body to drop away from the bar. As soon as your body moves from the bar, your swing slows down, and it is tough to make it up. Another problem is not shifting your grip enough. If you do not shift your hands around, then you are not in a position to pull down on the bar—fingertips on the bar is not a strong grip. Lastly, if you pike too soon you will not be able to generate enough momentum to get back up.

■

Spotting

Stand next to your student, on the same side of the bar as he starts. Your left arm reaches under and around the bar, so that as soon as he begins, your left hand will reach to the back of his left thigh. Your right hand reaches underneath the bar, and as soon as he passes under the bar, that hand goes to his back. So you are really spotting the last half of the skill; the first half does not need spotting. You just help him to stay close to the bar, because if his hand shift is not accomplished, he will not be in a position to hold his body next to the bar.

Straddle-on to Backward Sole Circle Dismounts

You can do a cast to a sole circle (so called because the soles of your feet touch the bar) in either an overgrip or undergrip, but I will describe an overgrip here as it leads into backward sole circle dismounts.

The straddle-on (also called a toe-on) is done from a cast, and you have to lift your seat somewhat high behind the bar (figure 12.16). Before casting to a toe-on, see if you can push up to a straddle-on slowly. If you can do this, the cast to toe-on will be easy. At just about the height of your cast, flex your hips, then straddle your legs, and place the back parts of the balls your feet on the bar. Keep your feet pointed as you circle—this will help you to keep your feet on the bar. Your legs should straddle no more than 90°, but your feet can come as close together as just outside of your hands. A variation of this is done with your legs together (called a stoop-on). This requires more height in the cast and good hip flexibility.

Undershoot (Figure 12.17)

The same sort of a shootout as the undershoot dismount is then done from a sole circle position whether straddled or stooped. Swing down from the sole circle support position, but as you swing underneath the bar and are beginning to go up, shoot your legs off in a forward-upward manner and pull the bar back, arching slightly as you fly to the mat. Look at the bar as you go down, but as you begin to swing up, look at the wall in front of you and watch it during your flight for orientation. Throughout your sole circle, push on the bar with your feet and push your lower back as far from the bar as you can to build up maximum swing. You will feel your arms pulling on the bar as well.

To feel the start of this move, you can get on a very low (just above the floor) bar on a safety cushion and fall to your seat while in a sole circle position. To feel the end, you can stand next to a low bar, jump up to put your feet on the bar, and swing forward into a low sole circle shoot dismount. Another valuable set of lead ups is done utilizing both uneven bars. With the bars close, you

Figure 12.16a, b, c, d

a.

b.

c.

d.

Figure 12.17a, b, c, d, e, f
Although she keeps good pressure on her feet, Cindy should point her feet more on the bar and in flight.

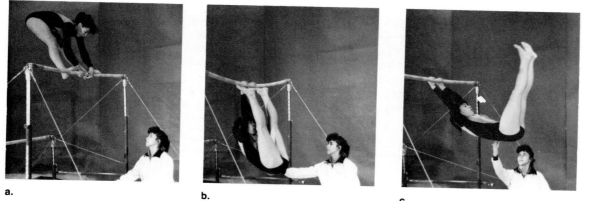

a.

b.

c.

d.

e.

f.

can hang from the high bar facing the low bar, straddle and pike to put your feet on the low bar, reach for the low bar with one hand, then reach with your other hand and begin a modified sole circle shoot dismount. In a like manner, if you do a straddled stand on the low bar facing the high bar while holding the high bar, you can push back a bit and grasp the low bar as you begin the sole circle shoot dismount.

A variation on the sole circle shoot (or the underswing dismount) is to do a jackknife action, which is a quick pike-open action in the flight phase. Just after you leave the bar in a stretched position, quickly pike, and immediately open from your pike into a stretched position again for the rest of your flight. When you do this, you must be careful that you do not overturn to your face, because by shortening your body (the pike) your rotation is sped up. You will have to learn how much you have to push on the bar to do this without over-turning, and/or learn to shoot a little higher so that your rotation is slower when you leave the bar.

Common problems are bending your arms or legs, not casting high enough, shooting off too soon, and dropping your feet from the bar as you pass below (because you hook your feet and/or do not keep pressure on your feet).

■

Spotting

This can be done several ways. If you have a student who is fairly strong, all you need to do is stand on the front side of the bar with your hands on her upper arms, and as she casts up, provide her with a bit of balance support. If she is not strong you must stand closer to the bar, again on the front side, but to her side. With your left hand on her left upper arm, if your shoulder is around bar height, your right hand will reach underneath the bar to her abdomen as she casts up so you can give her lift as well as stability. If you are on a block and over the bar (as shown in figure 12.16), reach over the bar to lift on her abdomen or hip. Since her legs are being straddled, in this particular skill you cannot stand on the side of the bar on which she begins—you will get kicked (unless her straddle is very narrow). As her downswing begins, move to the side so you are out of her way, and get back in under her as she does the shoot. Watch out for overrotation if she does a jackknife.

Three-quarter Backward Sole Circle to Jump Off (Figure 12.18)

For this dismount you ride a sole circle around until you are above the bar (the higher, the better), then you dismount by merely a jump off when you stop. It is as if you went for a full sole circle and missed it. Look at the bar as you circle down, then look back for the mat as you move up. At the end of your rise you are looking at the mat, and you merely let go with your hands, push off the bar by extending your body, and jump to your feet. Do not bend your legs to jump; all you need do is open your body.

The common problem here is jumping off too soon.

■

Spotting

Stand in front of the bar. Have your student attempt the sole circle by himself. As he comes around, reach underneath his shoulders to provide them with a little support, and let him come off the bar. You have to learn how to move in rapidly on him—these are straddled sole circle dismounts, so you cannot stand next to him.

Chapter 12

Figure 12.18a, b, c, d, e
Jim should not have a slight knee bend on
the bar.

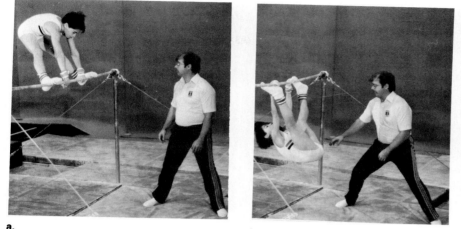

a.

b.

c.

d.

e.

Backward Sole Circle Shoot to One-half Turn (Figure 12.19)

This is directly related to the sole circle shoot dismount and the hip circle shoot with one-half turn. Your sole circle can be straddled or stooped. You do almost the same action as the dismount, but do not let go at the end of your shoot. Rather, as you shoot out, twist your body, and shoot toward the side you are turning around. If you turn on your right hand, twist to the right and shoot to the right. You have to move over a shoulder width to swing down straight. Look at the bar during this skill to see where to put your hands. Turning your head to see the bar outside of your right hand will also help to initiate your turn. If you begin straddled, bring your legs together as soon as you can after your feet

Figure 12.19a, b, c, d, e
Angela should have her legs together on the way down.

a.

b.

c.

d.

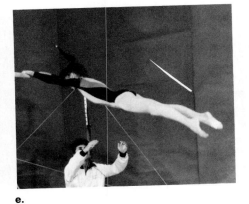

e.

leave the bar. After you push to the right side, release with your left hand and regrasp the bar on the other side of your right hand. You will finish in a mixed grip. Another method has you changing both hands—you release both grips as you finish the turn and regrasp in a double overgrip. For this method you do not have to move over. You can do both on the low bar at first or can try them directly on a high bar. If you are on a low bar, be ready to land on your feet once you complete the move.

Common problems are shooting too early, letting go too early, and, for the first method, not directing your feet (and body) to the side. If you have trouble twisting, hang on a bar and twist your body the way you want to go to feel how to push on the bar and turn your lower body, which then turns your upper body.

■

Spotting

Stand to the side in front of the bar and reach under your student as she does the turn. If this is done on the high bar of the unevens, be ready to slow her down if she is swinging into the low bar and has not practiced a bar beat.

Figure 12.20a, b, c, d, e, f
Aside from a slight toe hook, this single-leg
squat-through is done well.

a.

b.

c.

d.

e.

f.

Squat-on (Figure 12.21) and Squat-throughs (Figures 12.20 and 12.22)

If your cast is coming along well, you can learn how to do movements that bring your legs between your hands. These are a squat-on, a squat-through, or a stoop-through. All of these skills can be done in either overgrip, undergrip, or mixed grip, but generally they are done in an overgrip to start with because it is a stronger grip.

Single Leg

For the single-leg squat-through, cast up, flex your knee and hip on one side, and bring that tucked leg between your arms. This must be done very quickly. If you do not lift your hips high enough, you may land on your shin—that is quite painful. You will learn quickly not to do that. Finish in a stride support.

Another way to get to a stride support from a front support is to do a leg cut forward, just as boys do on the pommel horse. Lift your right leg to the side and lean on your left arm. Lift your right hand from the bar, and bring your right leg over and past the bar, regrasping the bar as you complete the cut (see chapter 7 for pictures).

Figure 12.21a, b, c
Maureen's leg and toe form needs
improvement during her squat-on.

a.

b.

c.

Figure 12.22a, b, c, d, e
Again, Maureen needs to improve her form
during her squat-through.

a.

b.

c.

d.

e.

Double Leg

A double-leg squat-through is done in a similar manner, and you will finish in a rear support. Before you do a double-leg squat-through, do a double-leg squat-on. See if you can do it without a cast at first—just push down on the bar to lift your body enough to put your feet on the bar. If you can get there, lift your feet off and return to a front support. This strength makes the squat-on and -through easy. Next, cast up, push down on the bar, and bring both legs to a squat stand on the bar. You can squat as your cast leaves the bar. If this is accomplished easily, then try to squat all the way through. At first, lift without a cast as just described. Once you are squatting on the bar, lift your feet off and lower to a rear support. Next, lift back to a squat stand and return to a front support. Then do this sequence from a cast and in a quicker tempo. A harder variation is to do these skills in a stoop position—not flexing your knee(s).

The biggest problem here is not casting high enough so that your feet or legs hit the bar. By the time this particular skill is attempted, you will have a little experience in balancing in this casting position, so you may have learned how not to lean too far forward or too far backward. You must push down hard. Doing these skills slowly without casts helps to build the strength you need.

■

Spotting

For the single right-leg squat-through, there are several methods. The way I prefer is to stand on the back side of the bar just to the side, and hold on to my student's left leg (that is not doing the squat). As she casts I can provide plenty of support, and hold her hips high enough to allow her right leg to clear the bar. Another way is to stand with the bar by your left shoulder, with your left hand on her left arm (reach under the bar). Hold her left thigh or knee with your right hand and lift her there. A third way is to stand in front of the bar and just make sure she does not fall forward as she attempts the squat-through.

For the double-leg squat-on or -through you do not have a leg to hold. So in these moves you have to be a bit surer that your student is going to be able to push up high. Be careful that she does not lean too far forward or too far backward, which would result in an unexpected fall below the bar. Stand either next to your student with the bar by your side, putting your left hand on her left upper arm and providing lift by pushing up on her abdomen or thigh with your right hand, or stand in front of the bar just to her side, putting your hands on her upper arms to assist in balance. She has to be strong enough to push down and clear the bar.

Single Knee Rise (Figure 12.23)

This easy mount is started from below the bar with one knee flexed so that the bar is in the back of that knee. Your other knee is straight, and your elbows are extended so that your body is hanging below the bar from your hands and one knee. Swing your free leg up and down, developing a whole body swing, and once this swing gets big enough, as your body rises behind the bar, pull down on the bar (at first with bent arms and eventually with straight arms) to pull it to your seat while extending your flexed knee. You will rise right up to a stride support. From this support, you can push back and hook your knee on the bar, swing down and forward under the bar, and then swing back up. This is called a drop back and single knee rise.

a.

b.

c.

Common problems are swinging with bent arms (which is a waste of strength), bending your free leg, and not developing enough swing to pull your body on top of the bar. Sometimes this move can grind up the back of your knee, so it is preferable to wear pants when first learning this.

■

Spotting

Stand by the performer's side in back of the bar. Reach under the bar with your left hand so you can push down on the thigh of her free leg. Your right hand lifts her back as she goes up. Notice that the bar will shift positions on the way up—it will go from her knee to her seat.

Stride Circle

Forward (Figure 12.24)

This skill might directly follow a single knee rise after you change your grip. It is often called a mill circle because your legs and body rotate like the arms of a windmill. Begin in a stride support with an undergrip. Split your legs as widely as possible, push down on the bar to lift your body off the bar, and then push forward into space. You can think of pushing your chin and front foot forward, but do not let your trunk round forward as you begin—it should stay straight. In doing so, the bar will move slightly back on the thigh of your back leg. You will begin to fall forward. You must keep your arms straight throughout this circle. As you go down the bar will move back to a position opposite your seat. Throughout the below-bar phase, do not let your body change position in relation to your arms—for example, do not let the bar slip up toward your front leg. On the way up, pull down on the bar (keep tension on the bar to prevent it from moving along either leg). You should be able to come back on top of the bar, finishing in a stride support. You can do a series of these if you wish.

Common problems are bending your arms upon starting the descent, not pulling with your wrists as you rise to get your palms on top of the bar, and allowing your body to drop away from the stable balanced position underneath

Figure 12.24a, b, c, d, e
A forward stride circle—Meggan's legs
could be split wider.

a.

b.

c.

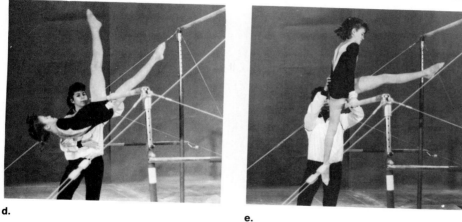

d.

e.

the bar—usually due to not pulling backward on the bar as you pass underneath. It is very important to learn how to do this skill without bending your arms, because if they are bent when you hit the bottom of the swing, they will most likely straighten out and result in a jerk, which might cause a fall.

Stand on the back side of the bar. Reach your left arm under the bar and then around it, holding just above the performer's left wrist with your pronated left hand (figure 12.25). When she begins, your right hand can be used to help lift her body by putting it on the underside of her front thigh. As she gets below the bar, that hand then reaches underneath her back. When she goes up on top, your right hand shifts to her back leg, and your left hand shifts to her front leg to stop her if needed.

■

Spotting

Figure 12.25
The spotting position at the start.

Figure 12.26a, b, c, d, e, f
Lindsay's legs could split more during this
backward stride circle.

a.

b.

c.

d.

e.

f.

Figure 12.27
The spotting position at the start.

Backward (Figure 12.26)

In a similar manner, you can do a stride circle backward. Begin in a stride support with an overgrip. Push off the bar in a wide stride position, and push your body back a bit so that the bar is below your front thigh. As you drop below the bar, pull on it to move the bar back to a position opposite your seat. As you pass through the bottom, freeze your position—do not let your seat move in relation to your arms. As you rise, pull down on the bar with your arms and wrists to shift your hands into a good support position. Finish in the same stride support that you started in. You can do several of these in a row.

Common problems are similar to the forward stride circle.

Stand in front of the bar next to your student. Reach under and around the bar with your right arm, and place your pronated right hand above her left wrist (figure 12.27). Your left hand can help her to lift and push back into the skill. As she passes under the bar, reach under her shoulder or chest with your left hand to lift her if needed. Your right hand will shift to her back leg or back to stabilize her finish position.

■

Spotting

Long Hang Swings and Turns and Hops

Moving to a horizontal bar that is high enough so you can hang all the way down without touching the mat, there are a number of swings and turns and hops that should be mastered for both boys and girls that are very helpful.

Stand near your student in case of a problem passing the bottom. Be sure to watch for bent arms or piked shoulders through the bottom. And be careful if your student's legs straddle for some reason—you may get kicked.

■

Spotting

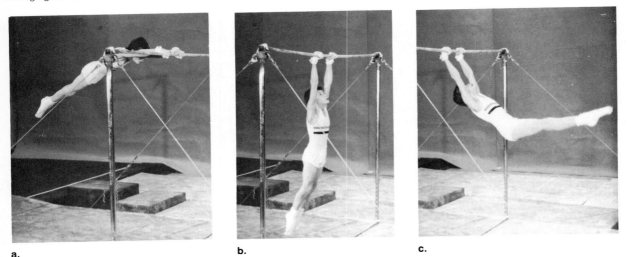

a.   b.   c.

d.

Stretched Swings (Figures 12.28 and 12.29)

Just hanging as long (lengthwise) as you can, feeling that position of stretch and learning it, is the first step. Next, hang in an overgrip, and start to swing back and forth by piking your hips and shoulders slightly in the front swing, then stretching until just before the back when you again pike slightly in your shoulders before stretching again for the downswing. If you continue to do this action, in effect rounding your body in the front (hollow your chest a bit, pike your shoulders and hips a bit) once you pass the bottom on the way forward, and stretching at the farthest forward point of your swing to let your stretched body swing back until you round again at the end of your backswing, you are going to eventually swing all the way up to a handstand on both sides. This will

Figure 12.29a, b, c, d, e
Lenny should not have a shoulder pike in
figure a as he begins to move down into his
backswing.

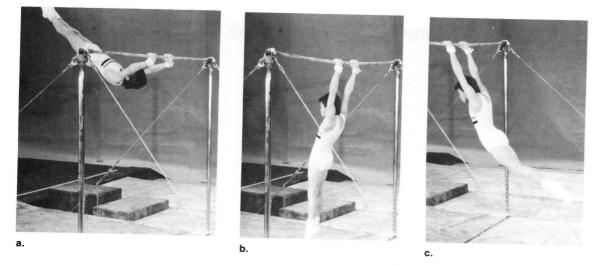

a. b. c.

d. e.

take quite a while, however. As you swing higher and higher, you will have to learn how to keep a solid grip. For instance, with an overgrip, when you start swinging forward toward horizontal, on the way up, instead of letting your hands slide around the bar, you can keep your hands in a solid position by squeezing tightly and letting your wrists flex (also called curling your wrists). Then, as you come back, your hands will still be on top of the bar giving you a firm grip rather than the weaker grip provided by your fingertips if you let your hands shift around the bar going forward. If you go higher than about horizontal, you will have to learn to shift your grip as you swing down in the direction your fingers point, or you will fly off the bar unintentionally (the "rule of thumb" applies here and says you will have a weak grip going this way). This swing can be done with a mixed grip or undergrip as well. With a mixed grip, as you go higher and higher, you will learn how to shift one grip when you swing down. For instance, on a forward swing, your overgrip hand will have a very solid grip, but your undergrip hand will tend to roll off toward your fingertips. So you learn how to regrasp. All of these swings eventually can be done right up to a handstand on both sides and are very helpful in learning how to do certain higher level skills. Each presents its own grip problems. If you want to come down from the bar, be sure that you do so only when you stop at the height of your backswing. This way you can see the mat, and your body will not be moving. If you let go to come down at any other time (unless you are doing a specific drill for a higher level skill), you are exposing yourself to a potentially dangerous landing situation.

As variations, swing in a hang rearways with an overgrip or undergrip, and swing in an eaglegrip or mixed eagle and undergrip. You will come across skills with these grips in the future as you progress.

Common problems are lifting your legs too early going forward, piking your shoulders on the downswing, and lifting with bent knees.

Turns (Figures 12.30–12.33)

As you are learning a stretched swing you can also be learning to turn around. This swing can be done in an overgrip, an undergrip, or a mixed grip. The overgrip is the strongest grip so it is generally how we start teaching swinging turns. For these turns your body has to change swing planes, that is, move to the side (to feel how you push to move over, hang without swinging and push your body to the side you will turn toward). To do a half turn on the front swing on your left arm, after you pass the bottom, push your body to the left (a hint often used is lift your toes to the left), and roll to your left by pushing the right side of your body forward (a left twist) while you still have two hands on the bar. Then your right hand releases the bar, and your body completes a half turn, finishing in a mixed grip. You can then swing forward, backward, and forward in a mixed grip and do the opposite turn around your right arm. In this way, you can do several turns in a series, but since this move travels on the bar (moves over), you will be limited as to how many you can do—you will run out of bar! If you want to train turning to only one side, switch your undergrip hand at the end of your backswing and proceed into another turn with a double overgrip. Doing a series this way does not move you over, so you can do as many as you like. This particular turn will help you to learn both a cross pirouette and a back pirouette from a giant swing. The same procedure is followed when doing a half turn on your backswing, starting in an undergrip. Move to the left on the way up, roll around your left arm by pushing the right side of your body back (a right twist), release with your right hand, and complete the half turn, finishing in a mixed grip. If you learn this half turn on the backswing, you will be on your way to a front pirouette from a giant swing. In doing these turns, I suggest you learn to look at the bar out of the tops of your eyes with your head held between your arms. I always found it comforting to know where the bar was when I had to let go of it and regrasp it. This practice will also stabilize your head so it does not wobble during the swings and turns. Later on you will learn to look at specific orientation points for certain skills. Eventually these turns can be done as hopping turns where both hands release and then regrasp

Figure 12.30a, b, c, d, e
A forward swinging half turn.

a.

b.

c.

d.

e.

in the same grip as they began. On the hopping turns, it is not necessary to change planes. Also, these turns can be done as high as a handstand when you master swinging.

Another variation is to turn from a double overgrip to a mixed eagle- and undergrip or double eaglegrip on your backswing. You move over just as you do for the others. At first, turn to the mixed grip—reach over your left hand with your right so that your left hand finishes in an eaglegrip. If you are flexible, go for the double eaglegrip, rotating your right arm to finish with your right

Figure 12.31a, b, c, d
End view showing the move over when doing a forward swinging half turn.

a.

b.

c.

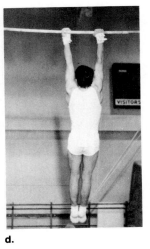
d.

Figure 12.32a, b, c, d, e
A backward swinging half turn.

a.

b.

c.

d.

e.

Figure 12.33a, b, c, d
End view showing the move over when doing a backward swinging half turn.

a. b. c. d.

Figure 12.34a, b, c, d
A first release-regrasp.

a. b. c. d.

hand in an eaglegrip as well. Keep your swing low until you can do the turn easily. You can hop out of the eaglegrip into another grip (an overgrip is safest) at the back end of your swing (hops are described next).

Common problems are not moving over, not turning enough, and arching as you turn.

Hops (Figures 12.34, 12.35 and 12.36)

You can learn how to do elementary release-regrasp movements where both hands let go of the bar. Use a small swing at first, then build it up. The simplest one is to start with an overgrip, take a swing, and as you rise up in the back at the end of the swing you will feel very little weight on your hands. Pull down a bit on the bar, let go with both hands, and regrasp again in an overgrip. Then swing forward keeping your eyes on the bar at all times. The next step is to begin in an undergrip and follow the same procedure.

Figure 12.35a, b, c
Hopping from undergrip to overgrip.

a.   b.   c.

Figure 12.36a, b, c, d
Hopping from overgrip to undergrip—Danny should not arch in figures b and c.

a.   b.   c.   d.

A harder release-regrasp can be done in the front. This is where you will most likely need a spot when learning it, because the finish grip does not feel as strong. When you swing forward with an overgrip, lift your toes as if you are doing a good swing (keeping your eyes on the bar). When there is a slight feeling of weightlessness in the front of your swing, when you are just about to stop, pull back on the bar a bit, then quickly release and regrasp in an undergrip. Extend your body as you pull back just before you release, but try not to arch. Stretch right away into a good downswing. As you get more proficient at these hops or hop changes, they can be done one after another on consecutive swings, eventually going all the way up to a handstand.

Common problems for both hops are not pulling down hard enough on the bar to give you that moment of weightlessness that allows you to let go of the bar (if you do not pull down enough, your body will continue to rotate or not get high enough above the bar to let go and recatch), hopping too soon (which may cause you to fly away from the bar!), and bending your arms while on the bar. A common flaw on the hop from overgrip to undergrip is to lift your toes and then stick out your belly.

Figure 12.37a, b, c, d, e
A beat swing going backward in an undergrip.

a.

b.

c.

d.

e.

Be ready underneath your student so that in case of a problem with his grip you can catch him and allow him to land on his feet. If possible, the bar should be only as high as needed to have him just clear his toes on an extended swing.

■

Spotting

Beat Swings—HB

To get a bit more upward power, you can learn a beat (or tap) swing going both forward and backward. This technique helps you to lift your toes upward, which aids in performing certain skills. Going backward in either an undergrip (shown in figure 12.37) or overgrip, as you approach the bottom of your swing, pike a bit, hold the pike through the bottom, and then snap into an arch as you rise. Keep your shoulders down (they are fully flexed) as you snap out so you have a whole body arch from your hands to your feet. You will change your shoulder position later for some skills. Going forward, round your chest on your downswing. Then, as you approach the bottom, arch and hold your arch through the bottom. As you move forward, snap from your arch into a pike and hollow (refer to figure 12.87b, c, d—even though this example is done during a giant swing and is subtle, it is a valid example). A good guideline is to perform this beat from cable to cable (looking at a horizontal bar from the side, the cables define this area below the bar). The actual timing will depend on the skill performed, but when you are learning to tap, use this guideline.

The common problem is starting and/or finishing the tap too early (it seldom happens too late). It may be useful to exaggerate the pike or arch passing through the bottom to feel the forces acting on your body and to feel where the bottom is. When doing the tap going backward, another problem is pulling down on the bar with your shoulders before you complete the snap into your arch.

Long Hang Swing—UPB

A long hang swing on the uneven bars precedes many kipping or circling skills, and eventually leads up to a giant swing, which is a difficult skill. One way to start is to sit on the low bar facing the upper bar (figure 12.38). Reach for the upper bar, and grab it in an overgrip as you push off the low bar and swing forward. To develop the swing, you have to lift your body very hard in the front by piking at your shoulders. This moves you toward what is called a front lever position, which takes a good bit of chest and shoulder strength (figure 12.38e). At the end of the front swing, open your shoulders and swing back to a seat on the lower bar. You can do this exercise from a squat stand on the low bar, then progress to a stand on the low bar. To learn a beating action (figure 12.39), which will help you to get lift as you swing up on your return, lift your feet as you approach the end of your front swing, and push into an arch from your hands to your toes as you swing down and back. Leave your hands back (flex your wrists) so that your grip does not slide around and make it necessary for you to regrasp on the way back. At the bottom, stretch downward, then pull on the bar while piking to help lift and rotate. You should be able to rise easily and return to a stand on the low bar. As an alternative, instead of returning to the low bar, do a fast pullover at the end of your front swing and finish in a front support on the high bar (figure 12.40). This is a lead up to a giant swing, which is mentioned later on in this chapter.

Common problems are not extending as you pass the low bar, and not pulling up hard enough at either end.

■

Spotting

Stand between the bars and be sure that your student does not fly off if she fails to regrasp on the way back. On the swing back to a stand on the low bar, you can lift on her abdomen to help her attain a stand.

Short Swing—UPB

A short swing can be done facing the opposite direction from the long hang swing described previously. If you swing forward into the low bar (figure 12.41), with the widths being used today, you will hit the low bar with your thighs (this is done in routines, and the rebound is used to get into the next skill). This can be painful, so if you want to try it, be sure to pad the bar and/or your legs first.

Figure 12.38a, b, c, d, e

a.

b.

c.

d.

e.

You can also lift your legs above the low bar, which leads into several harder skills. (See figure 12.52a, b, c for an example of a short swing done to a seat.) It takes a bit of strength to do this, so here are a few exercises you can do while hanging on the upper bar facing the lower bar. See if you can first lift your legs in a squat position above the height of the low bar, then do this straddled. Then do it with a swing—upon reaching the back of your swing, lift your legs quickly in either a straddle or a pike position above the lower bar, then swing forward, finishing with your legs or seat resting on the bar. This is a connection-type movement used in uneven bar exercises. Eventually you will be able to do these lifts from a large swing, even one that comes down from a cast from the high bar.

a.

b.

c.

d.

e.

f.

g.

h.

i.

Figure 12.40a, b, c, d, e, f

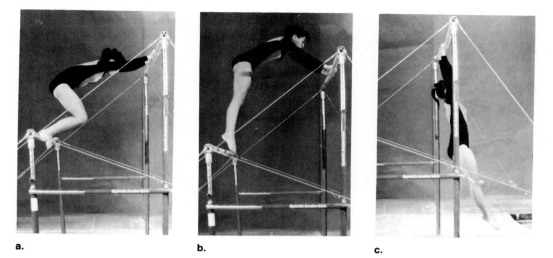

a. b. c.

d. e. f.

When learning skills that may result in contact with a bar, it is a good idea to pad the bar, or pad your legs. Your teacher will not know if you cannot lift your legs quickly enough until it happens, and then she usually will not be able to keep you from hitting the bar.

The common problems are not being strong enough to lift your legs rapidly, and straddling or piking too late.

Since you cannot stand next to your swinging student if she is going to straddle, come in from behind and lift underneath her legs if she needs help.

Spotting

Figure 12.41
A short swing into the low bar.

Cast to Back Uprise—HB (Figure 12.42)

A movement that does something with the long hang swing you have learned, is a lead up to a giant swing, and is useful in all areas of bar work, is a backward (or back) uprise. This usually starts with a cast, although it can be done from a high swing. It may also be done with either an undergrip or overgrip. I will describe an overgrip, as it often is used to begin a routine. Start with a small swing forward and backward, but as you finish your backward swing, pull down on the bar by chinning somewhat (do not pull the bar to your chin, just pull down on the bar with bent arms), then quickly flex your hips, bringing your feet around, and shoot them out forward and upward, at the same time pulling the bar back over your head. This will develop a swing. Remember to leave your wrists flexed so that your palms stay on top of the bar as you cast forward. If you slide your hands around the bar on the forward cast, when you swing backward you will go on to your fingertips and possibly fly off the bar.

It is obvious that the bigger your swing is, the easier it should be to go up behind the bar. In the beginning stages as you swing backward after your cast and after you pass the bottom of the backward swing, pull down on the bar and pull directly to a front support. As your cast gets higher and your grip strength increases, you will be able to do this uprise higher and higher, eventually going right up to a handstand.

There are two ways to perform this uprise, just as I later describe two ways to perform a giant swing. One is to generate your upswing by changing your shoulder angle. You start in a long swing with your arms aligned with your trunk. As your body rises in the back, pull down with your chest and arms, and round your chest a bit to pull your shoulders over the top of the bar. The other way to perform it uses an arch technique, often from a beat. Upon passing the bottom, arch hard. This also will shorten your body just as changing your shoulder angle did, causing your rotational velocity to increase, which gets you over the bar. If you do not get up to a handstand, pull your shoulders over the bar just before you stop. Both methods are valid and have many uses. Eventually, when you swing big enough, you can arch all the way up to a handstand without pulling on the bar at all.

Figure 12.42a, b, c, d, e, f, g

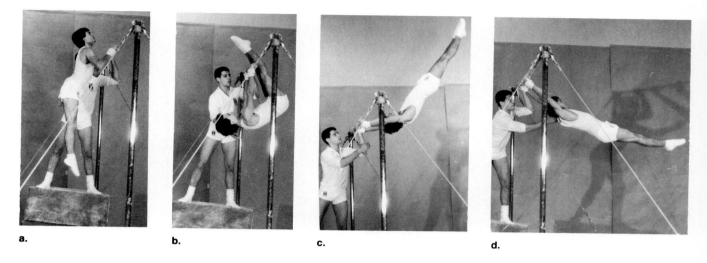

a. b. c. d.

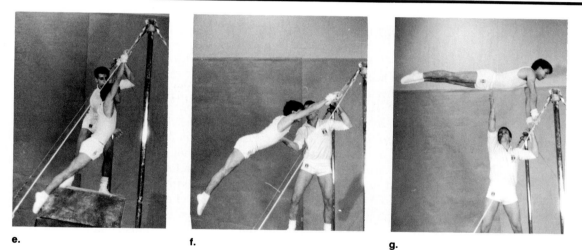

e. f. g.

Common problems are not casting high enough to generate the necessary backswing, not stretching out on the cast, and not pulling hard enough to get your shoulders over the bar.

Stand behind the bar to your student's side. Reach under him as he passes the bottom in case of a grip problem, and assist him in getting up if needed.

Spotting

Figure 12.43a, b, c, d
An overgrip stretched cast to handstand.

a. b. c. d.

Cast From a Front Support to Various Handstand Skills

To and Through a Handstand (Figures 12.43 and 12.44)

Earlier you began casting exercises to learn how to get your stretched body off the bar to begin various skills. Now it is time to carry that cast up to a handstand, which is one of the most basic skills for bar work. If you cannot do this, you will be extremely limited in what you will be able to learn. For boys this is considered so basic that it is not even rated as an A-level move, but for girls it is a B-level skill. The way you become strong enough to do it is by performing lots of casts. You have to learn how much to lean forward over the bar and how hard to cast to just reach a handstand or to pass it. You must be able to cast up with a double overgrip, double undergrip, and a mixed grip. Although you will leave the bar in an arch, you will straighten your body on the way up so that you arrive at a straight handstand. For a while you may find that you have to flex your elbows slightly to get to a handstand, but eventually you should do it with straight arms. For a beginner, just learning to get up to a handstand is the most important thing. Be careful about poor leg form and poor body position.

Sometimes you see a cast to a handstand where a performer's body is piked (figure 12.45). This is generally done when people are not strong enough to cast up with a straight body or as a variation on a straight body cast, and is seen more often done by girls than boys (it is an A-level move for girls). What happens is that just after leaving the bar you pike, which shortens your body and allows it to rotate more quickly to the handstand. Extend your hips as your trunk becomes vertical. This can be done in a straddle as well. On uneven bars you can jump to a handstand on the upper bar from a standing position on the low bar with a variety of grips.

When learning these casts to handstands, you also have to learn how to recover from an unplanned fall from a handstand. For instance, by the "rule of thumb," if you cast to an overgrip handstand you normally would swing down with the front of your body leading. But if you go past the handstand, you are

Figure 12.44a, b, c, d, e
An undergrip stretched cast to handstand.

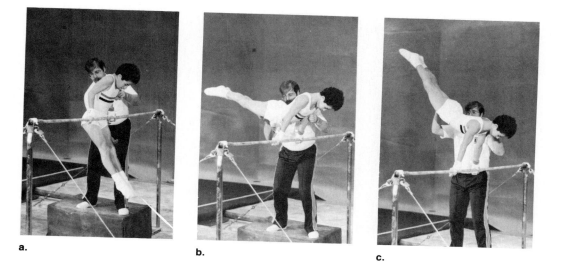

a.   b.   c.

d.   e.

in a situation where you could fly off if you swing through the bottom. So if you cast past a handstand, what can you do to avoid falling over with a weak grip? There are several recoveries. One is simply pirouetting off, doing a turn and landing on your feet. Another is changing one hand so that you are in a mixed grip and then swinging down. With one hand in an undergrip, you have a relatively strong grip, and you learn to shift your other hand around so that you pass through the bottom with a strong grip. A third way is to shift both hands— as you fall over, regrasp well before you pass the bottom, so that at bottom your palms and not just your fingertips are on top of the bar. As your training advances, you will learn how to do large swings (and maybe giant swings) with your hands in a position other than that dictated by the "rule of thumb."

Figure 12.45a, b, c, d, e
A piked straddled cast to handstand.

a.

b.

c.

d.

e.

Common problems are not casting up hard enough, not leaning forward enough, arching excessively, lifting your head rather than keeping it in line with your trunk, and bending your arms.

■

Spotting

Stand on an elevated platform next to your student just behind or just in front of the bar. If you are tall enough and the bar is low, you will not need the platform. Help him to get to a handstand if he cannot, and stop or slow him down if he goes past it.

Figure 12.46a, b, c, d, e, f
Casting with a mixed grip to a front pirouette.

a.

b.

c.

d. e. f.

To a Handstand and Forward Pirouette (Figures 12.46 and 12.47)

In learning a forward (or front) pirouette you learn how to do a turn that will later be done from a giant swing or a kip to cast. (It is also a recovery move if you miss an overgrip giant swing or go over by accident on a cast.) The forward pirouette can be done from a double undergrip, from a mixed grip, or from a double overgrip.

An important thing in doing a pirouette, regardless of which kind it is, is that when you do the turn, you always must push down as hard as possible with your support arm. You do not want your trunk-shoulder alignment to change

Figure 12.47a, b, c, d, e, f
Casting with an overgrip, changing one hand, and pirouetting forward.

a.

b.

c.

d.

e.

f.

during the turn. You want to be as straight from your hand to your toes as possible. That is your strongest position. As soon as your alignment is not as straight as this, your body can turn through a conical path rather than right on top of your hand, and your shoulder angle can change further, which will cause a poor turn.

Performing this skill involves a shift of the plane of your body. You should be able to do a pirouette on the floor mat with this action. To do a forward pirouette on your left arm from a cast with a double undergrip or mixed grip (left hand in undergrip), as you approach your handstand, move your whole body over your left hand. Look down your left arm, and keep it in line with your trunk and legs—as straight a line as possible. Push off with your right hand, turn around by pulling the right side of your body back, and regrasp in a double overgrip. For a front pirouette on your left arm from a double overgrip, you cast up and either change your left hand to an undergrip and then turn on that hand, or you turn on your left hand without changing it, resulting in a left hand eagle-grip before you change it back to an overgrip. The first method is the better of the two. To accomplish that hand change you have to lean over on your right hand momentarily to take the weight off your left hand, make your change, then push off with your right hand and turn your body around. This move is a B-level skill for girls.

Common problems are not moving over, not keeping a straight alignment during the turn, and beginning the turn after you pass your handstand.

Do as you would for a cast to handstand, providing guidance if necessary. You may stand on either side of your student.

■

Spotting

To a Handstand With Hop Change of Grip (Figure 12.48)

Another skill combining a cast to handstand and a grip change is a hop from overgrip to undergrip. When you first learn this, lean forward excessively so that the hop change is a bit easier to do, and so that you will fall over toward your back as you should. To get the lift necessary to make the hop easy, you must have a strong cast, and you must push down with your shoulders harder than you have for other cast handstand skills as you approach vertical, and thus get vertical lift, enabling you to take your hands off the bar and turn them around. Keep your eyes on the bar at all times so you see where to put your hands. As you regrasp, push into a stretched alignment and proceed into a fall with your back leading—put a safety cushion down below the bar so that you have a cushioned contact with the floor mats, or have your spotter hold you in a handstand and help you lower to the bar or into the fall. This is a B-level move for girls.

As a lead up, you can change one hand rather than two. Change your right hand on one attempt, then change your left hand on your next attempt. If you are fast, you can change both hands in sequence on one cast before changing them simultaneously.

Common problems are not pushing down on the bar hard enough, catching with bent arms, pushing back (due to not leaning forward enough), which makes the regrasp difficult, and not finishing in a stretched handstand.

Stand on an elevated platform behind the bar and hold your student as you would for a cast to handstand. Be ready to hold him up if he has a problem with the regrasp.

■

Spotting

Figure 12.48a, b, c, d, e, f
Aside from breaking form, Eli does this cast to hop change well.

a.

b.

c.

d.

e.

f.

Stem Rises—UPB

A single-leg (figure 12.49) or a double-leg (figure 12.50) stem rise on the uneven bars is a lead up to a kip. For a single-leg stem rise, hang in an overgrip on the upper bar facing the low bar, put one foot on the lower bar, and bring your other leg upward so that that foot is by the upper bar. Push on the low bar with your bent leg, hold your other leg up by the upper bar, and pull down with your arms, keeping your arms straight. Pull directly to a front support on the upper bar. It takes a good bit of strength to pull down, and you can practice the motion by extending your leg that is on the lower bar a few times to see what the swing feels like. Then, as you extend powerfully, yank down on the bar, keeping your

Figure 12.49a, b, c, d, e

a.   b.   c.   d.   e.

Figure 12.50a, b, c, d, e

a.   b.   c.   d.   e.

upper straight leg very close to the bar. The bar will move from your foot down to your hip area on your straight leg. Your lower foot will leave the low bar before your hips reach the upper bar.

The double-leg stem rise involves putting both feet on the lower bar and extending both legs while pulling down powerfully on the upper bar. Like the single-leg stem rise, your feet will leave the lower bar before your hips contact the upper bar.

The biggest problem with this skill is not having enough upper body strength. If you cannot pull the bar to your hips hard enough, you will not make it. Your arms should be kept straight, but probably in the beginning stages your arms will have to bend a bit, as you will not be strong enough to do it with straight arms.

The figures show spotting from the right. For both skills, stand below your student with your left hand on her lower back or seat and your right hand under her legs. Help her get to the front support by pushing her hips up to the upper bar.

■

Spotting

Kips and Combinations

There is a variety of kips done on both the horizontal bar and the uneven parallel bars. These moves bring you from an underbar hang to a support. They are done from a long hang swing, a short swing or seated start on the low bar (on the UPB), a drop, and a glide swing. The kip action described in the next section on a drop kip is the same used for all kips. With the exception of a kip going directly into a forward hip circle (which uses a high, stretched front support to start the circle) and a flying kip, all kips should finish—or at least pass through a position—with the bar touching your lower abdomen where your hips flex and with your hips flexed a bit. This way you will be in a position to cast directly from the kip (discussed shortly). All kips should be done with straight arms.

Common problems for all kips are being too weak to pull your body to the bar or to get your legs into position soon enough or to hold them near the bar on the way up, bending your arms, mistiming the start of your kipping action, and pulling your chest up too slowly (which will hinder any casting or grip-changing-at-the-bar combinations).

■

Spotting

Spotting a kip is very similar to spotting the single knee rise. From the left, put your left hand under your student's legs and your right hand on his/her lower back. If needed, push him/her close to the bar to help the kip finish in a front support.

Drop Kip (Figure 12.51)

A drill often done to develop strength for kipping is doing a series of drop kips. Start in a front support with an overgrip. Push back slightly, lift your legs by piking, and keep your trunk upright somewhat—you do not want to turn over a lot here. As you drop below the bar, your legs stay close to the bar, and the bar moves down your legs from your hips to your toes. Once you get to this position, you will find that you are swinging forward under the bar. Your legs may move away from the bar as you go under, but you will pull them back to the bar as you begin your kip. Keep your shoulder angle open as much as possible during this underbar period—it will allow you to have a full pull into your kip. Once you stop going forward and begin to swing back, do the kip by extending your hips rapidly and pulling the bar to your hips along your legs—keep your legs close to the bar. This action is like pulling your pants on with straight arms. You will finish in a front support. Repeat this several times to get the feeling.

Short Kip—UPB (Figure 12.52)

This kip is shown as done from a swing and straddle over to a seat. It is a bit easier to start than some others. Since you are starting from a seated position on the low bar, you can lift your legs up a bit more easily than if you were in a swing such as a glide swing. The kip action is the same as for the drop kip. You want to pull your feet to the upper bar rapidly so that they get there early in your swing backward.

Figure 12.51a, b, c, d, e, f

a.   b.   c.

d.   e.   f.

Long Hang Kip (Figures 12.53 and 12.54)

On the horizontal bar, this is simply called a swing to kip, as only women have to differentiate between long hang swings outward and short swings inward. From either a long hang swing forward on the UPB, or a forward swing on the HB, as you approach the end of your front swing, pike rapidly and bring your feet to the bar, then perform a kip. You will find that as you are able to swing higher and higher, you will begin your kip from higher up on your legs than your feet. This will allow you to control the greater swing that you will have before your kip.

The same sort of kip can be done from an undergrip. This is tougher because your hands are not on top of the bar when you are yanking down, so an

Figure 12.52a, b, c, d, e, f, g, h, i

a. b. c. d.

e. f. g. h. i.

undergrip kip is harder to learn. It will involve a shifting of your hands, so you have to be able to initiate this kip with a very hard downward pull. If you bend your arms at the start of this kip, the bar may head for your mouth (and you are not in a strong position to push on the bar), so be aware of this.

Glide Kip—UPB (Figure 12.55)

On the uneven bars, a glide kip is used as a mount or connection element. This is similar to what is done on the men's parallel bars. But on UPB, you can do a glide swing with your legs straddled or together. To start this, the lead-up exercise is simply a glide swing. Stand next to the low bar, place your hands in an overgrip on the low bar with your body piked so that there is a straight line from your hands to hips through your shoulders, then do a partial squat and jump up a bit off the mat or a vaulting board, pushing your seat back and lifting your feet in front of you. Swing forward with your feet only a few inches above the mat all the way out to an extended position in front, and then return to your starting position by flexing your hips as you swing back. If you are strong enough for this, do the glide kip—just after you extend (forcefully) at the front of your swing, flex your hips rapidly to bring your toes to the bar and kip.

Figure 12.53a, b, c, d, e, f, g, h, i, j

a.

b.

c.

d.

e.

f.

g.

h.

i.

j.

As a drill, just as drop kips can be repeated, you can do a series of casts and drops to glide kips. Instead of dropping directly down, cast back away from the bar and push into a partially piked position. When you pass through the position you were in when you jumped to the glide, proceed with your glide kip. As you finish each kip, cast directly to another drop.

Instead of starting while holding the bar, stand behind it and jump to the glide—as you jump, reach for the bar, then pull your legs forward into a pike position and proceed into the glide (figure 12.56). Smaller students will have to jump up more than larger ones. Then work on a switch-glide (figure 12.57). This is where you do a straddled glide swing and in front of the swing you cross your legs, causing your body to do a half turn. If you turn to the left, your right leg crosses over your left leg. Your hands do a rapid change from overgrip to mixed grip to overgrip or hop from overgrip to overgrip, and then another glide is done.

Common problems are being too weak to lift your legs at the end of the glide, bending your arms or not leaving your shoulder angle open at the beginning of your glide, and bending your arms as you kip.

■ Spotting

Stand next to the performer on the front side of the bar and assist in the glide if she is not strong enough to keep her feet from hitting the mat. You generally just assist her to lift her legs up to the bar and then provide a bit of lift under her lower back to help her to achieve a support. If her glide is done in a straddled position, you cannot stand in close in front of the bar during the glide because you will get hit by her leg. Move in to help after her leg passes by.

Figure 12.54a, b, c, d

a.

b.

c.

d.

Figure 12.55a, b, c, d, e, f, g, h, i, j

a.

b.

c.

d.

e.

f.

g.

h.

i.

j.

a.

b.

c.

Figure 12.57a, b, c, d, e, f

a.

b.

c.

d.

e.

f.

Figure 12.58a, b, c, d, e, f, g

a.   b.   c.   d.

e.   f.   g.

Jump With Half Turn to a Kip—UPB (Figure 12.58)

This method of starting a kip can be later done by jumping from a vaulting board over the low bar to a catch and kip on the high bar, which is a higher level skill. To perform it from the mat, stand facing the low bar and back a bit, so that when you jump and twist to catch the low bar, your body is extended. If you are too close, you cannot achieve this extension. As soon as you grasp the low bar, proceed with a kip. This happens fast, as you do not get to set up for your kip with a swing as you usually do.

Common problems are being too close to jump to a good position, and not twisting enough when jumping.

Kip to Cast

All of the casts covered earlier can be done directly from a kip. In fact, that is how you see them in a routine. Being able to cast to a handstand opens up a whole world of kip combinations for you. To perform them, you want to finish your kip in a piked support (until you learn more powerful kips). You pull up very hard, and learn to shrug your shoulders (elevate your shoulders) so that

a.   b.   c.   d.

the bar can stay where your hips flex. You may have to flex your elbows a bit at first to pull the bar to this position. Upon achieving support, extend your hips powerfully and continue into the cast. This can be done with an overgrip, undergrip, or mixed grip. When you first learn this, you may lay on the bar before casting, but as you become quicker you will not have to.

An additional common problem is finishing your kip with extended hips so you cannot cast.

Kip Change (Figure 12.59)

In addition to a kip and cast where your hands stay in one position, there is a variety of other types of kips involving hand changes. The first method is to do a kip change (this hand change is done at the bar). Do an overgrip kip and pull up so powerfully that as you yank up to a support position, the weight comes off your hands a bit. At this point, while your body is in a piked position, quickly change your hands from overgrip to undergrip, and then continue casting up to a handstand. It is sometimes easier to learn this hand-change action doing a forward hip circle and changing as you come on top of the bar in a pike. At first you may lay on the bar to do the hand change, but this will pass as you develop strength. If you have trouble changing both hands, change one, and then change the other. You can cast to a handstand with a mixed grip from a single-hand kip change as well. Although at first most students change with bent arms, eventually you will move quickly enough to do it with straight arms. That is the key—you must pull your chest up rapidly.

The common problems here are not pulling up hard enough and not changing your hands quickly.

Hop to Flying Kip (Figure 12.60)

I am combining two skills here. To do a hop to a kip, swing underneath the bar, and as you swing forward, lift your feet hard to perform a hop change from overgrip to undergrip (covered earlier), but continue lifting your feet and pressing back on the bar with your hands to get into the undergrip kip position. A flying kip, also called a straight body kip, is an undergrip kip that is done with a large

Figure 12.60a, b, c, d, e, f, g, h, i
Stephan should push on the bar to open his
shoulder angle more in figure d; otherwise
this is well done.

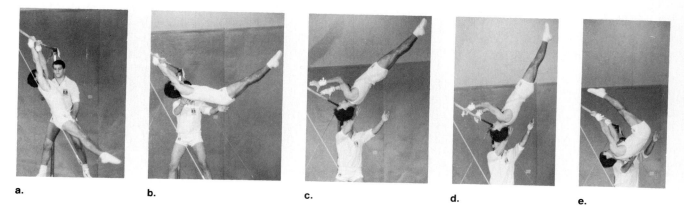

a.   b.   c.   d.   e.

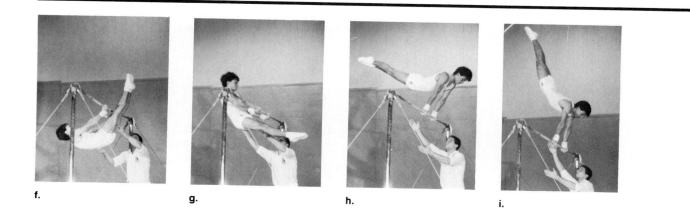

f.   g.   h.   i.

amount of swing. Here, once the kipping action is initiated, your body straightens
quickly and goes directly up to a handstand without passing through a piked
support position and without touching the bar. This is done by yanking down
very hard on the bar to achieve a support quickly and extending your hips rapidly.
When learning this skill, often you will not pull your shoulders over the
top of the bar enough and wind up shy of a handstand behind the bar. If you
do not pull down hard enough on the bar to keep the bar close to your body,
then the other general performance flaw comes in: You fly away from the bar
backward and often below it. This will not happen if you are strong enough,
but it sometimes takes a while to develop the strength to hold the bar in close.
As you swing higher in the front, you will have to pull the bar to a position
farther up your legs than your feet. This will help you to control the large swing.
When this kip comes from a swing near or at a handstand, in the USA it is
sometimes called a Weiler kip (pronounced: wy'-ler), named after Canadian
gymnast Willy Weiler, who performed a similar move from an undergrip giant
swing—although he was not the first gymnast to do such a move.

Figure 12.61a, b, c, d, e, f, g, h, i

a.   b.   c.   d.   e.

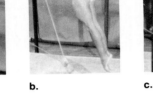

f.   g.   h.   i.

The common problem with the hop is not pushing back on the bar when you regrasp, which allows your shoulders to close and reduce your pull. For the flying kip, not pulling your shoulders over the bar enough is the usual problem.

■
Spotting

Stand below your student and assist if needed, combining the spots for a hop change and a kip.

Between-Bar Skills—UPB

Drop From the High Bar and Catch the Low Bar (Figure 12.61)

This is a connection used to get into a glide movement on the low bar from a hang on the high bar. If you are facing the low bar and have a small swing (it can be done from a still hang as well), as you swing away from the low bar, pull on the top bar to round your body and pike your shoulders. Then, as you start to swing toward the low bar, arch your body hard, throw the top bar back, and

Figure 12.62a, b, c, d, e, f

a.   b.   c.

d.   e.   f.

release your grasp. You will drop toward the low bar and will then grasp it in an overgrip and proceed to a glide swing and another movement. Try it first with a soft mat under the low bar, since if you miss the recatch you will land on your feet but if you come off during the glide you will land on your seat. Keep in mind that the farther your bars are spread, the stronger your throw will have to be.

The common problem here is not timing your arch and release well—if you throw off the top bar early you will not reach the low bar. Also it takes some strength to hold on and do a glide from this drop.

Kip Catch (Figure 12.62)

This skill requires a strong kip, as you will let go of the low bar and regrasp the high bar, so you need to have some lift. It is done with your back facing the high bar. As you perform your kip and yank down hard, look at the top bar and reach for it when you feel you are lifting above the low bar. If you miss your grasp, you will land on your feet under the top bar.

The common problem is a lack of kipping strength.

Figure 12.63a, b, c, d, e, f
Other than a form break, this straddle over mount is well done.

a.

b.

c.

d.

e.

f.

Spotting

Stand next to your student and help her reach the top bar if necessary. Otherwise, just see that she lands on her feet if she misses the recatch.

Jumps Over the Low Bar to the High Bar—UPB (Figure 12.63)

These mounts are done as you would do a squat or straddle vault, and they are done from a vaulting board. You should be able to perform those vaults safely before trying these skills. Begin facing the bars from the low bar side. Take a few running steps, hurdle to the board, reach for the low bar, and perform a squat or straddle over the low bar. As you do this, quickly shift your eyes from the low bar to the high bar. When your hands release the low bar, reach for the high bar and proceed into a long hang swing.

a.

b.

c.

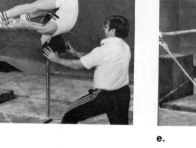

d.

e.

f.

Common problems are not jumping hard enough to clear the bar, not pushing down on the low bar to get your chest up and to facilitate the recatch on the high bar, and reaching late.

Stand under the high bar facing your oncoming student. As she goes over the low bar, watch to be sure that she clears the bar, and then catch her if she misses catching the high bar.

Spotting

Sole Circles (Figures 12.64 and 12.65)

I described casting up to a toe-on position and a sole circle dismount earlier. A sole circle, so named because the soles of your feet are in contact with the bar, can be done forward or backward. It can be done with your legs straddled or together (also called a stooped sole circle). A straddled backward sole circle

Figure 12.65a, b, c, d, e, f, g, h
Danny should not hook his feet during his cast and as he finishes his forward sole circle.

a.

b.

c.

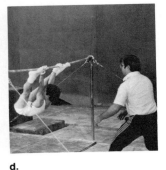
d.

e.

f.

g.

h.

starts from a position above the bar. Your legs are not spread very wide here; these circles are done with your legs somewhat close—no more than 90° apart, preferably narrower. Keep the bar just behind the balls of your feet. Push down on the bar with your pointed feet to lock into position. Your back will be rounded so that your lower back is as far from the bar as possible. You will feel pressure on the bottoms of your feet and on the insides of your hands. Push your seat back a bit to begin your drop. As you pass below the bar and start to swing up, you may have to bend your legs to pull closer to the bar to generate the velocity necessary to get back on top of the bar. Your spotter can help at this point. As you get better, you will cast up and not do a toe-on right away, but will drop around the bar a bit before doing the toe-on to generate more momentum than you would if you started your drop touching the bar. Eventually you will be able to cast to a handstand, start to drop far away from the bar, and toe-on as you drop to around bar height. With these bigger drops you will be able to keep your legs straight and still finish the sole circle. Eventually you will be able to lift off from the bar and push directly to a handstand from this circle. And much later you will be able to do this skill from a giant swing and to a giant swing (this is often called a toe-on toe-off).

The same sort of circle can be done forward in an undergrip. The same considerations and progressions apply. After passing the bottom of the swing, you will have to pull on the bar and maintain that pressure on the bar with your feet to keep from slipping off. Like the backward sole circle, at first you may

a. b. c. d.

e. f. g. h.

have to bend your legs to increase your rotational velocity to get back on top of the bar, but as you learn to toe-on later (eventually from a handstand) you will be able to get around with more ease.

The common flaw here is not having enough pressure on your feet to keep them on the bar, so that when you hit the bottom of the swing your feet fly away and you drop. (This can be a potential danger to a spotter, so the spotter should be aware there is a possibility that feet might be flying at him or her.)

Stand on the uprise side of the bar and reach underneath your student's rising body. Help him up to a support by lifting him. For the backward sole circle, reach under his shoulders as he rises. For the forward sole circle, reach under his seat or thighs.

Spotting

Drop Back and Overshoot (Figure 12.66)

The drop back and overshoot (or basket swing) is the start of a series of skills that circle around the bar in a piked rear support. (See the description of a peach basket in chapter 11 for a probable explanation of the name "basket

Horizontal Bar and Uneven Parallel Bars

swing.") Begin in a rear support with an overgrip. Lift your legs up through an L position, push down and back, and you will start a drop to an underbar swing through a piked inverted hang. After you swing forward (seat leading) in a tight pike, as you swing back, do the overshoot by pushing down on the bar and pushing your legs over the bar. Finish in a rear support with the bar by your seat.

Common problems are turning over either too much or too little when you push to initiate the drop portion. If your seat is too low on the drop it will continue to drop as you pass through the bottom of your swing and will either cause your legs to strike the bar or your feet to come through your hands. If your seat is too high, it will cause your body to turn over too much, and you will probably continue turning over once you hit the bottom of the swing and wind up in a hang rearways. Therefore, it is important to know where a balanced position is in a piked inverted hang—your legs should be horizontal when you pass the bottom of your swing.

■

Spotting

Stand behind the bar to the side. Keep your hands below your student to aid in positioning her throughout the move. If she needs help getting back up, provide lift. If she drops back poorly you can prevent her from flying off at the bottom.

Glide to Straddle-up to Rear Support—UPB (Figure 12.67)

This begins in the same manner as a glide kip. If you straddle your legs as you lift them from the glide, you should be able to pull them past your arms as you swing back. Once your feet are past the bar, push the bar down as if you want to push it below your seat. Keep your legs away from the bar at the start, but as you rise up you can let them come near the bar so that you finish in a straddled piked rear support or a straddled seat. From here, you can reach for the high bar and do a swinging skill. If you go past a support, be ready to regrasp or push off, since you will have the wrong grip for a forward circle.

Common problems are pulling your legs in too slowly, and not pushing down enough on the bar on the way up so that your seat drops and your legs hit the bar.

■

Spotting

Stand behind the bar and grasp your student's waist as she swings up behind the bar. You can stop her on top of the bar if you feel she is moving too fast to control the end of the skill.

Stoop-in From a Hang and Overshoot (Figures 12.68 and 12.69)

There are a number of stoop-in movements done on the bar, both from below and above. Stooping in under the bar is a bit easier than over the bar, since above the bar you have to support your weight, whereas under the bar you are in a swinging hang and mainly have to lift your legs. This underbar swing can be a hanging swing on a high bar with an undergrip, mixed grip, or overgrip, or a glide swing on a low bar with an overgrip. Although almost every gymnast

Figure 12.67a, b, c, d, e, f

a.

b.

c.

d.

e.

f.

hooks his/her feet momentarily as they pass the bar on a stoop-in, if you can learn not to do this, you will be a more refined performer.

As you swing forward, just as you reach the end of your swing, pike rapidly and bring your legs directly next to your body. Keep your arms overhead as much as possible to maximize the distance between your hands and your hips. This way you will be able to bring your legs between your arms as you begin to swing backward. As you continue going backward, turn over a bit and hold your legs next to your body so that they point close to horizontal by the time you pass under the bar. As you rise up in the back, your tightly piked body rotates around the bar so that as you get bar-high your legs are vertical. Push down on the bar with both hands, and push your seat over the bar, lowering your legs, to finish in a rear support. If you go past the rear support with an undergrip, just hold on and you can either do another overshoot from the fall forward (which is a forward seat circle and is covered later) or squeeze the bar to slow down, which will allow you to get off below. If you have an overgrip or mixed grip, be ready to regrasp. As a further challenge, you can do a hop change from overgrip to undergrip followed by a stoop-in to overshoot.

Figure 12.68a, b, c, d
A stoop-in from a hang swing on HB.

a.   b.   c.   d.

Figure 12.69a, b, c, d, e, f
A stoop-in and overshoot from a glide swing
on UPB.

a.   b.   c.   d.

e.   f.

Figure 12.70a, b, c, d

a.　　　　　　b.　　　　　　c.　　　　　　d.

If you are not strong enough to bring both legs through, try to bring one leg through. This will be a single-leg stoop-in and overshoot in a fashion similar to the double-leg action. As you swing forward, instead of flexing both hips, flex one and pull that leg between your arms (your other leg remains away from your body). Push down on the bar to force your leg over the bar, and pull the bar down toward your back leg. You will finish in a stride support.

Common problems are not lifting your legs fast enough, closing your shoulder angle (leaving full flexion) too much to allow your legs to come through, not pushing down on the bar as you go up, and not piking tightly enough through the bottom of your swing.

Stand just in front of the bar to the side. Put your right hand on the performer's back, your left hand on her seat, then assist her by pushing her body over the bar. Be ready to stop her in case she goes past a rear support, especially if she has an overgrip.

■

Spotting

Cut-Catch

Single Leg (Figure 12.70)

A few other stooping skills that lead to release moves are cut-catch skills. For the simplest, as you finish your forward swing, bring your left leg between your arms. As you rise behind the bar, push that leg to the outside and release the bar with your left hand, then regrasp right away with an overgrip. Do this with your other leg, too. If you can swing enough so that you rise over the bar a bit, your chest moves forward, making your recatch easier. There is slight downward push on the bar. This is a lead up to a straddled cut-catch, which is a movement where both hands are released and regrasped.

Common problems are not rotating your trunk forward as you cut, bending your leg as you stoop in, and not swinging enough.

Figure 12.71a, b, c, d, e, f

a.   b.   c.   d.

e.   f.

■

Spotting

For a left cut, stand behind the bar on your student's right. Support his lower back with your left hand and his right thigh with your right hand. Be ready to reach for his front side with your right hand in case he misses the regrasp.

Double Leg Flank (Figure 12.71)
The same skill can be done with both legs together doing the cut. (Flank refers to a sideward movement.) It can also be done from a drop back. The action, problems, and spotting are similar.

Straddled (Figure 12.72)
Here you combine the overshoot with a release-regrasp. This skill is usually done from an overgrip underswing or a drop back to overshoot swing, although higher level versions have it done with an undergrip and from a forward seat circle.

Figure 12.72a, b, c, d, e
A straddled cut-catch from a glide swing on
UPB.

a.

b.

c.

d.

e.

As you reach the end of your forward underswing, rapidly stoop your legs between your hands and start to overshoot. As you rise over the bar, spread your legs and pull your seat back, which rotates your trunk forward, while releasing the bar with both hands. Look at the bar throughout the skill. Regrasp as soon as you can. With a big swing you can begin the cut with your feet over and past the top of the bar, and you will finish with your shoulders above the bar. This is a B-level skill for girls.

Common problems are not swinging enough to get high enough to recatch, releasing too early, starting the cut when you are moving too slowly, and pushing your stoop-through too much so that you land on the bar.

Stand behind your student, and move in as she is rising. When first learning this skill, a performer tends not to rotate into the bar because she is not strong enough to accomplish that, so you stand with your hands on her back or on her waist and give her support to allow her to recatch.

■

Spotting

a.   b.   c.   d.

Straddled Cut Dismount (Figure 12.73)

If you go through the action of the straddled cut-catch and do not regrasp, it turns into an elementary dismount. As long as you are rotating forward a bit as you release, you will land on your feet behind the bar. If you do not rotate enough, you may land on your seat, which is usually not a dangerous fall.

Spotting

Stand as you would for the cut-catch. Guide your student to an upright landing if needed.

Seat Circles

If the overshoot movements are all mastered, then it should be easy to learn seat circles. These are called seat circles because your seat faces the bar.

Backward (Figure 12.74)

Start in a rear support with an overgrip. Lift your legs through an L to a tightly piked position and push backward a bit, pushing your piked body as far from the bar as you can on the way down, but keeping the backs of your legs facing the bar. The more you push away, the more momentum you will generate for your circle. Stay in that position until you are on your way up in front, when you pull on the bar a bit to bring your weight closer to the bar. This speeds up your rotation and enables you to get back on top of the bar, finishing in a piked rear support. If you want to finish in an open rear support, as you pass below bar height, pull the bar into your seat and rapidly open from your pike into an arch. This is the same action that is used to do a back kip, which is described next.

Common problems are not passing the bottom in a balanced position (which allows your trunk to tip either way as you pass the bottom) and not piking tightly enough on the way down so that you collapse into a deep pike at the bottom (which slows your swing).

Figure 12.74a, b, c, d, e, f

a.

b.

c.

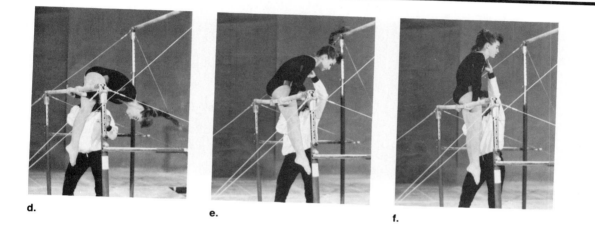

d.

e.

f.

Figure 12.75

The positions of the spotter's hands at the start of a back seat circle.

a.   b.   c.

d.   e.   f.

■

Spotting

Stand in front of the bar to your student's side. Reach under and around the bar with your pronated right hand and grasp her left wrist (figure 12.75). Your left hand can help lift her from the bar to start the circle. As the skill is finishing, reach under her chest or left shoulder with your left hand and push her up over the bar if needed.

Backward Kip (Figure 12.76)

The backward (or back) kip is an overgrip skill that combines a stoop-in, an overshoot action, and the end of a back seat circle. After you do the stoop-in, rise up behind the bar by pushing down on the bar and opening your body slightly. Your legs should be vertical, and you can rise so that your seat goes above the level of the bar. As your body begins to descend, push away from the bar to develop your swing. As you pass below bar height, pull the bar into your seat and rapidly open from your pike into an arch. In doing this you will circle around the bar, touching the bar with your seat in an arched position.

Common problems are opening too late, pulling the backs of your thighs to the bar instead of your seat (usually because you drop your seat through your arms too much on the way down), and allowing your seat to move away from the bar on the way up.

■ Spotting

I use two methods for spotting this skill. For the first, which is similar to the spot for a back seat circle, I stand in front of the bar to the left side of my student. As she drops below bar height, I reach under the bar with my right hand for her left thigh or knee and reach under her trunk or left shoulder with my left hand. Both hands push on her to keep her close to the bar and to key her on when to open from her pike to an arch. If I am concerned that she may have trouble under the bar, I may grasp her left wrist with my right hand, just as with a back seat circle. The second method is done behind the bar. As she begins her descent, I hold her legs with both arms (I wrap my arms around them) and keep her legs from circling too far under the bar while I hold her seat in a position close to the bar, so that if she opens up she will make the skill easily. If she does not open well, I have to hold her up and maneuver her to a rear support. This works better with small students than with large ones. It also makes them work their back and seat muscles, which tells them which muscles make them arch.

Forward (Figure 12.77)

A forward seat circle uses an undergrip. Begin in a seated position on the bar. Lift to an L support, and bring your legs up closer to your body so that you are tightly piked. Freeze in this position, and lean forward a bit to begin your circle. Push as far away from the bar as you can, bringing your legs closer to your body. Like the back seat circle, you have to be in a balanced piked inverted hang under the bar, because if you are not in that balanced position, your shoulder position may change, causing your seat or feet to drop and causing you to miss the circle. As you come up behind the bar, pull the bar down. You will finish in a rear support again—this can be an open rear support or a piked rear support. If you go past the rear support, just do another circle. Do not panic. Sometimes you start well enough so that you have enough momentum for several circles, and eventually you will learn to control your swing by varying your body position and squeezing the bar. As you progress, you will start from a higher position by lifting your seat and pushing down hard on the bar to start far from the bar, and you will come up with enough power to shoot out toward a handstand and go through a dislocate action with your shoulders, which results in an eaglegrip, and is often seen on the horizontal bar (this is covered later).

If you can stoop-in from a support (figure 12.79), this ability will lead you into a more powerful seat circle. Cast up, and as you bring your legs between your hands, pull them into your body so they point down, and go directly into the seat circle. It often helps to think of pointing your legs forward and down. You will learn to do this stoop-in from higher and higher positions until you can do it from a handstand. Be sure to push hard on the bar to keep your shoulders from falling forward early and to maximize your hand-to-hip distance before your legs come in.

Common problems are starting too close to the bar so you do not develop momentum, pointing your legs back and down at the start, starting too open so that you compress at the bottom (which reduces your swing), not maintaining a solid position as you circle underneath, and not pulling on the way up.

a.

b.

c.

d.

e.

f.

Figure 12.78
The position of the spotter's hands at the start of a front seat circle.

Figure 12.79a, b, c, d
A cast to a stoop-in.

a. b. c. d.

Stand on the back side of the bar next to your student. Reach under and around the bar with your pronated left hand, holding your student's left wrist just as you did for a stride circle (figure 12.78). As he begins the circle, your right hand can be used to put his legs in a proper position or help push off the bar. As his circle passes the bottom, your right hand reaches underneath his seat or lower back to assist him in getting over the bar. At the finish on top, your hands go underneath him to stabilize his position.

Sometimes it is helpful for a beginner to just try to circle the bar in a solid L position, without thinking of piking tightly, to get the feeling of circling. This requires assistance from his teacher, as it is doubtful that he will get around.

Forward Straddled (Figure 12.80)

Just as you learned to do a sole circle forward and backward, you can learn a straddled seat circle, which is the lead up to higher level moves called an Endo shoot and a Stalder shoot (named after the great gymnasts Yukio Endo and Josef Stalder), which usually start and end in a handstand. In fact, these circles are often referred to as Endo circles and Stalder circles. (Since Stalder did his move first, some refer to the Endo as a front Stalder.) The principle governing these circles is the same as the one governing all circling movements: If you start away from the bar on the downswing, and then come in toward the bar on the upswing, you will generate the necessary rotation to get back over the bar and will successfully complete your circle.

For the Endo (forward) circle, begin in a straddled L support with an undergrip. Lift your seat up and bring your legs as close to your shoulders as you can. Lean forward and begin your circle. As you pass the bottom, pull the bar toward your seat and pull your shoulders over the bar. Looking over the bar will help. Keep your legs far from the bar, and hold them up as you go over the bar.

Common problems are not compressing enough on the way down so that you collapse into a tight pike at the bottom (which reduces your swing), not being in a balanced position at the bottom so that you tip forward or backward (which often kills your swing), and not pulling down hard enough as you rise.

Figure 12.80a, b, c, d, e, f
Aside from flexed knees, Maureen does this
Endo circle well—to generate more
downswing, she will learn to push farther
away at the start.

a.

b.

c.

d.

e.

f.

■

Spotting

Stand behind. As your student rises, reach under her seat or grasp her waist and push her up if needed. Before introducing my student to ideal technique, I have found it helpful for some to simply try to go around the bar in a bent-legged straddled seat circle without trying to push away from the bar, just to get the feel of the move.

Backward Straddled (Figure 12.81)

The Stalder (backward) circle is done in a similar fashion. Begin in a straddled L support with an overgrip. Push up and back from the bar to start the circle, pulling your legs as close to your shoulders as you can. As you drop, keep pushing on the bar so that you compress well before you hit bottom. At the bottom, turn

Figure 12.81a, b, c, d
Jill's legs could be farther from the bar at
the beginning.

a.

b.

c.

d.

over more so that your feet are pointing at the floor as you rise. Pull your seat over the bar with straight arms. You will have to pull with your wrists as well in order to shift your hands over the bar.

Common problems are bending your arms as you finish the skill, not compressing enough on the way down, not turning over enough to pass the bottom in a balanced position, and not continuing to turn over as you rise.

Stand on the front side of the bar, reaching under your student's shoulders or grasping her waist as she rises to push her up if necessary. If she comes out early, watch out that you do not get hit by flying feet. Like the Endo circle, it sometimes helps to go around the bar without refined technique to get a feel for the move.

■

Spotting

a.

b.

c.

d.

e.

f.

Flyaway Dismounts—HB

Flyaways are generally taught from a bar-high swing first, then from a near-handstand swing (perhaps from a support cast), and finally from a giant swing. They can be learned well before a giant swing is learned, but with a giant swing preceding them, they can go quite high and be spectacular. I use a method that teaches you to orient yourself in the gymnasium visually, and do not teach a tap swing until later on to simplify matters. Some students tap naturally, without instruction.

Backward (Figures 12.82, 12.83 and 12.84)

A back flyaway is a back salto done with an overgrip on the forward upswing from the bar to a landing in front of the bar. While you are swinging, find a point to look at on the wall in front of you that is 10°–30° above horizontal at

Figure 12.83a, b, c, d, e
A piked back flyaway from a large swing.
Note the toe hook in figure c.

a.   b.   c.

d.   e.

the height of the bar. Keep your eyes on this point during your swinging both forward and backward. This gives you an orientation point—a place to spot— for a large portion of your swing. You will be able to see your toes pass through your point as you swing up in the front. Then all you have to do is swing up and kick your feet through that point, let go of the bar when your feet pass your point, and rotate around to your feet. When you release the bar you can look back for the mat (after you see your feet pass your point). I prefer to teach this flyaway in a pike position so that you learn to lift with straight legs, although it is less difficult to rotate in a tuck and many coaches teach it tucked, having

Figure 12.84a, b, c, d, e
A layout flyaway from a giant swing.

a.

b.

c.

d.

e.

you lift your knees rather than your feet. I feel it is easy to do a tucked flyaway after a piked lift, and the piked lift lends itself to learning a layout flyaway better than a tuck.

After you feel comfortable with a small swing, try a big swing or a cast to a swing. Learn to look for your spot when you pass by bar height on the way down, and you will be able to see it for a good portion of your large swing or giant swing. If you are getting a good swing, you can do a flyaway in layout position. As you lift your feet and release, instead of continuing to lift into a pike, extend your body into a layout. If you are doing this very well and from a big swing or giant swing, you may find that you have a tendency to overrotate. This is caused by a strong kick. To counteract this, you may have to push back on the bar just as you release to reduce your rotation a bit. A good guideline is to land 6–8 feet from the bar when doing your flyaway from a big swing or giant swing.

The most common problem is not letting go at the correct place that will give you lift and rotation but not bring you close to the bar. It is very important to not let go before you see your toes pass that orientation point. If you let go too early, you will fly out and possibly down. If you let go too late, way past that, you will come close to the bar. Other problems that are often encountered are kicking too early, and bending your arms or breaking your straight shoulder angle just prior to release, which again brings you in closer to the bar. You do not want to do that—the spring steel bar is hard! If you swing lower than the bar you can still do a flyaway, but it will not lift or rotate as well.

Spotting

This can be hand spotted (easy with small students) or spotted with an overhead belt. Standing to the side in front of the bar, put your left hand under your student's back and your right hand on his abdomen. You can lift and guide him to a landing. With the overhead belt, you can hold him up easily and observe his technique from a distance. For dismounts, the overhead belt should be attached to the ceiling so that it hangs around 6–8 feet along the mat from the bar. When your student can do giant swings (discussed shortly), you can spot the flyaway from giants by wrapping the ropes around the bar an equal number of times to the number of giants he will do prior to his flyaway. **NOTE**: Be sure to wrap the ropes the opposite way that his giants go! Check the situation out carefully before he goes for the combination.

Forward (Figure 12.85)

A front flyaway is a little harder than the back flyaway, as the release position is a little weaker, and the landing is blind—it follows a front somersault. It is learned from a high swing first, then from a giant. As you swing up in the back with an undergrip, arch hard to lift your heels, just as you did when you did a back uprise. Keep your eyes on the bar to see when you are level with the bar. At the point that you pass bar height, release the bar and perform a forward somersault in a tuck, pike, or layout. As you turn over, if you pull your head forward to look for the bar or the wall beyond the bar (you will be able to see it once you turn over), you will be able to orient yourself for the landing. Although the flyaway can be done with less swing than going over the bar level, obviously it will be tougher to rotate and lift with less swing. As you release, do not pull down on the bar at all—this will slow or stop your rotation. If you constantly underrotate, you may have to push up on the bar as you release.

Common problems are releasing too early, bending your arms (which pulls you in toward the bar), not arching hard into your release, or pulling down on the bar as you release (which will slow your rotation and may bring you in toward the bar).

Spotting

This can be hand spotted (easy with small students) or spotted with an overhead belt. Standing to the side in back of the bar, put your right hand under your student's abdomen and your left hand on his back as he swings up. Lift and guide him to a landing. With an overhead belt, you can hold him up easily and observe his technique from a distance. Read the previous section (on a back flyaway) for advice about spotting a flyaway from a giant swing with an overhead belt.

Figure 12.85a, b, c, d, e, f
Stephan should lift his heels more prior to release when doing this tucked front flyaway from a big swing.

a.

b.

c.

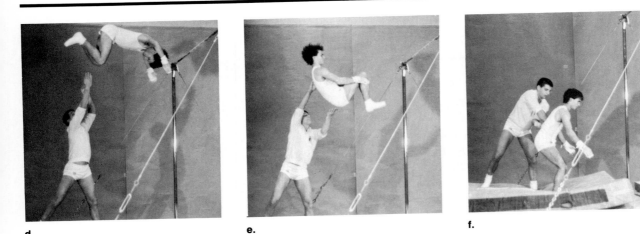

d.

e.

f.

Lead up to UPB Giant Swing

For girls, the giant swing is a high-difficulty skill, although for boys it is a basic skill. However, since you worked on long hang swings earlier, I will present a lead up for an overgrip giant swing on UPB, which has become a standard move in uneven bars routines these days. A similar lead up is used for boys on the horizontal bar and, in fact, girls are working more and more on the horizontal bar and/or high single [uneven] bar to develop these skills that originated as horizontal bar moves.

As you progress and want to work toward this giant swing on the unevens, spread the bars as wide as they go (or remove the low bar and either put a piece of foam where it was or just leave a space). Begin in a front support on the high bar. Cast off backward, being sure to pike (you can straddle as well) as you pass the low bar position—look for it (or where it would be) under your body to see where it is. (This is assuming you are tall enough to hit the low bar with your legs if it were there.) Stretch as soon as you pass it, and proceed to the swing and fast pullover. As you cast higher and higher and become stronger, you will find that the pullover becomes easier and that you will be able to do it like a free hip circle. Then you will be ready to challenge an overgrip giant swing on the unevens.

Giant Swing—HB

If you can cast to a handstand and have mastered a number of the circling skills so that your grip strength is good, it is time to start working on giant swings. Although giant swings are advanced skills for girls, for boys they are the basic skill for horizontal bar routines and can be done in an overgrip, in an undergrip, and eventually in a mixed grip. There are other grip variations that are higher level skills. Giant swings are often referred to as simply "giants."

Although an undergrip is not quite as strong as an overgrip, the undergrip giant swing is perhaps the safest one to learn. This is because if you do not complete one, it is easier to recover and land on your feet than if you do not complete an overgrip giant. However, if you learned recoveries (in case of over-casting) when you learned to cast to a handstand, you will know what to do if you miss the overgrip giant, and either giant will be good to begin with.

For lead ups, kick to a handstand on a safety cushion and fall over to either your back or front keeping your body straight. You should be able to land flat going in either direction before you try a giant swing. The next step is to cast to a handstand on a low bar and fall onto soft mats piled up to the level of the bar. See if you are in a straight position when you hit the mats. Another way to practice the start of a giant is to have fellow students standing in the downswing area next to the low bar, and have them gang-catch you as you fall from a handstand. If you can do these lead ups, you are ready to learn giant swings. A way to experience giants without worrying about your grip is to use wrist straps, which hold your hands on the bar. Use of these devices requires specialized instruction and equipment, but I mention them as they are quite useful and gaining in popularity.

Once you learn them, you should do a series of giants, and learn how to slow down as you go over the top so that you can lower to the bar. The more giants you do, the more comfortable you will feel going around and around in space. It is actually a very pleasurable feeling once you learn to do it. I still remember how good it felt to do my first giant swing.

Undergrip Giant (Figure 12.86)

For the forward (or front) giant, before doing a complete giant swing, do a three-quarter giant as a further lead up. Cast to a handstand, stretching to get as straight as you can. Keep your head in line between your arms so you can see the bar out of the tops of your eyes. (You can watch the bar the entire way around.) Fall over forward (toward your back) without changing position. Once you are about 45° past the bottom, pull up to a support, doing a back uprise. The next step is to cast and fall again, but as you rise and pull your shoulders up and over the bar, push into a handstand position again. Look over the top of the bar to see where you have to pull your shoulders. I suggest doing your giant without piking your hips. Many years back, a piked giant swing was the style, but I prefer teaching this without hip piking because it gives a much longer body line and has mechanical advantages. Later you will learn to round your chest in addition to pulling with your shoulders, which gives a smooth, curved

Figure 12.86a, b, c, d, e
Stephan arches a bit coming into his front giant; otherwise it is well done.

a.   b.   c.

d.   e.

look leading to more polished performances. As you rise above the bar, you will feel less weight on your hands, and you will be able to shift your wrists around to get your palms on top of the bar for a good support. If you pull with your wrists (into hyperextension) while you are pulling down on the bar, they should shift easily. If you do not make it past a handstand you can pull to a support and try again. If you go past a handstand, do another giant. To stop, just do not pull as hard. You can lower to the bar, or push off once you stop moving upward.

Common problems are not casting to a good handstand, not stretching on the way down, arching through the bottom, wiggling (making several body position changes) on the way around, lifting your head as you come up, and not pulling far enough to get your shoulders over the bar.

A second technique of performing this giant swing is to use an arch method rather than a shoulder pike method, just as you learned when doing a back uprise. For the arch method, rather than pulling with your shoulders once you are past the bottom, arch hard.

■

Spotting

You can hand spot or use an overhead spotting belt. For the hand spot, stand on an elevated platform behind the bar and to your student's side with your left shoulder just below the bar level. Reach under, around, and over the bar to hold his left wrist with your pronated left hand as he starts to fall. The critical point is just past the bottom, where the greatest force is on his hands. That is where there is danger of flying off the bar. As he passes the bottom and starts to lift, reach in under his abdomen or chest with your right hand and give him a boost. If he does not make it to a handstand he can either come back to the bar or push off because he can see the mat. As soon as you feel confident that he will not rip off of the bar, allow him to try giants with a spotter standing down below just in case a hand comes off. When spotting giants from the floor, always stand on the uprise side of the bar perhaps 5 feet back, as this is where your student will fly if he rips off. If you use an overhead belt, be sure you have wrapped the ropes around the bar the correct way (the opposite way that the giant will be done), and leave some slack so his cast is not hindered by the ropes. Then take up the slack, and as he passes under the bar keep a light tension in the ropes through this critical point. You can give him a boost to get over the bar by pulling on the upswing, and can lower him if he does not make it. Only do single giants using the overhead belt system!

Overgrip Giant (Figure 12.87)

The learning progression for a backward (or back) giant is similar to that for a front giant. There is a three-quarter giant swing here, too, which is also called a baby giant swing and can be done from an underswing or a cast from support. This is the lead up I described for an overgrip giant on the UPB. If you do a large forward swing, as you go up in front, do a backward pullover to a support. Then, from a support with an overgrip, cast out as high as you can and swing down, looking at the bar out of the tops of your eyes with your head between your arms. After you swing about 45° past the bottom, lift your body over the bar and perform the back pullover again. You may move so well that you do not touch the bar. This will teach you the pulling action necessary for a back giant swing.

Once you are ready, start in a support and cast to a handstand. Look at the bar all the way around on the giant (this gives you a point of orientation). As you descend, push on the bar to get as stretched as you can. Once you are about 45° past the bottom, pull your body over the bar by piking your shoulders a bit. Try not to pike your hips; rather, change your shoulder position to pull over. As you feel yourself rising up over the bar, open your shoulder angle to pass through a handstand. Your wrists will shift here as well. As with the front giant, if you pull back with your wrists as you rise, they will shift automatically when you lift, reducing the force on them. If you finish short of a handstand, either

Figure 12.87a, b, c, d, e
If Stephan were straight in figure a and
rounded instead of piked in figures c and d,
this well-done back giant would be better.

a.

b.

c.

d.

e.

regrasp with both hands on the way down, or change one hand to an undergrip and swing down, or pirouette off. If you go past a handstand, do another giant, or push off.

Common problems are not casting to a good handstand, not stretching on the way down, kicking through the bottom (too early), wiggling (making several body position changes) on the way around, lifting your head as you come up, opening from your shoulder pike into an arch, shifting your wrists late, bending your arms as you shift your wrists, and not lifting your feet far enough to get over the bar.

Figure 12.88
Spotting a back giant from the ground—
stand where the gymnast would fly if he
came off.

You can hand spot or use an overhead spotting belt. For the hand spot, stand on an elevated platform in front of the bar with your right shoulder just below it. Reach underneath, around, and over the bar with your pronated right hand, and hold your student's left wrist. As he passes the bottom, reach under his back with your left hand and give him a push to go over the bar. Again, the critical point is just past the bottom. If he is ready, allow him to do the giant with you spotting on the floor. Stand about 5 feet in front of the bar, and be ready if he comes off (figure 12.88). Also be ready in case he does not make it over the bar and has trouble with a recovery method. With the overhead spotting belt, follow the same guidelines as discussed for the front giant.

■

Spotting

Pirouette From a Giant Swing—HB

Once you learn how to do giant swings, a whole new world has opened up for you. Next you should learn how to turn around so that you do not have to do giant swings facing one direction the whole time. If you have learned how to do a pirouette on the mat, and then on a low bar, or a cast (perhaps from a kip) to a pirouette, or a pirouette from a back extension on the mat, you have an idea of what it is like to turn around in a handstand position. If you have learned swinging turns as discussed earlier in this chapter, you are ready to learn pirouettes from giants. In fact, those swinging turns become giant swing pirouettes when they are done from and to a handstand.

Forward Pirouette From Front Giant to Back Giant (Figure 12.89)

To do a forward (or front) pirouette well on the horizontal bar, you have to learn how to change your plane of rotation during your giant swing. This is done as you uprise in the back. As you pull downward on the bar during your upswing, move your whole body over the arm that you are going to do the turn on, changing the plane of your giant. You have to shift sideways by a shoulder width to do

Figure 12.89a, b, c, d, e
Stephan should start his turn earlier, so that
his pirouette finishes at or before a
handstand.

a.   b.   c.   d.   e.

a pirouette well. It is important to move your whole body—if you just move
your shoulders, your feet will go in the opposite direction, and you will not accomplish the plane change. If you pirouette on your left arm, what actually
makes you change planes is that you push out of your right shoulder and pull
in a bit with your left shoulder while pulling down (do this while hanging still
below the bar to see how it works). As you move over, start to turn by pushing
the right side of your body backward. Then release with your right hand by
opening it and pushing off. Once you are on your left arm, push against the bar
to stretch your body, and reach for the bar with your right hand. Your pirouette
should be completed by the time you pass through a handstand position.

The most common problem is a late pirouette, a turn completed past a
handstand. The reason it is usually done poorly, past the bar, is that many performers are not confident enough of their giant swings to know that they are
going to go over the bar if they let go early. So you have to feel confident about
your giant swings. If you do not shift your hands so that your palms go on top
of the bar as you pull for your giant, you will not feel a good support, and you
will be wary of turning early without firm support. Another problem often seen
is not moving over well so that you go around the side on your turn. This happens when you do not push off well.

■

Spotting

Either stand on an elevated platform next to the performer on the upswing side, or
use an overhead rig with a twisting belt. Assist him in moving over, and be ready to
lower him if he goes so early or so slowly that he does not make it to a handstand.
Use the overhead belt as you would for a giant.

Figure 12.90a, b, c, d
By opening into an arch, Stephan is slowing
his back pirouette and regrasping in an
incorrect position.

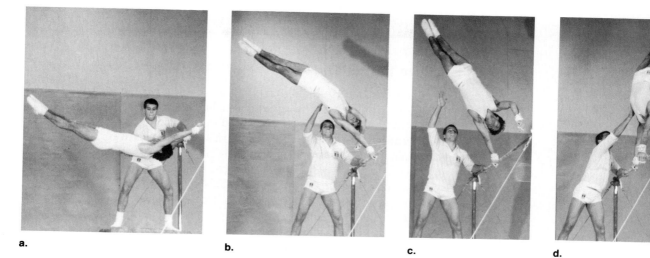

a.   b.   c.   d.

Backward Pirouette From Back Giant to Front Giant (Figure 12.90)

Although this is a B-level skill, you need to know how to turn around this way so that you can do both front and back giants connected by pirouettes. A back pirouette (which, in the USA, is often called a blind change) begins in an over-grip. I suggest that if you do a front pirouette on your left arm, learn a back pirouette on your left arm also, as then you will not walk all over the bar when doing several turns in a sequence. Often students are asked to do a flat cast from a support into a large swing to provide not quite enough swing to make a giant but enough to perform the turning action. After the turn, in this learning stage, you can either push off once your swing has stopped, or pull to the bar as in a back uprise, or change to a double over-grip and do another.

In a similar manner to a front pirouette, as you rise up in front, at the same point where you lift for a giant, shift to your left (like a swinging turn) and turn over to your left by pushing the right side of your body forward. You will have to move over the width of your shoulders. Open easily from the lift as you would for a giant. At that point, your right hand releases by pushing off from the bar. As you turn, stretch away by pushing on the bar with your left hand to get as long as you can. Your turn should be finished just prior to passing a handstand. I teach my students to look at the bar throughout the turn (to see the regrasp). Another method is to look at a point to the left on the way up and lift your feet toward it. However, this method has you looking away from the bar and then looking at it again in a short time span, which is less desirable from my point of view.

Common problems are turning too early or late, not moving over enough to finish in the correct plane, lifting your head, and kicking into an arch as you open into your turn.

Stand on an elevated platform on the upswing side, or use an overhead rig with a twisting belt. Just as you do for a front pirouette, reach in and help your student turn and change planes, and be ready to lower him if he does not make it to a handstand. Use the overhead belt as you would to spot a giant.

Shoot to Handstand—HB (Figure 12.91)

This mount (also called a high start) can be done with an undergrip, overgrip, or mixed grip, and leads directly into a giant swing. The action is practically the same for each. I will describe the undergrip shoot. Each of these mounts should eventually be done with straight arms on the upward phase, but it will take a while to become strong enough to do this. A good drill to learn this skill is to begin as if you were going to do a cast to a back uprise, but instead of casting out, do a fast backward pullover. This will get you used to pulling your feet and lower legs over the bar, which is necessary to perform the move to a handstand. A simpler drill is to do a fast pullover on a low bar.

To push this mount up to a handstand, you begin as I just described for the drill. Keep your eyes on the bar as you start the pullover action. Drop your shoulders quickly under the bar, and watch for when your feet and the lower half of your shins come over the bar. At this point, pull the bar toward the floor, which will push you over the bar and up toward a handstand. You will bend you arms when you first learn this, but as you gain strength you will be able to keep your arms straight on the way up. When that time comes, you will have to turn over farther and faster to perform the straight-armed shoot than you did to perform a bent-armed shoot. This mount is often done directly to a forward giant swing.

Common problems are not pulling your feet over the bar enough, not rotating your shoulders under the bar quickly, throwing your head back, and pushing to a handstand too slowly. Sometimes you may hit your shins on the bar if your timing is off on the way up.

■

Spotting

Stand in front of the bar and to the side and help your student turn over if needed. This skill often is not spotted, as doing it by gradually pushing a fast backward pullover up higher and higher is relatively safe. Should your student overshoot (that is, go the wrong way after the shoot), he can drop off to his feet.

Stoop-in From a Front Giant to Seat Circle and Shoot to Dislocate—HB (Figure 12.92)

Now you will combine some of the skills covered earlier. Before you work on this sequence from a giant swing, get on a low bar to do some preparatory drills. First, start in a rear support with an undergrip. You may want to spread your hands to facilitate your dislocate action if your shoulders are not flexible—try some dislocates on a broomstick or similar bar to see where you can do this action (part of the warmup I suggested in chapter 3). From the rear support, arch with your seat in contact with the bar, then rapidly lift your legs in front of you through a V support position and push your body in front of the bar. As you do this, extend smoothly and push into a dislocate (figures g, h).

Figure 12.91a, b, c, d, e

a.

b.

c.

d.

e.

Next, see if you can shoot (push rapidly) into a dislocate as you come up behind the bar from a front seat circle. At first, do the shoot just above horizontal, and go higher as you feel comfortable. Eventually you want to do this shoot directly upward, which is a higher level skill. The more momentum you have in your seat circle, the easier it will be to do the seat circle and shoot. To build up momentum, start from a high piked position—lift your seat and push down on the bar to get your center of gravity as far from the bar as possible before starting your seat circle, or cast up and do a stoop-in (as described in the earlier section on a front seat circle). On the way down, point your legs

Figure 12.92a, b, c, d, e, f, g, h
Aside from hooked feet in figures b and c, this is a good sequence.

a.

b.

c.

d.

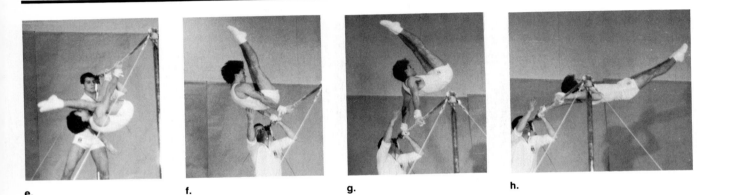

e.

f.

g.

h.

directly down at the floor and pull them as close to your body as you can. Passing the bottom, if you are in a balanced piked inverted hang, you should be able to shoot out well. Pull the bar behind you as you rise to initiate the shoot. You will want to lead the dislocate action with your seat—do not shoot out into an arch; rather, you should shoot out with your body staying somewhat piked at first. Later, you will learn to open from a pike to a stretch as you approach the end of your movement outward. By not opening from a pike at first, you will emphasize the push back on the bar to get away from it. If you can finish the sequence in a stretched eaglegrip swing downward, you are ready to take it to the high bar.

The stoop-in from an undergrip giant covered here is an early stoop-in. This is so called because it happens before a handstand is reached. If you stoop-in from a handstand, it is a higher level skill (and gives you more momentum to work with). As you rise behind the bar from an undergrip giant swing, once you pass above bar level, push on the bar to stop your shoulders from moving forward, pull your straight legs between your hands rapidly, and point them at the mat directly below. If you look at the mat below as you stoop-in, you will have a spot to point toward. Once your legs are in position, proceed with your seat circle and shoot. This will happen fast, so be ready to act quickly. Push into an eaglegrip swing and come through the bottom. You will watch your body extend as you shoot to your dislocate, then look for the bar as you approach the bottom of your swing. As you rise behind the bar, pull down on it to lift a bit, watch the bar, and hop your hands from an eaglegrip to an overgrip (like hopping from an undergrip to an overgrip). Later on you will learn to pull over the bar in this eaglegrip, doing an eagle giant swing, or hop over to a front giant, both of which are higher level moves.

Sequences to Practice

On a low bar:

1. Using an overgrip—back pullover, cast and return 3 times, cast to back hip circle, drop kip, front hip circle, cast, undershoot dismount
2. Perform a series of at least 3 in a row—free hip circles, front sole circles, back sole circles, front seat circles, back seat circles, Endo circles, and Stalder circles

On a single (uneven) bar or horizontal bar just high enough to swing without scraping the mat:

3. Swing forward with an overgrip, kip, forward hip circle, cast to straddle-on, undershoot with one-half turn changing both grips to finish in an overgrip, stoop-in to straddled cut dismount
4. Swing rearward with an undergrip, one-half turn to mixed grip, change to overgrip at back end of swing, swing forward, swing backward, swing forward and hop change to undergrip, swing backward and hop change to overgrip, swing forward, kip, cast to handstand and pirouette off as a dismount

On UPB:

5. Facing the bars on the low bar side—glide, single-leg stoop-through to stride support, change hands to undergrip, stride circle forward to stride support, cut front leg back to a front support, cast and squat on, stand and grasp high bar, long hang swing out and return to low bar, repeat long hang swing out and pullover to front support on the high bar
6. Facing the low bar under the high bar—straddled glide-switch-glide, kip, cast back to glide and straddle-up to seat, reach for the high bar and long hang kip, cast to free hip circle, undershoot with one-half turn dismount
7. From a hang on the high bar facing the low bar—drop to glide kip, forward hip circle, cast back into glide, kip catch, swing forward and straddle over the low bar, short kip

On HB:

8. Cast to back uprise, free hip circle, undershoot with one-half turn, swing forward, stoop-in to straddled cut-catch, kip change, cast to front sole circle, stop just before going over, change hands to overgrip, three-quarter back sole circle dismount

9. From a forward swing close to horizontal—one-half turn to mixed grip, swing forward, change to undergrip and flying kip to handstand, one and three-quarter front giants, hop change to overgrip, one and three-quarter back giants, lower to a support, drop kip, cast to piked back flyaway

10. Begin with an undergrip—shoot handstand, one and three-quarter front giants, front pirouette, one and three-quarter back giants, back pirouette, three-quarter front giant, hop change to overgrip, free hip circle to handstand, front giant, giant flyaway in layout position

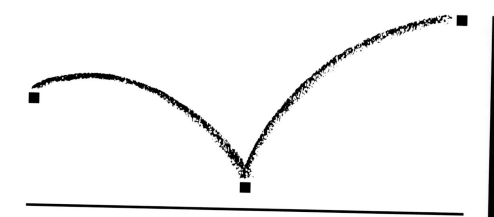

Although trampoline is not a competition event in artistic gymnastics, it is a useful event on which to learn many of the skills of artistic gymnastics, as it provides a good deal more air time than you can get by jumping off a mat or vaulting board and has a relatively soft landing surface. It also provides a great opportunity to develop kinesthetic (body position) awareness during flight. I described some trampoline drills in chapter 10 (**Vault**). (Note: These devices are not often found in public schools, but are often used in private clubs and universities.)

Beginners can learn many nonsomersaulting skills before they go on to somersaulting skills. These nonsomersaulting skills should be emphasized to develop a feel for what the trampoline does. George Hery, a former world champion on trampoline, composed a "no flip" trampoline program that was printed in the December, 1984, issue of *International Gymnast* magazine. He lists over 150 nonsomersaulting skills in a progressive manner, and these should provide any beginner with challenges to overcome before advancing to somersaults. Jeff Hennessey has an excellent book entitled *Trampolining*, published by Wm. C. Brown Publishers, that covers trampoline setup, performance area requirements, teaching and performing progressions, and spotting. Jeff also wrote the section on trampolining in the US Gymnastics Safety Association's *Gymnastics Safety Manual*, published by the Pennsylvania State University Press.

Rather than describing many of the beginning skills, I direct you to one or all of these sources. You will learn about various jumps, how to control your bounce, various bed contact positions, and you will eventually combine the skills you learn into sequences. You will be able to do all of the jumping skills that you learned on the mat with greater height, and therefore more air time.

A minitrampoline is a single rebound device that provides you with much greater air time than a vaulting board will. Landings are done on a mat just as if you were jumping from a vaulting board. Spotting for the minitrampoline is done just as you would for a tumbling skill done from the mat or a vaulting drill done from a vaulting board, but of course the student is generally much higher so you have to be more careful of landings.

The American Alliance of Health, Physical Education, and Recreation published a position statement in 1978 with guidelines for trampoline use in physical education classes. These guidelines include a suggestion that somersaults generally should not be taught in physical education classes. Of course, a gymnastics school program or team is not the same as a general physical education class, but the basic skills still must be taught before heading into somersaulting skills. The entire text of the AAHPER position statement can be found in the *Journal of Physical Education and Recreation,* October, 1978.

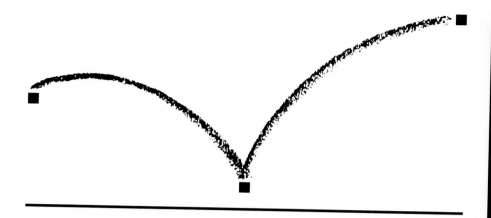

Once you have learned a number of gymnastics skills and can put them together into routines, you may want to participate in a gym meet to see how you compare to others who are also training on the same level that you are. If you become a competitor, you will be evaluated by a judge. Who are these judges, and how do they come up with their scores? What kind of training do they take to be able to evaluate your gymnastics? Who writes the rules?

The rules governing competition on the international level are written by the members of the men's and women's technical committees of the International Gymnastics Federation, whose acronym is FIG. These rules are contained in books called the *FIG Code of Points* for men and women. The US Gymnastics Federation, the National Gymnastics Judges Association (men), and the National Association of Women Gymnastics Judges adopt these rules for domestic competitions, occasionally modifying them for domestic use. The judging associations also publish rules interpretations to clarify or augment the international rules. High school associations often further modify the rules.

A judge is often someone who has had previous gymnastics experience as a competitor or coach. Judges must separate performers so that different levels of performance may be recognized. The duty of a judge is to evaluate a performance according to objective criteria that have been universally taught and accepted, so that evaluation everywhere should be uniform. A judge must study and know the *FIG Code of Points* and any supplemental materials that are used by the judging organizations. Just as gymnastics evolves, judging evolves as well. As performers reach and surpass the limits of performance described by the rules, the rules are reevaluated periodically to keep up with (and to try to get ahead of) the gymnasts. To become a judge, you will have to study these materials, attend a course, and pass both theoretical and practical judging tests. You may train for a particular level of judging—usually beginning judges start with the lowest levels of competition and work their way up the ladder as they acquire experience. Judges take courses each year to improve their skills and often attend seminars at gymnastics meetings to keep up with current news.

International (elite) competitors perform both compulsory routines (that are designed by the FIG technical committees) and optional routines (that each performer makes up, often with the help and advice of a coach). Elite-level compulsory routines are produced by the FIG technical committees and used in our elite program. For our age-group programs, various committees compose scaled-down compulsory exercises for use by the many levels of competitors found in our domestic programs. Optional exercises are used at many levels also.

For optional exercises, the main areas of evaluation are execution, difficulty, and combination. These areas account for the bulk of a score, and the bonus categories of risk, originality, and virtuosity are used to separate very good performances from superior ones. As of this writing (1990), in men's gymnastics, execution is worth 4.4, difficulty 4.0, and combination 1.0. This adds up to 9.4, with the balance of 0.6 divided between the bonus categories, and gives a final possible score of 10.0. In women's gymnastics, execution is worth 5.10, difficulty 3.00, combination 1.50, and bonus 0.4.

When judging a compulsory exercise, the judge is not concerned with combination or difficulty. He or she knows what is coming, as judges are supplied with the text, a set of drawings, and a table of special areas of concern to which they can refer. In addition to these special areas, a judge knows that the same criteria that are used to evaluate execution of an optional exercise are used for compulsories. The bonus area of virtuosity is used as well, but it is a small part of the score.

When judging an optional exercise, the judge must record what he or she sees and keep track of the combination requirements, execution flaws, difficulty, and bonus areas as the performance unfolds before his or her eyes. Once the routine is finished, all of this information must be evaluated and a score, representing the quality and level of the work just seen, delivered in about 30 seconds.

If there are two judges evaluating a performance, their scores must be within a certain range, depending on the value of the average of the two. If four judges are used, the high and the low are dropped, and the two middle scores are averaged. Again, the spread of these two scores must be within a certain range, which is dependent on the average. For important international competitions, women use a panel of six judges plus one or two superior judges who oversee the judging panel, and the score is the average of the middle four scores from the panel, whereas men use a panel of four or (in individual finals) six judges plus one or two superior judges. (I have heard of possible changes coming in international judging panels, so when you read this the situation may be different.) As an example, if a four-judge panel arrives at scores of 9.1, 9.1, 9.2, and 9.3, the exercise's score is 9.15.

A judge has to be able to recognize each move that is performed, to know what it should look like when performed correctly, and to know what penalties to assess when a performance is less than perfect. It is a tough job and often a thankless one, but those who judge gymnastics do so because they love our sport and want to contribute to the development of the many fine people involved in it.

Anyone who coaches should also learn to judge, as it teaches you the rules governing gymnastics and the proper way to perform skills. Gymnasts should also learn these rules so that they can understand how to construct competition routines and how they will be evaluated.

If you want to know more about judging, contact your local gymnastics program for information on how to begin. Once you have contacted your local judging organization, you will learn what criteria are involved with the different levels of judging, where you can obtain the necessary material to study, and where there are training courses you can attend.

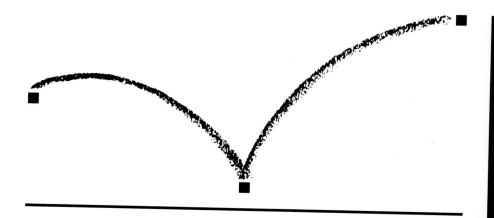

All students who take part in a gymnastics program should be given a physical exam by their family physician or the team/program physician and should be cleared for participation. A medical history should be kept on each student in a program, so that in case such information is needed, it will be readily available.

Due to the nature of gymnastics, accidents and injuries happen occasionally. In a beginning level program, the nature of most of these is relatively minor, and a teacher must be prepared to treat minor problems and to get help in the case of major ones. Taking a Red Cross first aid course is a good idea, and undergoing further training in health areas will help a teacher to be prepared in case of a major problem.

Keep first aid supplies handy in the gym, so that if minor problems arise you will be able to take care of them quickly.

A plan of action should be known to all teachers in case of an injury that cannot be treated at the gym. Post the phone numbers of your team or school doctor, trainer, local ambulance, police department, fire department, and hospital by the phone so that any teachers can find them and will be able to call any of these emergency personnel should the need arise.

Some of the common minor problems found in a training program are:

1. Hot hands, blisters, cracks, and rips. When you constantly stress your hands as you do in gymnastics, your skin becomes irritated. When your hands feel hot, this is a warning signal from your body: You should stop doing whatever it is that is irritating the skin on your hands, so that it can heal. A nice aspect of working on all of the events is that when your hands hurt, you can go to an event that does not stress them. When I was a training gymnast, I would often wash dishes after a workout, since this made my hands feel good. Some gymnasts hold ice in their palms, which also soothes their hands. Others put lotion or ointment on their hands to keep their skin pliable and moist.

   If you push your skin beyond its elastic limit, you may suffer a blister, crack, or rip. Should this happen, you will have a longer healing period to deal with. A blister, crack, or rip has to be cared for specially, as you will have done a bit of destruction to your skin. Should you crack or rip, you must treat this as an open wound—clean it and keep it from getting dirty so that it does not become infected. There is a variety of preparations to apply to your rip. I used to cover a cleaned-out rip with adhesive tape directly, as this acted as a protective layer and allowed me to train on my rip somewhat. Other protective measures include using "Second Skin," an artificial skin substitute, and using antibiotic ointments or other ointments in conjunction with bandages. An excellent article on hand care written by Dr. Jim Campbell, a member of the USGF medical committee, can be found in the magazine *USGF Gymnastics,* January/February, 1983 (this magazine is now titled *USA Gymnastics*). Among other things, Dr. Campbell discusses the use of urea cream to keep hands in good working shape.

2. Sprains, strains, and bruises. If the nature of these is minor, just a little ache, you can treat them with the R.I.C.E. method: Rest, Ice, Compression, and Elevation. The sooner you can apply ice, the better your chance of a quick recovery. Use a plastic bag of crushed ice if it is available, and apply it at 20-minute intervals. In between the treatments, move your injured part as much as you can without pain to promote blood flow into it. You can continue treatment at home easily. Keep your injured part above your heart to promote drainage and reduce swelling. An elastic bandage applied over the injury site will help reduce swelling, and if the wrap is long enough, the inner wrappings can cover the injury site and the outer wrappings can hold an ice bag in place.

Both the *USGF Safety Manual* and the USGSA *Gymnastics Safety Manual* have chapters on medical responsibility. I recommend that you read them.

16

Other Sources of Information and Supplies

National Governing Body

United States Gymnastics Federation
Pan American Plaza—Suite 300
201 South Capitol Avenue
Indianapolis, IN 46225
(317)237–5050

NOTE: The USGF sponsors gymnastics safety certification courses many times and at many locations during the year. Coaching clinics are also sponsored periodically. Contact them for a current listing of these courses. The USGF marketing department carries publications, videotapes, and other items of interest. Within each region of the country, coaching and judging organizations sponsor educational sessions. A list of regional and state directors can be obtained from the USGF.

Another Organization Sponsoring Educational Sessions and Materials

US Association of Independent Gymnastic Clubs (USAIGC)
235 Pinehurst Road
Wilmington, DE 19803
(302)655–2627

Magazines

International Gymnast
225 Brooks
Oceanside, CA 92054
$18/year
USA Gymnastics
published by the USGF, address above
$12/year

Books

A source of information is:

Frederick, A. Bruce. "Gymnastics: A Guide to the Literature." *International Gymnast* 24:7, July, 1982. (This is the "IG Technical Supplement #9.")

Some of the instructional books that I have in my library are:

Brown, James and Wardell, David. *Teaching and Coaching Gymnastics for Men and Women.* New York: John Wiley & Sons, 1980.
Cooper, Phyllis. *Feminine Gymnastics.* Minneapolis: Burgess, 1980.
Drury, Blanche and Schmid, Andrea. *Gymnastics for Women.* Palo Alto, CA: Mayfield, 1977 (4th ed.).
Frederick, A. Bruce. *Gymnastics for Men.* Dubuque, IA: Wm. C. Brown, 1969.
Frederick, A. Bruce. *Gymnastics for Women.* Dubuque, IA: Wm. C. Brown, 1966.
Fukushima, Sho and Russell, Wrio. *Men's Gymnastics.* London: Faber and Faber, 1980.
George, Gerald. *Biomechanics of Women's Gymnastics.* Englewood Cliffs, NJ: Prentice-Hall, 1980.
George, Gerald (editor). *USGF Gymnastics Safety Manual.* Indianapolis: USGF, 1985.
Gula, Denise. *Dance in Gymnastics.* Original publication—Newton, MA: Allyn & Bacon, 1986. Now published—Dubuque, IA: Wm. C. Brown.

413

Hennesey, Jeff. *Trampolining.* Dubuque, IA: Wm. C. Brown, 1968.

Kaneko, Akitomo. *Olympic Gymnastics.* New York: Sterling, 1975 (2nd ed.).

Klaus, Marshall. *A Teacher's Guide to Gymnastics.* Palo Alto, CA: National, 1967.

O'Quinn, Jr., Garland. *Teaching Developmental Gymnastics.* Austin, TX: University Press, 1990.

Ryan, Frank. *Gymnastics for Girls.* New York: Viking, 1976.

Sands, Bill. *Beginning Gymnastics.* Chicago: Contemporary Books, 1981.

Szypula, George. *Beginning Trampoline.* Belmont, CA: Wadsworth, 1968.

Tonry, Don with Barbara Tonry. *Sports Illustrated—Women's Gymnastics 1*; *Sports Illustrated—Women's Gymnastics 2.* New York: Lippincott & Crowell, 1980.

USGF Education Subcommittee. *Sequential Gymnastics for Grades 3–6.* Indianapolis: USGF, 1988.

Wettstone, Eugene (editor). *Gymnastics Safety Manual.* University Park, PA: Pennsylvania State University Press, 1979. (2nd ed.)

Some books that are of general interest and are helpful for all who are beginning their involvement in gymnastics:

Conner, Bart with Paul Ziert. *Winning the Gold.* New York: Warner, 1985.

Krements, Jill. *A Very Young Gymnast.* New York: Alfred A. Knopf, 1978.

Martens, Rainer; Christina, Robert; Harvey, John and Sharkey, Brian. *Coaching Young Athletes.* Champaign, IL: Human Kinetics, 1981.

Thomas, Kurt and Hannon, Kent. *Kurt Thomas on Gymnastics.* New York: Simon & Schuster, 1980.

Also check your local bookstore for instructional books on gymnastics and entertaining books by gymnasts.

Videotapes

Mulvihill, Dick and Linda. "The Foundations of Gymnastic Excellence Series." Dubuque, IA: Wm. C. Brown Publishers, 1990.

Posner, Steve. "Rolling, Twisting and Turning Your Way to Fitness." North Palm Beach: The Athletic Institute, 1989.

Other videotapes may be purchased from the USGF or USAIGC. Also check the ads in the magazines.

Visual Aids, Posters, Supplies, Personal Gear

My suggestion is to get an issue of *International Gymnast,* which has ads for anything you will need in our sport.

Index

BB = balance beam
FE = floor exercise
HB = horizontal bar
PB = parallel bars
PH = pommel horse
R = rings
UPB = uneven parallel bars
V = vault

Note: when describing movements, front = forward; back = backward

Other Books from
Wm. C. Brown's Championship Series

☐ **DRILL TO SKILL: TEACHER TACTICS IN PHYSICAL EDUCATION**
by Connie Blakemore and Nena Hawkes both of Brigham Young University and Evelyn Burton of the Alpine School District-Aspen Elementary School

1991/288 pages/Paper/ISBN 04457/$15.00

DRILL TO SKILL is a book of teacher tactics purposely designed for those who teach a variety of sport activities. This book is focused on sports that are most often taught by teachers in middle, junior, and senior high schools

☐ **CHILDREN'S GAMES FROM AROUND THE WORLD**
by Glenn Kirchner

1990/202 pages/Paper/ISBN 11738/$19.95

CHILDREN'S GAMES FROM AROUND THE WORLD is a unique publication that includes traditional games and introduces new games that the children from all countries have created for themselves.

☐ **VISUAL ATHLETICS: VISUALIZATIONS FOR PEAK SPORTS PERFORMANCE**
by Kay Porter, Ph.D. and Judy Foster

1990/210 pages/Paper/ISBN 10987/$13.95

Develop the elite athlete in yourself; find out why the best athletes use mental power to maintain their competitive edge. VISUAL ATHLETICS helps recreational as well as elite athletes attain their peak performance through guided visualizations.

☐ **DANCE IN GYMNASTICS: A GUIDE FOR COACHES AND GYMNASTS**
by Denise Gula, Former Dance Coach of the U.S. Gymnastics Training Center, Connecticut

1986/196 pages/Cloth/ISBN 6833/$19.95

Denise Gula organizes the basic principles and techniques of dance and applies them to the gymnast. She'll help you teach your advanced gymnasts the dance movements that are both appropriate for their level and suitable for performance in competition.

ORDER FORM

TO ORDER ANY OR ALL OF THESE TITLES:

1. **CALL Toll Free 1–800–338–5578**

2. Send check or money order plus appropriate state tax and $1.00 shipping and handling for each book ordered along with a list of the books you would like to receive (include ISBN numbers) to:

Wm. C. Brown Publishers
2460 Kerper Boulevard
Dubuque, Iowa 52001

SHIP TO: _____   Book Total $ _____

_____   Tax $ _____

City _____ State _____ Zip _____   Shipping $ _____

Total $ _____

REMEMBER TO ASK FOR A **FREE** SPORTS PAGE CATALOG LISTING ALL OF OUR TITLES